Bricks and Mortar

BRICKS AND MORTAR

The Making of a Real Education at the STANFORD ONLINE HIGH SCHOOL

Jeffrey Scarborough
Raymond Ravaglia

CSLI
PUBLICATIONS
Center for the Study of
Language and Information
Stanford, California

Center for the Study of Language and Information
Leland Stanford Junior University
Printed in the United States
18 17 16 15 14 1 2 3 4 5

Library of Congress Cataloging-in-Publication Data

Scarborough, Jeffrey, 1976-

Bricks and mortar : the making of a real education at the Stanford Online High School / Jeffrey Scarborough, Raymond Ravaglia.

pages cm

Summary: "The rise of online learning is rapidly transforming how and what teachers teach, and even who-or what-teachers are. In the midst of these changes, the characteristics that have historically defined a high-quality education are easily lost. Not only content knowledge, but also ways of thinking and habits of mind are the hallmarks of the well-educated individual, and these latter qualities are not so easily acquired online. Or are they? This volume shows how a group of online-learning believers built the best high school in the world without laying a single brick: the Stanford Online High School (SOHS). By chronicling SOHS's distinctive approach to curriculum, gifted education, and school community over SOHS's first seven years, Bricks and Mortar makes the case that the dynamic use of technology and the best traditional methodologies in education are not, in fact, mutually exclusive. Indeed, while SOHS has redefined what is possible online, a great education is ul timately the product of an interactive community of teachers and students"– Provided by publisher.

Includes bibliographical references and index.
ISBN 978-1-57586-739-7 (paperback) –
ISBN 978-1-57586-741-0 (electronic)

1. Stanford Online High School (Stanford, Calif.) 2. Web-based instruction–California–Stanford. 3. Gifted children–Education–California–Stanford–Computer-assisted instruction. 4. Educational innovations–California–Stanford. I. Ravaglia, Raymond, 1965- II. Title.

LD7501.S9147S33 2014
373.794′73–dc23

2014017798

CIP

∞ The acid-free paper used in this book meets the minimum requirements of the American National Standard for Information Sciences—Permanence of Paper for Printed Library Materials, ANSI Z39.48-1984.

CSLI was founded in 1983 by researchers from Stanford University, SRI International, and Xerox PARC to further the research and development of integrated theories of language, information, and computation. CSLI headquarters and CSLI Publications are located on the campus of Stanford University.

CSLI Publications reports new developments in the study of language, information, and computation. Please visit our web site at
http://cslipublications.stanford.edu/
for comments on this and other titles, as well as for changes and corrections by the author and publisher.

To the Pixels

To Rebecca, for showing me the wonder of teaching.
And to Helen and Anne, whom I love to watch learn.

J.S.

To Renzo and Maisie, for providing a never-ending source
of education and amusement, and to the BSG, my muse,
for sharing her vision of a perfect little world.

R.R.

Contents

Acknowledgments

Full and proper acknowledgement should go first and foremost to the students and teachers who have invested themselves in the school and without whom we would have had nothing more than a collection of virtual courses. You are truly the secret sauce.

Next to the parents and families who have trusted their children with us over the years. We hope that we have returned them to your satisfaction, no worse for the wear, and perhaps slightly improved.

Also to the administration of the school for doing the thousand tasks that when properly done are never noticed. We have noticed and we are grateful.

Then to the Malone Family Foundation, without whose enthusiasm and generous financial support the Stanford Online High School would not have been possible.

And to Stanford University, for providing the fertile soil at the Farm in which to cultivate this garden.

And finally, to the countless individuals whose contributions we have received and incorporated into the school and into our thinking about the school. You are too numerous to mention and any attempt to name you would require arbitrary distinctions and inevitably result in regretful omissions. As we have always said, any successes that may have resulted from our efforts are surely due to having had the right combination of ingredients. We can take credit only for the failures.

Preface

1 Twenty-Five Years of the Next New Thing in Education

I took my first two computer-based courses in 1984 while an undergraduate at Stanford and have been working actively in this area since finishing my undergraduate degree in 1987. I played a central role in building what was arguably the first online Advanced Placement (AP) course, an AB Calculus course that we first used with students in Summer 1988 and which was offered with great success to advanced middle-school students in the 1990-91 academic year. I was the cofounder of Stanford's online program for gifted students and I was also the founder and principal architect of Stanford's Online High School, having sketched the initial draft of the school grant proposal while sitting at an airport in Tucson back in Spring of 2005.

So while online learning may seem to many to be the next new thing in education, for me it has been the next new thing for most of my adult life. And if one searches back through the literature, one can find evidence that it has been the next new thing since the early 1960s.

It used to take me five minutes to explain to people what I was doing. I would say 'I am working on computer-based education' and they would ask if that was teaching people programming. I would say 'No, I am teaching them mathematics.' And they would say 'Ah yes, you are teaching them mathematics by teaching them how to program.' And on it would go. Or they would ask if I was writing a new version of Math Blaster or some such thing. These days when I say that I am working in online learning people get it immediately, but the problem is that what comes to their minds is not the way we are doing it. So whereas before a five minute explanation could suffice to give people the idea of what we were doing, these days it takes somewhere between a chapter and a book. At this time of considerable innovation and ferment in online education, Jeff and I think that the story of our school, how it operates, and how it came to be that way can help to clarify understanding of what it can mean to educate students online. Furthermore, this story can provide a basis for assessing developments and directions in the field, as well as a clear illustration of why online learning does not need to be at odds with the best aspects of traditional education—one might say that we show how one can use twenty-first century technology to delivery a twelfth-century education.

Raymond Ravaglia
May 2014

Introduction

1 A School, not a Technology

In writing a book about our school, we have written a book about hope. Hope that children everywhere will find the education they need. Hope that this education will bring students and families together regardless of where they might live. Hope that those passionate about teaching will have the opportunity to share that passion with students longing to learn. For it is in bringing together the right teachers and the right students that the magic happens.

This is not a book about technology. While technology certainly figures prominently within this book, it is first and foremost about a school. That the school exists only because of the technology is true, though this is not the most interesting thing about the school. Rather, what is interesting is the realization that compared to the importance of getting the interaction between teachers and students right, and providing them with a rich and fertile environment in which this interaction can occur, the technology is only a small piece of the puzzle.

And while this is a book that tells a particular story of a particular school at a particular time (even if not in a particular place), it is more than that. It is a story of how what began almost twenty-five years ago as an investigation into how to use technology to teach advanced courses to individual students online led to a reaffirmation of seminal truths about good education and the importance of community and engagement to this education. It is a story of how a relentless focus on these values, and the goal of making it possible for like-minded students everywhere, regardless of exigent circumstances, to come together to receive the education they deserve, provided the insights necessary both to solve the particular problem at hand and to light the way to a future of possibilities.

2 How to Use this Book

We have structured this book as a narrative of the School's experience and development, arranged by topic. So while it is held together by the story it tells and the broad argumentative questions it addresses throughout, it is also organized to provide relatively self-contained treatments of central aspects of the school as they pertain to broader pressing questions in education. Interwoven are arguments, about the school in its 'schoolness', about what is important in online education, about curriculum and pedagogy for talented students, and about directions in curricular innovation. Accordingly, this book should be useful and of interest to a variety of audiences.

First, as we have mentioned, this book chronicles the creation and first eight years of a new, innovative, and dynamic school. It presents a picture of the conception, opening, growth, discoveries, and development of a new school, played out in a fundamentally new environment. In this story, somewhat unexpectedly given the unique medium of the school, the students and teachers figure prominently as the real source of the school's interest and vitality. But it also depicts the events and considerations that have informed the school's curricular, administrative, and cultural evolution, providing a telling of how a vision rooted in years of experience in online and gifted education interacts with the realities and discoveries of a unique school in a quickly changing technological terrain.

Within this discussion is a reflection on what makes for compelling, effective, engaging education for precollegiate students in online courses and the design decisions we have made in building the school that have been driven by these insights and that are central in the realization that the product of our efforts is not a suite of technologies, but educated students.

Embedded in the story of the school are hard-won lessons and best practices across the spectrum of questions in which the school represents an innovative approach, as well as some lessons in areas where the school's very traditional emphases are also informative.

The Stanford Online High School (SOHS) is, of course, online. We have been teaching talented high-school students in online classrooms, in the context of a demanding curriculum for eight years—a short tenure as a school, but a virtual epoch for a school online. In that time, during which we have been responsible for making the school work as a school for each of its students, we have accumulated deep experience in what works, and does not work in this setting. But the SOHS is not just a venerable online school; it is an online school that participates in the educational mission and traditions of one of the top universities in the world. And so the lessons that the school has accumulated in what works in online education are filtered through the standards for academic excellence and impact that have shaped Stanford University.

Our assessment of success online and in the classroom, then, does not equate to what is financially profitable, nor to what is scalable or represents an incremental gain in instructional efficiency, nor to applications of technology that look good at trade shows. Our duty is first and foremost to be the best school for our students. In doing so we have found ourselves becoming a demonstration school—a demonstration not of technology per se, but of how schoolness can emerge from technology. Our story is one that shows how it is possible to take a blended, flipped classroom approach, and using commercially available tools create an online school that provides a quality of education and level of engagement characteristic of the best schools in the world. In this regard it is a celebration of what can actually be accomplished and sustained over a period of years, rather than one of the more common celebrations of the promises that technology makes possible in the abstract or the gross generalizations from particular examples of short-term success. We are long on delivery, even if a critic might say we are short on promises. As to the moral of our story, it is one that will make neither online learning partisans nor online learning skeptics entirely happy. The partisans will shout that this does not scale, that it is insufficiently disruptive, or that it turns its back on the true potential of the technology. The skeptics will view it as overreach, saying that even if it seems in all regards to advance values that they subscribe to in the abstract, this school since it is online cannot be real. In this context, our story offers general perspective and a middle ground for those interested in the direction and possibilities of online education, in the midst of both explosive growth in online learning and at a moment of great interest and controversy regarding education reform.

Here, the first chapter's historically informed situating of the SOHS in the trajectory of computer-based learning, and the more detailed discussion in Chapters 3 and 4 of the preeminence of the discussion seminar at SOHS, offer the experience of the school in support of live, interactive seminars led by talented teachers as the gold standard in secondary education, online or not. These chapters also offer a picture, furthered in the future-looking conclusion of Chapter 8, of how technology can be used to support these priorities in a range of settings, from the fully online school setting of SOHS to a traditional brick-and-mortar context.

Thoughtful skeptics of online learning rightly stress the importance of community to learning and social and emotional development. Having labored at every juncture to bring our students and teachers together in every conceivable way, we find the now-common pictures of students in physical classrooms sitting next to one another as they work individually (with headphones) on their own computers, to be not portraits of a wondrous future, but rather illustrations of almost tragically wasted opportunity. In Chapter 6, we recount the efforts of the school and our students to build and sustain what has been from the start an unexpectedly vibrant and supportive community at the very heart of the school's success in its academic mission and as a real school. The formative and motivational impact of working in a school setting with talented and compassionate peers and teachers is affirmed by reflections from our alumni in a wider-ranging assessment of the school's outcomes for students in Chapter 7.

Just as it is not the school's motivating purpose to be online, but rather to meet the educational needs of a certain population of students, so are the implications of the school not just those to do with how to be, and not be, online. The school, then, as well as the account of it offered in this book, enters into questions of reform in curriculum and pedagogy with views thoroughly shaped by the experience of our unique academic program, chronicled in Chapters 3 and 4. Our experience bears most immediately on curriculum and pedagogy for gifted, passionate students. As it stands today, the SOHS reflects a view, acquired in work in gifted education prior to the SOHS as well as during its conception and early years, that the optimal academic environment for talented and dedicated students is one in which they engage difficult material *with* similarly situated peers and teachers who have the academic background to inspire and challenge them. Notably, such a picture recommends against reliance on (computer-based) private acceleration and early matriculation into college or community college. The SOHS, its seminar setting, and a curriculum focused on courses sufficiently challenging and finely targeted to our students, are designed to make such an approach to education for talented students possible. In Chapter 8, we consider ways in which the model of the SOHS might be applied to different populations and in different online and in-situ contexts.

But the relevance of the SOHS academic program is not limited to gifted education. In the experience of the school, the kinds of academic and thinking skills that help drive particularly talented students to excel are not fundamentally different than those seen as essential for all students. We describe in Chapter 3 the strategies the school has developed to foster habits of mind and skills of critical thinking across the curriculum. Of special note is the unique four-year Philosophy Core sequence of courses that focuses on critical thinking skills in the context of a range of subject matters, teaching students how to ask questions about foundational concepts, methods, and argumentative strategies in those fields. More broadly, the school has worked toward development of courses designed for focused pedagogical objectives, rather than the broad content surveys that flow from standardized programs like the Advanced Placement (AP) curriculum. Ultimately, we skirt sweeping formal prescriptions, having developed a framework in which teachers with rigorous academic backgrounds are able to develop and teach courses that provide *their* students with the training in a subject that will prepare them well for academic and professional inquiry.

In building a program that does all of this, the SOHS has arrived at a keen understanding of all that is involved in supporting students in an online setting. It is this apparatus, described in Chapter 5, that alongside our rich school community distinguishes the SOHS from programs that are ultimately collections of courses, and makes it instead a real school.

We hope, then, that this book, like the school, can provide a basis for further consideration of these broad issues in the capacity of a demonstration. To be sure, the arguments we offer, the evidence we cite, and the population we serve are all limited. Where we offer depictions of outcomes, they are based on our small (but growing!) body of alumni and students. And where we enter into literature surrounding some of the features of our school, it is to situate our experiences in some of the many possible relevant discussions—typically those that have figured directly into the design of the school and its programs. The force of our account lies in the richness of the example it describes: the intensity of student and teacher experiences in the classroom, the extreme demands made of the academic program and technology alike, the diversity of cases that emerge in such an environment, and the completeness of the community and independent-school support that have developed at our school.

1

Keeping it Real While Going Virtual

1 Introduction

While much of this book will look at different aspects of the Stanford Online High School (SOHS) in great detail, there is some value in beginning with a quick discussion of some of the key lessons we have learned over the past twenty-five years of research and program activity—including eight since we created the school—and that have led to the development of the school in its current form. And because our school does not conform to the expectations that readers have when they hear the phrase 'online high school' it is important for us to take the time to dispel certain misconceptions that the reader might have and to provide a basic sense of how the school operates. Furthermore, for the reader who lives by Francis Bacon's admonition that some books are meant to be tasted and set down, this chapter will provide that taste and will leave you with some important points to take away. For those who find that this is a book to be devoured whole, there will be an opportunity to come back and savor these points again in much greater detail and with the expected garnishes in the later chapters. And for those whose taste still remains unsatiated after that, there will be a second volume in this series that will provide wider-ranging perspective across the disciplines, providing, one might say, an opportunity to make a meal out of every course.

Before diving into the whys and wherefores underlying the school, we begin by describing how the school operates. It differs markedly from the current received conception of an online school in a number of significant ways.

2 What the Stanford Online High School is not

When people hear the phrase 'online school', different images come flooding into mind about the school and the students who would seek it out. Skeptics might think 'Pshaw! Surely this must be a fundamentally unserious enterprise. Anyone doing this must have no reasonable alternative. Imagine those poor students having to settle for an online school.' Others may imagine defects of family or students, assuming that students must be doing this because they have no friends and are incapable of 'learning in a normal way' and that the family must be using the school to hide some sort of social or emotional dysfunction. Those more sympathetic might worry for those poor students, toiling alone asynchronously, with no human contact, no opportunity to make friends, sentenced to a lonely life online.

Next the hearer's thoughts will race to questions of technology and its use. Is it a school composed entirely of online-education components? Perhaps the students come as avatars, and their virtual selves sit around a seminar table. Perhaps the *raison d'être* of the school is to affirm the use of technology in every way possible. Maybe books are seldom seen and all interactions are mediated, digitized, and recorded. And what about the teachers? Are they certified? Are they certifiable? Are there even teachers at all? Perhaps the teacher is not a teacher, but a very clever instructional apparition, a veritable electronic Aristotle who always does the right thing. Perhaps the students are simulations as well, and everything has been carefully constructed to provide each student exactly what is needed, when it is needed, without ever requiring interacting with another live person. Or perhaps the school embodies a vision of education after 'disruption', with the distinction between 'teachers' and 'students' long gone. It could be that everything has been individualized, accelerated, and engineered to the point where the motto of lifelong learning has become 'personalization and acceleration from cradle to grave'.

Or maybe the images that come to a hearer's mind are extrapolations from popular media. We have all seen commercials for online education showing students sitting at kitchen tables, smiling at mom while she prepares dinner, reading online and posting to discussion groups. The narrator touts the virtues of online schooling and the freedom it affords. Or does one imagine a news show exposé, and now the image is one where the kitchen table has been replaced by a side table crammed into a corner and the student is disengaged, distracted, watching YouTube videos of cartoons, periodically zapping aliens or buying shoes, unclear on what the assignment even is.

Utopian or dystopian or simply mundane, the preconceptions that people have of an online school tend to be driven first and foremost by their conceptions of the technology, either of technology as savior or of technology as the thing that will lay waste to all that was wonderful.

And for all but the most enthusiastic supporters of technology there tends to be a deep-seated feeling that the students in an online school could not possibly be getting a world-class education.

In fact, the Stanford Online High School is nothing at all like these people think.

3 How the Stanford Online High School Works

> The course in Democracy, Freedom, and the Rule of Law meets at Stanford at 2 PM. Unless you are in New York City, where it is 5 PM. Of course if you are in London, it is 10 PM, while in Seoul, it is 5 AM, the next day. From the energy of the students in the class you would be hard pressed to tell what time of day it is, or to know that these students are scattered across the globe. And from listening to the familiarity expressed in the lively banter going on between students, you would not guess that most students have never met face to face. You also would not guess, from the quality of the discussion that the students were not undergraduates—though the cynics might suggest that it is precisely the lively pace of discussion that gives this fact away.[1]

At its core, the Stanford Online High School is like any other mid-sized independent school. With 533 students, it emphasizes small discussion-based class meetings, prizes student-teacher interaction, and offers a deep curriculum along with extensive counseling and academic- and college-counseling support. It has a student government, a robust array of clubs and academic teams, assemblies, and homerooms. Admission to the school is competitive, with high academic standards and expectations of strong intellectual passion and work ethic.

That it is online does not fundamentally alter the SOHS's academic program: the school is accredited by the Western Association of Schools and Colleges and offers diplomas to students who meet its academic requirements; teachers are largely full-time employees (of the University) and hold superlative academic qualifications in their disciplines; and students are called upon to complete all manner of assignments, projects, and presentations that are subject to extensive evaluation and feedback from teachers.

Full-time students at the SOHS typically take five classes, though unlike most schools, the SOHS welcomes a diversity of enrollment statuses, with part-time students and single-course students common as well. Full-time students pursue a complete course of study with the

[1] R. Ravaglia, 'An Online High School at Stanford University', *Understanding Our Gifted* 19, no. 4 (2007): 6-9.

SOHS; part-time students take two or three courses and are typically enrolled in a brick-and-mortar school as well as at the SOHS and are using the SOHS to pursue advanced study in an area of strength; single-course students are usually either testing the waters before going part-time or full-time, or they are students in the last year or two of high school who are looking for particular advanced opportunities.

The model for a standard course is one that blends synchronous seminars with asynchronous lectures and interactive online components in a 'flipped' classroom model. In a typical course, seminars occur twice a week for sixty to ninety minutes in a real-time shared-whiteboard virtual classroom environment, complete with voice and video. During seminar, students and instructor can see each other and the shared whiteboard presentation space. The main channel of interaction during seminar is similar to that of a traditional college seminar, with conversation happening between members of the class talking one after another and occasionally several at the same time. Unlike a traditional classroom, there is also a text chat that unfolds concurrently with the seminar and that serves several purposes. Students can ask their questions or type their critiques without interrupting the speaker, and the instructor can use it to ask everyone the same question at the same time or to choreograph class by talking privately with students

Lectures are similar to seminars in that they have audio, video, and shared whiteboard presentation space, but they differ in occurring without students in attendance. Lectures provide an opportunity for instructors to elucidate certain points, comment on the readings, show sample solutions, or otherwise provide background and frame conversations that will take place in seminar. A typical course might have several intense but efficient lectures per week, though many will have fewer consistent with pedagogical best practices in the subject or grade level. Lectures occupy a role similar to that of texts and other static instructional resources that students consume outside of class.

In addition to seminars and lectures, students in a given course will also have interactive online resources, homework, and out-of-class readings; students will complete problem sets, write papers, conduct experiments, do group work, and make presentations—exactly what one would expect to find in any brick-and-mortar school.

The SOHS school day begins at six o'clock in the morning (Pacific time) with first period and ends at a quarter past ten at night. Because of the flipped classroom and the focus on seminars, the SOHS follows a college-style schedule with classes (seminars) meeting live only twice a week, except for languages and courses in select other subjects, which meet up to four times per week. This structure affords students remarkable flexibility of schedule to accommodate both academic and outside pursuits during the day, but also requires that students be disciplined managers of their time if they are to get all of their work done. With students in forty-three states and twenty-one countries, the sun never sets at the SOHS.

The SOHS does not schedule classes on Fridays in order to provide students with the opportunity to engage in clubs, presentations, colloquia, and assemblies within the school and to be active in their local communities. It is a busy and fruitful day.

In addition to the interaction students have online at the SOHS, they also have opportunities to meet each other face-to-face. These occur during an optional two-week residential summer session that occurs on the Stanford University campus as well as at informal, student- and parent-organized meetups.

4 Technology and the Human Element

Understanding why we explore online technology is important. Someone developing educational materials to send to a region that has none necessarily has a different perspective than someone developing materials for people who have choices. Bringing technology into contexts where students have historically had a wide variety of high quality offerings poses a particular challenge and demands a higher degree of scrutiny.

Many efforts in online education have been driven by either an impulse to democratize learning or a desire to bring free resources to the world so that those who need courses can find them. These impulses have been behind efforts as diverse as MIT's Open Course Initiative, Udacity, and the Khan Academy.

One thing that such efforts often overlook is that to the average man on the street, or person with aspirations for economic advancement, given a choice between on the one hand a head full of the learning that one acquires at MIT but no degree, and on the other hand an empty head but also the piece of paper that says he has this knowledge, the average person will choose the piece of paper every time. It is the rare individual who is willing to toil for knowledge for its own sake and not have any recognition. This is why places like MIT can give free access to their content without worrying that people will stop showing up, and why those who are giving it away for free are trying to find solutions for documenting what students have learned, whether it be by certificates or badges or credit from other institutions.

Efforts to bring courses to those who would not otherwise have access to them can arguably measure their success by the number of students they reach, viewed absolutely, as well as the number of students making it successfully through a course, again viewed absolutely. So that if one offers a course on artificial intelligence that has 150,000 students start the course and has 7,000 students finish the course, one can look at this as a grand success. No one would ever expect to have 7,000 students complete such a course, and it may be that even the other 143,000 got something more than they would have otherwise.

The advantage that universities have here over secondary schools is that a university, unlike a secondary school, does not need to explain to the parents of those 143,000 students why their sons or daughters did not successfully complete the course. The objectives of reaching large numbers and producing unusual results differ markedly from what has historically been seen as the objective of secondary education, namely to develop the talents of particular individuals.

Losing sight of one's essential objective is an easy trap to fall into. This is particularly true with educational programs offered to students but conducted in a research-university context. It is natural for students and parents to look upon such programs first and foremost as delivering something educational, and as such to assume that the organization's mission must be to educate, when in fact it is often the case that a research university's mission is to produce generalizable knowledge, and that the educational activity of the project is ancillary to this mission. While educational institutions must attend to the needs of the individual students, research projects must keep their eyes fixed on the general. This misalignment of fundamental interests has proven fatal for many a student over the years.

In the 1990s and 2000s we spent a great deal of time at Stanford building and offering individualized online courses that were highly personalized and adaptive.[2] We had in mind that every kid could be Alexander the Great working with his own personal, albeit electronic, Aristotle.[3] It was a vision that had its appeal. Learning could occur anytime, any place, and more importantly, the best students would be allowed to go running ahead of the pack, while those students needing extra time and attention could get all the attention that their available time allowed. This electronic Aristotle could lope along and steer students out of trouble.

---

[2]R. Ravaglia, P. Suppes, C. Stillinger, and T. Alper, 'Computer-based Mathematics and Physics for Gifted Students', *Gifted Child Quarterly* 39 (1995): 7–13.

[3]P. Suppes, 'The Uses of Computers in Education', *Scientific American* 215 (1966): 206-220.

The design of our early courses was one that was committed to using the computer as an intelligent agent that could assess student work and provide immediate feedback, not just looking at whether answers were correct, but using symbolic computation to allow students to enter complex expressions and to analyze answers under a set of author-specified equivalences.[4] This allowed us to ask more intricate questions, to give partial credit for responses, and even to gain some insight into student errors.[5] We coupled these self-paced lessons with an opportunity for students to interact with an instructor via phone or email in the event that they had questions that the program was unable to answer. In essence, we provided our electronic Aristotle with human teaching assistants.

That such an approach had potential was bolstered by the first offering of our AP calculus course. The initial motivation for the course was the fact that at the time, only 20-25% of the high schools in the United States offered calculus. We thought that a self-paced computer-based course would provide a cost-effective way of getting the course out to students who were ready for it but were at schools that did not have calculus, either because there was no one able to teach it, or because the school lacked a critical mass of students to take it.

When we went to test the course in the 1990-91 academic year, we found that all the students who were a convenient drive from Stanford already had calculus available to them. So instead of going further afield we shifted our focus to students in middle school or the first year or two of high school, who for whatever reason had been accelerated in their mathematics education. Obviously, middle school is not a place where one typically finds a calculus course. That year we had one seventh-grader, five eighth-graders, four ninth-graders, and three tenth-graders. All thirteen students took the Calculus AB AP exam in May 1991, with six scoring the top score of 5, six scoring 4, and one scoring 3 (where 3 is considered passing). Of particular note was that the seventh-grader and four of the five eighth-graders scored 5.

Looking at this result we thought that there was clearly a good match between these students and this course. Looking more closely at the students we determined that they were representative of the top 2–3% of the population, but nothing more extreme. We went back to

---

[4]R. Ravaglia, 'Design Issues in a Stand Alone Multimedia Computer-based Mathematics Curriculum', in *Fourth Annual Multimedia in Education and Industry* (Asheville, NC: Association for Applied Interactive Multimedia, 1995), 49-52.

[5]R. Ravaglia, T. M. Alper, M. Rozenfeld, and P. Suppes, 'Successful Pedagogical Applications of Symbolic Computation', in *Computer-Human Interaction with Symbolic Computation*, ed. Norbert Kajler (New York: Springer-Verlag, 1998), 61-87.

the National Science Foundation, which had funded the development of the initial course, and asked them to fund wider distribution, pointing to this success. They declined, and so we reinvented ourselves as a tuition-based program within Stanford University.

Over the next two years we built out courses in mathematics down to the Kindergarten level and also began work on eighteen university-level courses in mathematics and physics supported by a grant from the Alfred P. Sloan Foundation.[6] Our goal was to make it routine for the best students to begin Algebra by fourth grade and calculus in seventh or eighth grade. If they did so, and if they took one course a quarter during the academic year and two during the summer, they would be able to finish high school with an undergraduate degree in mathematics in hand and be about four courses shy of an undergraduate degree in physics. This way, when they got to university they would be ready for serious work.

We expected to see increasing numbers of students work through this sequence and had anticipated that by the year 2000 we would have a steady stream of such young Alexanders landing at universities across the United States. Needless to say, the actual result was not what we expected.

While we did have plenty of students start these courses, and while we did have some students work through the sequence, we had significant attrition at every step of the way. Fewer than half of students who began a course would ever complete it. Moreover, even students who were finishing courses and doing well were leaving the program. So while there was much beautiful about what we were doing in creating this style of asynchronous, computer-guided, self-paced course, there was clearly much that was not working for our students. Unfortunately, because we were overly focused on the underlying technology, because we thought of ourselves as a research project developing technology rather than as an instructional endeavor developing educated students, we missed what was clearly in front of us. And we were not just missing it with the students. Our instructors were also leaving at what would have been an alarming rate if not for the fact that we had a steady stream of people wanting to teach for us.

At the same time that this was going on, we had two other projects underway that were producing strikingly different results. But because neither was thought of as developing new technology, neither received much attention.

---

[6]For a history of the projects that the Sloan Foundation supported in the early days of online learning see A. F. Mayadas, R. Gomory, and W. Patrick (unpublished manuscript in production, Hudson Whitman/Excelsior College Press).

The first was our effort to teach student writing, ranging from a middle-school-level composition course through AP English Language and Composition. Because production costs to create this sort of course were high, especially to develop machine-evaluation techniques to assess student writing in the manner in which we were evaluating their mathematics, we decided instead to use real-time shared-whiteboard, desktop voice- and video-conferencing programs to create a virtual classroom in which we would conduct the courses as live seminars. We also decided that students would just write traditional essays and that we would subject them to peer and instructor review. This type of synchronous course posed a number of logistical challenges, for since it was not self-paced and not anytime, anywhere, students would actually have to come together at a particular time of day in a virtual classroom. Moreover, the instructor would need to be there as well during class, and since there was no electronic Aristotle, the instructor would have to do a great deal of work to evaluate and comment upon student writing.

In spite of these obstacles, the courses were extremely successful from the point of view of student and instructor performance. Attrition was typically below 3% and while the instructors often complained about the workload, they tended to stay in the job for years and years. So while the course was logistically more challenging, and required more work on the part of the instructors to teach and more commitment on the part of the students to attend, and while it was in no sense self-paced, it served the purpose of educating students much better.

The other example of success was the three-week residential summer program that we were running. This was a program, similar to those found at many colleges across the country, in which academically able and curious students come on campus, live in the dorms, and pursue intensive study of subjects not typically offered to younger students. For students who participate in such programs, the effect can be life changing. In our own programs the median overall program satisfaction rating hovered between 4.6 and 4.7 out of 5. The single most common comment one would see in evaluations was 'This was the best experience of my life.'

What was also interesting was that the ratings and the comments tended to be the same regardless of the age of the student or the subject that was being studied. This success was not due to the effect of a particular instructor or a particular course. What made the program work was the fact that what these students really wanted was to come together with peers who shared their interests and their passions and to have the chance to work with instructors who also shared these passions and whom the students saw as later-stage versions of themselves.

Could it be that students did not want or need an electronic Aristotle after all? Could it be that what they really wanted was to be in the Agora with Socrates *and each other?*

5 'Anytime, Anywhere' Often Means 'Never'

In developing the SOHS we settled on a blended, flipped-classroom approach to teaching in which asynchronous and synchronous components were combined to provide students with a model of education that takes as its centerpiece the real-time virtual seminar (think 'online Harkness table') and blends it with asynchronous lectures and interactive course materials. In our discussion, two important dimensions for comparison are whether the course is synchronous (i.e. occurring in real-time) or asynchronous, and the degree to which the course is interactive. Rather than give formal definitions for what are at times fuzzy concepts, we will just give four quick examples to illustrate the differences:

Large lecture class in auditorium—synchronous and non-interactive

Lecture class on video—asynchronous and non-interactive

Small seminar class—synchronous and interactive

Self-paced adaptive online course—asynchronous and interactive

The large lecture class and the small seminar are both synchronous because they are happening live and the students are there at the moment of creation. A recorded lecture, a recorded seminar, or an adaptive self-paced online course are all asynchronous in that they are being consumed by students after the fact. As for interactivity, it comes down to whether the experience of the student participating in the event can be altered substantially by the behavior of the student. In a large lecture class, anyone can fall asleep and generally not be noticed. In a seminar, online or offline, it will be noticed and a piece of chalk, virtual or real, may be delivered. If a student has a question during a non-interactive event such as a lecture, she may need to write it down and ask it during office hours, or submit it online to the crowd and await a response through an alternative channel such as a text chat, while during a seminar a student can just interrupt whoever is talking and ask her question.

Asynchronous courses are typically touted as enabling 'anytime, anywhere' learning. Since the student is not there at the moment of production, the moment of consumption can be any time. And similarly since the course is online the student could be taking it from anywhere. Most asynchronous courses are developed around some model of self-pacing or adaptability. Students are expected to watch lectures, do readings, do exercises, and have those exercises evaluated. In some cases the evaluation will be by humans, in some cases it will be by machine. In some cases the results of evaluation will cause dynamic branching of the course, in others it will just cause branching of the student's grade. Some courses are designed to provide students with an immersive world that they can explore and discover, others are driven by a model of student understanding that ensures that exposure to new ideas occurs at optimal moments. While a discussion of the taxonomy of online courses would be interesting, it is one that we leave for elsewhere.

Most asynchronous courses make one fatal assumption that seems obvious to course designers but laughable to students, namely that a necessary condition of 'being in a course' is 'doing all of the work assigned for the course'. Asynchronous courses are relentless in this way, in that the only way one is able to demonstrate that one is actively working in a course is by actively working in the course. This is very different than the way that one demonstrates that one is in a course in the traditional academic world. There, being in a course is all about showing up when the course meets. Sometimes one shows up not having done the work or having read the book and so one needs to bluff one's way through the particular class session, but on those occasions what matters most is that one shows up, engages, and keeps at it. This is not a defect of traditional instruction, as it is often identified in discussions of the comparative benefits of online learning, but is instead both an important life skill that students must learn and an inescapable truth about how students work.

With a purely asynchronous course, students run the constant risk of falling into bad faith from having set it aside for too long. Perhaps a student is swamped in other courses, or other school commitments interfere with getting work done in this course. After a week or so they might get an email from the course or from the instructor checking up. But inevitably in such cases, students find themselves in a dysfunctional relationship with the course. Anyone who has ever stopped playing a musical instrument will have experienced this pattern. Rather than going at it thirty minutes a day every day, one starts practicing only in marathon bursts the day before, or of, the lesson, trying to cram a week into a morning. Next comes a week or two in which lessons are missed and before long it has been a while since a lesson occurred. Picking up the instrument again becomes harder and harder as time passes until finally one pushes it into the back of one's mind and it becomes forgotten.

In a synchronous course this does not easily happen. If a student fails to come to class, his absence is noticed. His friends reach out to him and say 'Hey man, where were you?' Moreover, seeing friends and being in the class pulls him in even if he has not done his work. Maybe he saves the work up and does it over a long weekend, or maybe for certain things he never does the work. But he makes his way through the class and finishes it.

This is not the only positive reinforcement going on in the synchronous environment that is lacking in the asynchronous one. Students working alone in an asynchronous class are deprived of the experience of showing off how clever they are, which while it may seem trivial can serve as a great motivator for students. Take this away and class is suddenly less compelling. Indeed the complete absence of a social-emotional dimension in most online learning is a tremendous defect.

The same holds true for teachers. In our asynchronous model for courses, the electronic Aristotle was responsible for the bulk of the instruction. The human instructors would intervene only when students were having difficulties that went beyond what the computer was capable of addressing. While efficient, it served to deprive the teachers of the joy of working with students who were doing well. Few people become teachers only to work with students who are failing. Contrast this with the synchronous class where the teachers see all the students and have plenty of opportunity to work with students across the success spectrum.

Another factor pertaining to instructor attrition is rooted in the apparent efficiency of anytime, anywhere instruction. Due to the nature of supporting an asynchronous course, the teachers had significant control over their days. They would develop stock responses to common email questions received and make their jobs more and more efficient until inevitably they would lose interest and quit. While people would begin with a lot of enthusiasm, the enthusiasm would wane as they realized that they were basically reducing the job to teaching by algorithm.

This was in stark contrast to the experiences of both online instructors in synchronous courses and instructors in the residential summer program. In both of these cases, even though a great deal more work was required on the part of the instructors, and in the case of the online courses there were greater logistical challenges as well, the instructors did not suffer from the burnout of those in the asynchronous courses, but instead kept working year after year.

When we sat down to design the SOHS, we began to take a serious look at these factors, and realized that there is something fundamentally unsatisfying about being the teaching assistant for the electronic Aristotle. Moreover, there is something fundamentally unsatisfying about being his student. Again our thoughts returned to Socrates in the Agora.

What is compelling is getting the right teachers and the right students together and getting out of their way. What the technology needs to be about is making this happen. This is not to say that one cannot make wonderful use of adaptive analytics to personalize the process of working through textbooks or for making the asynchronous components of learning more efficient and engaging. Rather, it means only that in taking the broader course perspective, one needs to keep in mind that what students need to get from their courses is different from what authors tend to think about putting in. This is the difference between a good teacher and a good textbook author.

Now this is not surprising when one thinks about it. One can easily imagine a student saying 'The Stanford Online High School—it is fabulous. The teachers are so smart. The other kids are so interesting. The technology, ah, it falls down sometimes but overall the school is great.' One cannot so easily imagine someone saying 'The teachers are not as good as those at my old school, the other students are sort of boring, but the immersive video conferencing technology is so wonderful, you just have to be in this school.'

In education the human element dominates. This point can be made as well in the context of textbooks. The effort to create our electronic Aristotle was akin to developing a perfect textbook. But even the best textbook is not an antidote for having a poor teacher. The textbook is perhaps 20% of the effect. To appreciate this point, consider how a great teacher can do an excellent job even with a poor text. In fact, such a teacher can use a poor textbook to illustrate a variety of points by getting metacritical about how textbooks are written, the right attitude to have to secondary sources, and so forth. On the other hand, even a great textbook is not going to redeem a poor instructor.

In approaching online learning, one needs first and foremost to get the learning right. It is the 'schoolness' that is essential and not the 'onlineness'. It is the educated student that should be the end result of the process and not just facility with the tools that are purportedly being used to educate the students.

6 A Course is More than its Content

As we began to look more critically at the role technology properly played in delivering our courses, we also began to think more critically about what we were calling courses and what we were trying to accomplish in moving from being a university-based program offering courses in certain subjects to talented students, to being a school.

Much of the current conversation about online learning takes a very content-centric view of courses and learning. Courses are equated with their content, the management of courses and instruction of courses is equated with managing content and vectoring students through knowledge states, and the instructional process is often thought of as a process that moves the content knowledge from the course into the heads of the students.

That this view would be propounded is no surprise. Firstly, the textbook publishers naturally have a very content-centric view of teaching and learning, for after all, their business is one steeped in the creation and distribution of content. This view is furthered by university faculty who see online course production as a natural extension of textbook authorship, and who see online courses as their avenue to teaching significantly more students. It is certainly more gratifying professionally to think of this effort as being one of teaching, rather than as a mere extension of textbook authorship.

Software publishers and online learning companies tend to further this view as well with a focus on things like content management systems and learning management systems; that the two phrases are often used interchangeably underscores this perception that content and learning are the same thing.

If one looks at the recent trends in large-scale course development, the fact that these efforts grow out of engineering and computer science departments should come as no surprise, for in these disciplines there has long been a healthy need for graduates to refresh their understanding of content in their rapidly advancing fields. Engineering schools have been pioneers in the field of technology-driven professional development since the 1950s with such activities as Stanford Instructional Television Network beaming classes to Hewlett Packard via microwave,[7] and success in MOOCs correlates with already having a degree and having specific content needs.[8]

However, this view is fundamentally limited in its applicability to K-12 students. Content knowledge is only a small piece of what we expect our students to take away from their education. It has long been a favorite line about education that 'an education is what remains when we have forgotten everything we have learned'. That this has

[7]A. Dipaolo, 'The Stanford Instructional Television Network: A Partnership with Industry', *European Journal of Engineering Education* 20, no. 2 (1995): 243-246, doi:10.1080/0304379950200217.

[8]E. J. Emanuel, 'Online Education: MOOCs Taken by Educated Few', *Nature* 503 (2013): 342, doi:10.1038/503342a.

a certain resonance suggests that there is clearly something more at stake in learning than content knowledge. Indeed, the incompleteness of the content-centric view has significant implications for how we should approach online learning.

While content knowledge may be readily obtained online by working through standard courses in the same way that one can read through a textbook on one's own, less well established is how one engenders the ways of thinking and habits of mind that are the hallmarks of the well-educated individual. This is something that the best schools do well, and that shows in their graduates. And it clearly involves teaching them how to think and how to learn and not just facts about the world. The fact that most universities have residency requirements above unit requirements for graduation is rooted in the belief that if they are going to put their stamp on a student as being 'a Harvard man' they want to make sure that the student has had the Harvard experience, and has the skills and requisite behaviors associated therewith, and not just that the student knows as much as the typical Harvard graduate.

We would argue that this type of knowledge is best acquired in the intimate seminar settings in which students work closely with instructors—exactly the type of approach to education that independent schools have historically prided themselves on, and that has been the canonical example of excellent education since Socrates sat around the Agora or Plato ran his academy. This is not to say that individual instruction does not have a place—there are times and places where the best way for students to learn is to work individually with an instructor. But this is an unforgiving sort of learning, and often what works best is being around other students, not just for the underlying learning, but for the motivation of the students as well. As noted above, when one is always in the spotlight, one must always be ready to be in the spotlight, and this is simply something that even the best students are not always ready for. Moreover, there are certain things, collaboration, argumentation, and conflict resolution, to name a few, that students learn best from each other.

6.1 Content Centrism and MOOCs

Since late 2011 a significant amount of attention has been paid to the rise of the Massive Open Online Course (MOOC) and the potential that such courses have for disrupting education as we have known it. While we will steer clear of this discussion for the most part, the phenomenon provides an opportunity to illustrate some important points.

The first is that the decision to call these things courses was a stroke of marketing genius. For if we look at what is there, one has the content, wrapped up with a certain amount of social media, but lacks the context and the live interaction with instructors and peers in a collaborative effort that is characteristic of a course. They are much more textbooks than courses. But had they called themselves textbooks 2.0 or textbooks with lectures and social media, or any number of things that are more descriptive of what they actually are, they would not seem so exciting.[9]

A course is content, plus context, plus the record surrounding the endeavor that one has engaged in while traversing the course. A course properly provides exposure to content along with the opportunity to engage with others around the communal experience of learning the content. It provides the opportunity for students to become excited, engaged, and to develop relationships. Ideally too a course provides an expert who guides one through the process and who helps to light the fire. In this way we can think of hell as a course for Dante, since he has Virgil to walk him through it and answer his questions about it. Without Virgil, all Dante would have had is hell. The same can be said of many traversing MOOCs on their own.

Now to be fair, many MOOCs are better for the most part than textbooks—or certainly have the potential to be—but they are nowhere near what one thinks of when one thinks of good education. They are, however, fine exemplars of the content-centric view of learning. And any course designed primarily around its content, and not around the reality of student engagement as an essential driver of learning, is doomed to being inadequate.

Two other points about the content-centric view of learning merit brief mention.

The first is that equating content-knowledge acquisition with learning has the distinct advantage of making learning easy to measure. If one knows what one wants a student to learn, any number of summative assessments can be used to determine whether or not the student has learned it. This becomes increasingly important as efforts are made to scale learning and the instructional context becomes one where the instructor is no longer paying attention to her individual students. In such contexts, unless there is something to measure, there can be no hope of quality control. Moreover, without something to measure, one will have a much harder time conducting meaningful research into the activity.

[9] And perhaps had they been called 'Massive Open Online Texts', or 'MOOTs', they would not have generated such buzz.

The second point worth noting is that our model of small seminar instruction is common in two sets of institutions that have long been heralded as bastions of good instruction and good education: independent schools and small liberal arts colleges. This bears notice because the professors who have been driving the development of MOOCs have generally not been coming from contexts renowned for the quality of their teaching but from large research universities where teaching quality is not revered in quite the same way.

6.2 Flipped Classroom 2.0

In the current talk of online learning a lot of attention has been paid to the flipped classroom and the potential that it affords for making class time more productive by moving lectures—fundamentally a passive, receptive form of encountering a subject—outside of the classroom. Lecturing, as commonly practiced is more akin to supervised reading, and as such is something that can be best done by students on their own before coming to class. In an online course, synchronous time is precious and should not be squandered; forcing students to sit in a room listening to a presentation that while perhaps adequate for everyone has been optimized for no one is not the most productive use of time. This is not to say that there is no value to seeing a lecture live or in a community. After all there are significant differences between watching something by yourself on DVD and seeing it with a group in a movie theater, or even seeing a live production of a play. In each case what one is getting is somewhat different, and a teacher who is attuned to her students, even if lecturing, can deliver something distinctive and of value if she is willing to go off script and adapt to what the class needs.

All this said, when one is bringing students together in a live, online environment, one needs to recognize that seminar time should be used in a way that makes appropriate use of the live, dynamic quality of it. If an instructor is just giving a monologue to set the stage for discussion, that monologue should have been given ahead of time. Here is the value of the flipped classroom.

Now the notion of flipping the classroom can often cause anxiety among the faculty. One hears stories of how instructors feel threatened by the process, even going so far as to speculate that no one would come to class if students could see the lecture at home ahead of time.

It is important to keep in mind that the first great flipping event occurred with the advent of the printing press. Prior to printing, lectures were literally that: a professor would read to his students from his manuscript and the students would frantically take notes. One can easily imagine professors in the middle ages sitting around the faculty lounge decrying how this new invention of printing would spell the end of the university. 'Why would anyone come to class if they can just read the book?' Of course printing did not spell the end of the university—in fact the number of universities exploded with the advent of printing.[10] What it did do was shed light on the difference between the dissemination of texts and the dissemination of knowledge. Or rather, it shows that having access to textbooks, while perhaps a necessary condition for education (and one correlated with the flourishing of universities), was not a sufficient one.

7 Good Instruction Attends to Process, not Just Outcomes

This discussion of the limitations of the content-centric approach leads us to a key point that must be stressed and which poses a significant challenge to asynchronous courses, namely that good instruction pays attention to the process of students' learning and not just to outcomes.

Consider two examples to motivate this point. Suppose someone, say Jeff, decides that he really wants to improve his golf game. One way he might do this would be to sign up for an online golf course. Such a course might show videos of Tiger Woods swinging the club and then ask Jeff to repeat what he had seen. It might even be a course that is designed to take input from external examination and individualize instruction based on the result. So Jeff might take his tablet or phone down to the driving range and hit some balls, input where they land, and then the program would suggest adjustments, after which Jeff would hit additional balls, working toward improving his score. In this way Jeff might actually gain some insight into golf and improve his game.

Contrast this with the experience of taking lessons from a golf pro. The pro might take Jeff out to the driving range and ask him to hit a few balls. The pro will likely be less interested in where the balls are landing than in how Jeff is holding the club, the mechanics of his swing, and the overall process of hitting the ball. And after watching a few tries the pro might step in and make some adjustments.

In the former case, the attention is being paid to the outcome, and the system uses statistical methods and general theories to suggest particular changes. In the latter, the teacher attends to the process involved and evaluates it knowing ultimately that if the right process is established, the desired outcomes will follow.

---

[10] J. Etchemendy, 'Online Education' (presentation to Stanford Board of Trustees, February 7, 2012).

Taking a more academic example, anyone who has ever taught a mathematics course has had the experience of a student coming into to office hours, confused about some exercise. And often the confusion is so great that the student has trouble even articulating a question. The thing to do is to send the student to the board to write out the problem and start the solution. And often just by seeing how he writes the problem, and how he stops and starts when working, one can immediately grasp what the confusion is.

In mathematics courses we ask students to show their work so that we can gain insight into the process. An important part of any serious instruction is attending to the details of process. This is something that is very difficult to tease out sending emails back and forth to a student, but is very natural to do in a synchronous, shared-whiteboard environment.

The most impactful forms of teaching are not just about preparing students for post-course evaluations, but actually teaching them something, and seeing them actually learn it, by watching the process of learning unfold and shaping it as needed.

In looking at how online courses are designed, we frequently see the technology driving the pedagogy. So courses are designed around what is easy to do on the computer rather than what is the best way to teach students. This is not to say that there are not interesting things we can do with technology that are not possible in a traditional class, nor to say that those things should not be done. It is only to say that we really need to think through what we are doing, and that we should not let the tools we have to get it done change our goals or objectives about how we want to teach.

To be fair, this is not a limitation inherent in asynchronous courses. It is a limitation that is also present in any type of mass instructional effort. Once one gets to the point where it is no longer feasible to attend to the needs of particular students, the temptation becomes to not pay attention to any student during the teaching process, but to instead regularly assess the results of the teaching activity and to make adjustments accordingly. This is inevitable in the move from bespoke to factory production, where one cannot attend to process per se but must instead resort to statistical sampling of the process to determine whether the success or failure is within acceptable limits.

While this move may be inevitable, it is not ideal. It is a strategy that comes with a decision that the process is out of reach. But how can we pay attention to the details? In building our school we have taken a road that relies on human expertise and student engagement and a fundamental faith in the capability of both. This is not to say that technology has no role in an online school. Rather the technology needs to be subordinated, kept as a tool used to accomplish particular objectives. The technology cannot take the place of the teaching or the learning; it should take the place of the facilities. The place instructional technology has the most promise is in providing the space in which students are working and mechanisms for students and the instructors to keep tabs on what they are doing, providing additional resources when necessary, and for making sure that the balls are not dropped and that the promissory notes can be cashed.

8 The Right Conditions for a School to Emerge

In designing the SOHS we kept the image of Socrates and his students in the Agora firmly in mind. We knew that community would be important, but we did not know what shape that community would take, nor did we dictate to students how they should act. We believed that if we could provide an environment that supported authentic interaction among students, and provided them with the right curriculum and the right instructors, the community would emerge naturally. The only unknown was whether the environment we had would be rich enough to allow the community to flourish.

We knew from our experience with residential summer programs how such communities emerge when students are in the right environment. As students arrive, move into rooms, start talking with roommates and counselors, and realize that everyone is as smart and accomplished as they are, they rapidly discover the common bonds that brought them there, become familiar with each other, and form enduring friendships.

In the case of the SOHS, we wanted to ensure that students had the right assortment of semi-structured experiences so that they could discover each other in this same way. We were committed from the inception to all students having video in the online seminars so that they could see each other during class and realize that they were not working in isolation, nor surrounded by bots lurking in some simulation of a classroom, but that they were in a class consisting of actual embodied other selves who just happened to be in different locations. Also important was providing students with an understanding that the space inside the classroom was but a part of the broader space of the school. This was accomplished in two ways. The first was providing students with access to the classrooms before and after class so that they might engage each other in the less formal interaction that occurs in those contexts. The other was to use the same environment as the basis for clubs and extracurricular activities. Our hope was that by providing opportunities for students to learn facts about each other outside of class, we would be providing them with opportunity to discover common bonds.

The final factor driving the emergence of the community was the commonality of need and desire. These were all students who wanted to be there and who were willing to brave the unknown to challenge themselves. The initial meetings of SOHS classes were for many of these students the first time they had ever been surrounded by other students who were like themselves, and with whom they could be authentically themselves.

This is not to say that the students were friendless loners before they came to the school. Many came to this school because they did not want to sacrifice local social bonds that they cherished. Rather, they were students driven by the common vision of what education could be. Nor is this to say that all students showed up with a perfect understanding of what it would be like to be a student in the SOHS. While many had taken online courses before, few had experience with this type of synchronous model. We were pleasantly surprised when we saw how quickly they adapted to the model and how readily they made the conceptual shift to thinking of themselves as being in a classroom rather than being on their computers. These were tendencies we noticed in our first class of students and which we have continued to observe in the subsequent groups.

As the structure for the school emerged and observers saw that we were succeeding in educating our students, and that we were doing so not just to our own satisfaction but to that of accrediting bodies and college admissions officers, we saw the number of applications to the SOHS rise dramatically. With this also came rising expectations from the students and their families.

In the first year of the SOHS we knew that for our students we were the last best hope. The students who immediately flocked to us were those who had already exhausted the alternatives and who were desperate for an academically rigorous high school that could accommodate students of high ability. In conversations with parents that first year, it was clear that they were so happy with the academic program they had found that they were willing to endure the Spartan nature of the school, not to mention the occasional day of outage due to technical problems—we called these 'snow days'—in order to receive what we were offering.

With success, however, we began increasingly to draw students who were selecting us from a menu of viable alternatives, rather than turning to us out of necessity. And increasingly, it was the schoolness that was helping to draw them. With this change came expectations that in addition to a first-rate academic program we should also be offering the broader range of services and opportunities that academically minded independent schools afford their students.

This transition led to some scrambling on our part to anticipate what those services were and to think about how we might implement them online. Over time, we developed teams for college counseling, academic advising, and counseling and psychological services, as well as an office of student life tasked with the mission of thinking ever more seriously about extracurricular and cocurricular components of the school, as well as issues like service learning and social-emotional learning.

What has been important throughout this process is that the growth and the success of the school has more often been driven by attending to the schoolness, first and foremost, and the onlineness only secondarily. The steadfast refusal to compromise standards and sacrifice quality has enabled us to approach challenges from a different perspective than many other online-learning endeavors. Often the design and execution of online courses reminds one of the old joke of a man searching for his lost contact lens under the streetlight rather than in the alley where he lost it, because the light is better there. Having spent almost fifteen years looking where the light was good, we decided instead to refocus on the more difficult task of solving the problem we were handed, the one driven by the needs of our students, and not the one we wished to solve. And while it has often been frustrating, it has been worthwhile, and the success of our graduates is testament to the emergence of the school.

9 Summing it Up

In creating the Stanford Online High School we had in mind a diverse set of students whose needs and desires placed them outside the boundaries of where good traditional solutions were possible. These included rural students, younger, gifted students, students who had been homeschooled, students overseas, students living in multiple locations, or students whose passions required that they devote significant amounts of time during the day to external pursuits. We wanted to provide these students with options and flexibility so that they did not have to sacrifice their education just because of their circumstances or radically uproot their lives just to get the education that they deserved. We wanted to see if it would be possible, in a technology-mediated environment, to provide a quality of education and level of engagement typically seen only in the best schools in the world. We knew that doing this would be a matter of getting the curriculum right and finding the right students and instructors. We knew we needed to use technology to get this done, but we knew from our long experience developing such courses that we needed to take a different approach, and that ultimately the school would be about its students and not about the technology.

We knew that the first students who would come would be those who had no other comparable solution, and who would be patient with us as we built up services around the core academic program. In fact, in the first year of the school people did not even care if we were accredited. We also knew that as the school grew, and our students started having good results, people would come to us earlier in their decision process, and in doing so they would come with higher expectations for the nonacademic components of the school, and that if we were to remain viable we would need to surpass those expectations.

When we first created the Stanford Online High School we used to joke that our goal was someday to have students say 'Phillips Academy, yeah, that would be great, but where I really want to go is the Stanford Online High School.' The goal was not just to be the best online school—an uninterestingly low bar—but to be among the best schools of any kind, with the onlineness being a fact of the school, but no different than the way that for Phillips Academy being located in Northern Massachusetts is a fact. It was thus fitting that eight years after our founding we would find ourselves addressing the assembled trustees of Phillips Academy to talk about online learning. After telling them this story for almost an hour, we showed them an eight-minute film about the Stanford OHS that was made during the 2012 graduation. As the film ended, we turned to the trustees and said 'More than anything this film shows that you can use this style of instruction to produce among students the level of engagement and community that defines an institution like Phillips Academy.' And when we said it, we saw in their faces that they knew that it was true.[11]

[11]'Trustees Convene for Winter Meetings: Teaching—both high-talent and high-tech—was a centerpiece of the winter trustees meeting', Andover Phillips Academy Newsroom, February 13, 2014, https://www.andover.edu/About/Newsroom/Pages/Trustees-Convene-for-Winter-Meetings.aspx.

2

People

1 A School is not its Bricks and Mortar

Rarely does the bare fact that a student is enrolled at a school say as much about the student as it does at the Stanford Online High School. Many schools, of course, are highly selective, such that a student's acceptance indicates a high level of achievement and ability. More independent schools still are expensive, or are subject to other demographic constraints that tell stories about students' unchosen characteristics. While the SOHS is indeed an independent school that relies on tuition, and while its academic program is designed for talented students, it is a school of choice to a unique degree. And the choice it represents speaks to deep and compelling features of students' character, creativity, and priorities. SOHS students have sought out an encompassing intellectual challenge in a context—middle school and high school—where it is the overwhelming convention to take what one is given. This challenge is not just one of academically difficult material: it is strenuous to the verge of being all consuming, requiring dedication and sustained commitment. But it is not just the challenge, of course, that makes the choices of SOHS students so notable. These students have pursued this challenge in the face of what most would see as obstacles; online education is never easy when it is done in a meaningful way, and life at SOHS involves social challenges, technical hurdles, and a complex deviation from familiar norms and routines. And nothing about such a school is 'safe': it is a new school; it is a school at which academic success cannot be assumed in the face of difficult courses, high expectations, and universally talented peers; and it represents a model of education whose nuances even the most informed candidate cannot wholly anticipate. SOHS students, especially those who are fully committed and for their entire careers, have to really want the challenge and the opportunities that the school presents.

A unique process of self-selection, then, does much of the work in assembling at the school a population of students who are equipped and disposed to drive a vibrant academic program and intellectual community. And the character of the student population, and of the teachers and administrative staff as well, is of special importance to the school. As we will argue in characterizing each aspect of the school, the medium and technology of the school are not its essential qualities. However much it is true that the school would not be possible without this technology, it is the mission, curriculum, and community of the SOHS that make it worthwhile. And essential to each of these features of the school are the people whose goals, abilities, and commitment animate it.

When the school works best, when it fosters educational opportunities that are simply hard to find elsewhere, it does so through the collaborative work of the unique members of the school community. In its pairing of teachers and students, SOHS excels at challenging extremely talented students and at inspiring them to achievement through that challenge. The type of student who goes on to work with distinction as an undergraduate at Stanford, the type of student who had always gotten As on papers without much comment, embraces the critical feedback he gets from teachers who can evaluate his work by standards more common for advanced undergraduates. Similarly, the type of student who is always trying to excel, who is looking for sustained, serious criticism of her work, not with an eye toward raising it to 'A' standards, but to making it the best that it can be, once having received this level of attention, cannot imagine going back to lower standards. Close relationships between students and teachers can also point to new opportunities, both for the students and for the teachers, and sometimes shape the school in return. This has been seen in the case of one student, who entered the school as a self-identified humanities specialist. The mentorship of an AP Biology teacher ignited a passion for biology that led him to spearhead the student initiative for a new post-AP biology course and has continued into his undergraduate study and work in a college lab. And on more than one occasion, a student will fall in love with the humanities or Philosophy Core in a way that will shape her college and professional career.

In its diverse, passionate community, SOHS also fosters a dynamic intellectual environment. It is a school where debates about politics spill outside the classroom and return again, much transformed; where students relish making connections in courses across disciplines (everyone knows about panopticism, and that it is relevant to nearly everything); and where Nobel laureates, professors, entrepreneurs, and writers speak to students about their work and careers, some of them at the invitation of enterprising students and student clubs. And drawing on its singular geographic and cultural diversity, the school fosters a rare community of perspectives. In discussion with students who are the products of schools and academic programs around the world, students and teachers profit on a daily basis from the different strategies, curricula, and traditions each student brings with her. Students experience international events and discussions about core values as they are seen through peers encountering those ideas in a different context: they know about the real impact of Hurricane Sandy or Typhoon Haiyan because their friends were flooded or threatened, and they have unique access to fundamentally different traditions and politics surrounding concepts like the rule of law through the testimony of a student in China discussing how that elusive value is conceived there. And, perhaps most powerfully, SOHS students learn to draw on and adjudicate those divergent perspectives in truly cosmopolitan collaboration, as did the students charged with creating the student government's constitution. Convening from England, South Korea, Hong Kong, Canada, Maryland, and California, these students considered adaptations of comparative mechanisms for controls on tyranny to draft a creative (if not always transparent) system that has shaped the school culture for their successors. When students say of such situations, as they often do, 'Only at OHS', they are usually pointing to the results of the school's rare collection of talents, experiences, interests, backgrounds, and perspectives.[1]

If the people of the SOHS are ultimately what make it a special, successful school, then an account of the school should begin with them. Who are the members of the SOHS community, and how do their qualities underpin the distinctive features of the school? Why, and in what capacity, are these students and teachers drawn to the school? And has the development of the school affected the constitution of the school community; in turn, how have changes in the community's composition affected the school's own development?

2 Students

Upon revealing where they go to school, students at the Stanford Online High School are frequently met with some degree of incredulity: 'You go to school online?' Now, the explosion of online learning, with particular prominence at the college level, has removed some of the incomprehension about the concept of online schooling. But the notion

[1]While we refer to the school throughout by its full name and the attendant acronym, students and teachers often speak of it internally as the 'OHS'. We have preserved the expression in quoted comments.

that a real high school student—a good student—would choose to attend an online *school*, not just take a couple of asynchronous courses on the side, remains an imaginative hurdle to many. It is not the premise of the school, of course, that such a choice is the right one for all students, or even for certain students at all times. So in considering the impact of the SOHS on its students, the nature of the school's curriculum and pedagogy, and the broader lessons of the school's experience to online, gifted, and traditional education, a nuanced picture of these students is vital.

2.1 Who the SOHS Students Are

The SOHS is a little more than midway in its journey to the effective size of a standard independent school. In our eighth year, we have 533 students at the school, a far cry from the 30 students present on the first day of school in 2006. In the 2013-14 academic year, 47% percent of students are female, and 53% are male, a slight skewing from numbers in the general population that has been in evidence since the beginning of the school, though the disparity has shrunk somewhat over time.[2] But this is about the point at which the school's enrollment ceases to be ordinary in any way. Of those 533 students, about 44% are enrolled at the school on a full-time basis, meaning that they take at least four courses at the school and will most likely receive an SOHS diploma. Meanwhile, 18% of students take two to three courses at the school, and are considered part-time students who are in many cases currently pursuing diplomas at different schools. Many more students—38%—are taking only a single course at the school, using it primarily to supplement their work at a local school of record. (As we will discuss below, the balance of these types of enrollment has fluctuated over the life of the school. See Figure 2.3.) Given these different types of enrollment, the effective size of the school can also be usefully assessed for many purposes in terms of 'full-time equivalences' (FTE), a measure which better captures the number of classes being taken. In a typical school composed primarily of full-time students, the course enrollments of the SOHS would represent about 335 full-time students, some ways shy of a rough eventual target of 600 FTE.

If the mix of enrollment levels is an uncommon feature of the school composition, the geographic diversity one might expect from an online school is also striking. SOHS students live in 43 states and 21 countries.

[2]This skewing is in line with that at the University. See K. Sullivan, 'Stanford Welcomes Class of 2016 and Incoming Transfer Students', Stanford News, September 17, 2012, http://news.stanford.edu/news/2012/september/new-student-orientation-091712.html.

TABLE 2.1 Student location by state and country, 2013–14

State	Students
CA	168
TX	38
NY	22
IL, NJ	17
WA	15
CO	14
FL, MI, NC, OR	12
VA	11
CT	10
AK, TN	9
MD	8
MA, MN, SC	7
PA	6
IN, ME, NV, OH, WI	5
AZ, GA	4
LA, MO, UT	3
AL, NH, RI	2
AR, DE, HI, IA, KY, MT, NE, NM, OK, VT	1

Country	Students
Sweden	10
Canada	9
China	7
United Kingdom	6
India	5
Japan, Mexico, South Korea, UAE	3
Singapore	2
Australia, Brazil, Denmark, Ecuador, France, Indonesia, Ireland, Malaysia, Portugal, Taiwan, Saint Kitts and Nevis	1

International students constitute 11% of the student body, though given the advanced level of courses, most of these students are expatriates or have other intensive English-language backgrounds. Some regional influence is manifest, with 32% of students hailing from California and another 7% from the far west. (Stanford University's own regional draw from California is 38%.)[3] Students from the Mid-Atlantic constitute the next largest demographic group, at 14% of the student population. Texas (38 students), Illinois (17), Colorado (14), and Florida (12) are also well represented at the school. These numbers reflect a geographic diversity comparable to that of national research universities and that is rare among independent schools. To be sure, the fact that the school does not have to displace these students in order to achieve this diversity is significant. But as we will stress, the embeddedness of students in their local communities throughout their careers at the SOHS also

[3]Sullivan, 'Stanford Welcomes Class of 2016'.

importantly shapes the impact of geographic diversity on the life of the intellectual and social community at the school.

A school with a rigorous academic program designed for academically talented students will also attract a student population with a unique testing profile. SOHS does not, as part of its curriculum, emphasize extensive standardized testing or standardized national curriculum in the form of the AP courses and exams. In addition, collection of data for students who are not graduating from our school is a manual and voluntary process. Nonetheless, our graduating students' scores are consistently exceptional. Graduates in 2012-13 passed 99% of their AP exams, with scores of 4 or 5 on 89% of their exams. The same graduating seniors had mean combined scores on the SAT of 2218, including 763 in critical reading, 728 in math, and 726 in writing. It is a high mark of achievement that the mean exiting student at SOHS shares a testing profile with admits from top colleges, including Stanford (730 in critical reading, 745 in math, 740 in writing, 2215 combined).[4] Certainly it is not the case that all of these students will be admitted to a school like Stanford; admission processes among such schools draw on characteristics far beyond test scores and reflect internal considerations of composition. However, these numbers do suggest that once admitted, the average SOHS graduate would be at home in classrooms at a university like Stanford. And while our own admissions data remain too variable to give an objectively quantifiable characterization of our own entering students, these exiting-student data give a good sense of the capabilities of the general student body.

Construed more qualitatively by their projects and accomplishments, SOHS students are equally distinctive. In sports and the arts, they exhibit the diversity to be expected from students who have carefully chosen their school environment, participating in a range of standard and eclectic sports from archery, badminton, and baseball, to equestrian, fencing, skiing, track, and water polo. SOHS students perform in theater, dance, in bands, and in voice, while also engaging in visual media like photography, filmmaking, drawing, painting, and sewing. Outside the classroom, students volunteer at hospitals, libraries, museums, and outdoor education programs; they tutor and mentor, participate in youth groups and social campaigns; they pursue research, train for mathematical and science contests, and de-

---

[4] M. Rosenberg, 'The 25 Colleges with the Highest SAT Scores', *Business Insider*, April 1, 2013, http://www.businessinsider.com/colleges-with-the-highest-sat-scores-2013-4#8-stanford-university-tie-18. Sullivan, 'Stanford Welcomes Class of 2016', gives median scores of 730 for critical reading, 740 for math, and 740 for writing.

sign robots; and they debate, cook, juggle, game, and play competitive chess and scrabble.

But while the diversity of activities speaks to a healthy, active, and balanced student body, what is perhaps most indicative of the nature of the intellectual environment at the school is the intensity and accomplishment with which students engage in these activities. SOHS pianists have won competitions at Carnegie Hall and been recognized as National YoungArts Foundation Winners. The gaming enthusiast writes the *Minecraft for Dummies* book, in eighth grade. Participating in a science fair can mean winning the BioGENEius Challenge or being named 'America's Top Young Scientist' by Discovery Education and 3M. There is no school football team, but a fencer is on the United States Development Team for the 2016 Olympics, and several of the ballerinas dance professionally. Scientific research is done in university and museum labs, is published, and occasionally eventuates in patents. And the programmers write top-selling iPhone student-organization apps and get invited to the Apple Worldwide Developers Conference. Early accomplishment, of course, is not the measure of an education. For many students, accomplishment and recognition outside of the classroom might come later, in the application of their hard work and talent to careers and projects. But all of our students work in an environment in which a grade or a score is at most a tool for something else; the school supports and encourages students to engage in the world in the course of their education. And there is, inevitably, a high bar for achievement. SOHS students encounter early the sort of attainment they will find among their peers in elite colleges and in their careers.

2.2 Why They Come to SOHS

In the founding vision of the school, the SOHS serves as a school solution to gifted students with a particular need that local schools are not positioned to meet. Prospectively, such students were anticipated to include those doing advanced math or science not offered at their local schools, but also students in search of more than a single course: students in rural areas with limited access to rigorous or advanced programs, students looking for a *school* that allows flexibility for advanced work and acceleration, current or former homeschool students with particular curricular needs in an accredited setting, expatriates seeking an American education, frequently dislocated students hoping for a consistent school environment, and broadly gifted students who otherwise might need to pursue early matriculation to college or a family move to areas with one of a few specialized programs. Fundamentally, the SOHS was created as a school for talented students on the premise that they had a unique need for academic freedom and challenging curriculum. What we have found has not always matched this conception: while curriculum is the central motivation for new students, a deep need among these students for academic connectedness—to their teachers and fellow students—consistently supersedes interest in certain kinds of flexibility the school had envisioned as points of emphasis. One current student expresses the spectrum and ordering of priorities precisely:

> When I was in eighth grade, I worried that I would not be able to find a high school that would provide challenging classes taught in a way I would enjoy. I considered home schooling, which I had tried in fourth grade, but I wanted structure, friends, and gifted teachers. I also wanted to take college-level science and math courses, but not on a college campus.

That the attraction of the school lies mainly in the curriculum it makes available, in the context of the people it brings together, has been the general lesson of the school's early life and is legible in the trends in enrollment, in student profiles, and in students' own words.

Alumni offer a candid assessment of their reasons for choosing to come to the SOHS, with all of them listing 'challenging courses' as important in shaping their decisions to attend, and 92% singled this out as very important. 'More advanced courses (AP, university courses)' (73%) and 'challenging peers' (62%) were next, considerably lower, though still significant and ranked ahead of logistical factors like local access (42%) and flexibility of schedule (52%). Actual course enrollments tell a similar, if more complicated aspect of the story. Enrollments among single-course and part-time students show a considerable narrowing of focus to math and science in eleventh and twelfth grades. These enrollments are concentrated in high-level courses, such as post-AP and university-level courses, that are not commonly offered elsewhere.

These students, it seems, come seeking coursework to which they would not otherwise have access, and whose lack is manifest. In disciplines like history, English, and philosophy, advanced courses are infrequently taken by single-course students, but are slightly more common among part-time students. Here one might speculate that students who know of the school and opportunities in these disciplines already, through past experience with the school or interest in math and science, seize upon those opportunities for advanced work in these disciplines as well. Enrollment among single-course students at lower grade levels is decidedly more mixed across disciplines, perhaps representing broader interest in alternatives not driven by a limited need for particular classes.

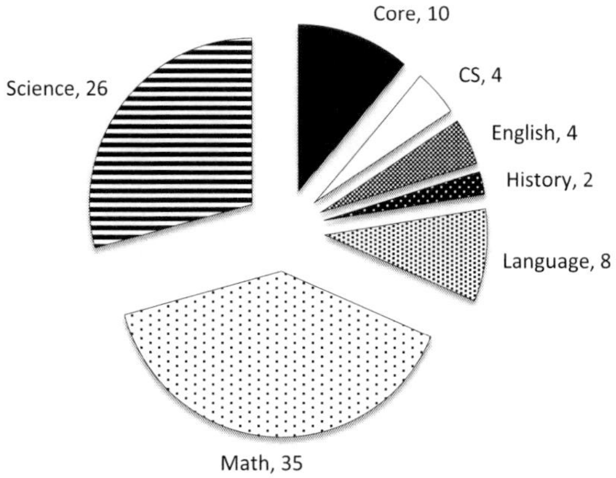

FIGURE 2.1 Single-course enrollment by discipline 11th–12th grade

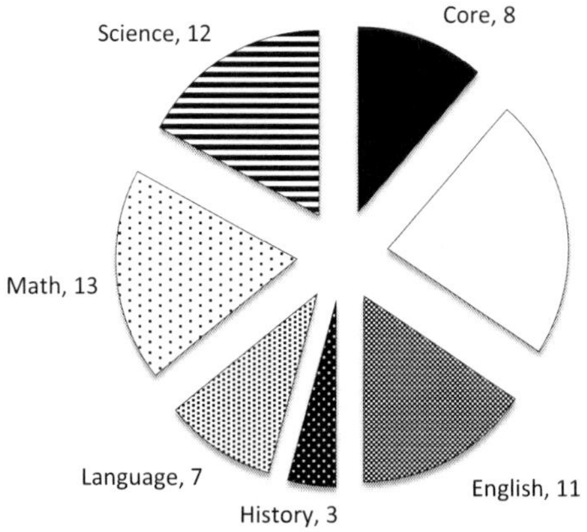

FIGURE 2.2 Single-course enrollment by discipline 9th–10th grade

Such enrollments are likely closer in character to the interest that motivated many full-time students and eventual graduates. And indeed, students who begin as single-course or part-time students in the early years of high school often progress to full-time enrollment.

While the academic program has emerged as the paramount attraction of the school, certain types of flexibility remain critical to the school's mission. Features of the school and school policy that provide flexibility focus on ensuring the accessibility of a rigorous curriculum to a range of able students. Most notably, the flexibility that these students need is built into the logistics of the school—where, when, and how the classes are taught—as well as some policies for accommodating the diversity of enrollment levels (graduating and non-graduating) made possible by the medium. Where flexibility has narrowed over the life of the school is wherever it might compromise the academic experience the school envisions for students, and where reasonable constraints could better support the emerging community learning environment. Indeed, as we will describe in the discussion of curriculum further on, students themselves have repeatedly chosen community and social learning environments despite some concurrent sacrifice of flexibility. Given a choice of self-pacing in the manner online gifted programs had been offering for many years to thousands of students, or of learning in cohorts, for instance, they favored cohorts. Providing for collaborative learning requires fixed meeting times, a common schedule for material that complicates acceleration, mandatory and regular attendance, and an intensified regime of prerequisites and placement exams, along with other encumbrances common to a conventional school. But these are tradeoffs that students generally make willingly, and that have driven growth and enthusiasm in the school. The flexibility that does attract students to the school, then, occurs within the parameters set by the mission and community environment of the school.

Apart from independence from geography, the primary logistical attraction that SOHS offers for some students is the opportunity to take *some* courses at the school while continuing work at a local school. Students have a variety of reasons for coming to the SOHS as non-graduating students, whether they are dipping a toe in early in their careers, supplementing courses not present at their local school, or pursuing intellectual curiosity in addition to their regular programs at local schools. These arrangements need not be simply temporary: students frequently continue in a single-course or part-time status for a number of years. One such student explains his part-time arrangement in this way:

> I began my high school education at my brick-and-mortar, public school. By the middle of my sophomore year, though, I so desired greater academic intensity that I began to consider leaving my high school altogether. The OHS has afforded me the enjoyment of a rigorous intellectual experience and helped me meet my goal of participating in academic work that deeply challenges me. Moreover, as a part time student here, I only take three of my academic classes online and am able to continue the rest of my education at the local school from which I will graduate. Despite pursuing just half of my education at the Online High School, I have grown to feel a part of an intellectual community of curious learners. With peers and professors equally passionate about intellectual debate and dialogue, I've discovered Edward Said, Virginia Woolf, and Michael Sandel while immersing myself

> in literary criticism, historiography, theories of justice, and American novels. My graduation this June will mean the realization of two important goals: a truly challenging high school education, and a committed involvement in my local community.

Whether driven by deep investment in local schools or specific but constrained need, part-time and single-course enrollments constitute significant segments of the school population.

At the same time, the school offers even full-time students the flexibility of a college-like schedule that is compatible with a variety of significant pursuits outside of the classroom. Classes meeting mainly twice a week at times scheduled according to student availability, supplemented by asynchronous lectures and exercises, potentially provide students with longer blocks of unstructured time, which can in turn be directed to serious academic or other training. Students use this time, of course, to complete the considerable self-directed study involved in their coursework; savvy management of this time is a critical element of success at the school and is one of the first skills new students acquire. But they also use the freedom to arrange sustained research time in local labs, to pursue careers in acting and modeling, or to train in sports and the arts. While this demographic was unanticipated in the design of the school, the fit has frequently proven to be a good one. The school was never, and does not intend to be, a flexible alternative schooling arrangement for students more focused on their sports and careers than on their academic work. However, among the very focused and talented students who are in a position to pursue such careers at this point in their lives, there are more than a few who are unwilling to sacrifice academic rigor. If they are able to meet the participation and curricular requirements, these students often flourish at the school. One such student, who has danced professionally for much of her time at SOHS and who recently agonized over the decision of whether to go to Princeton or to the University of Virginia as a Jefferson Scholar, illustrates the extent to which a strategic choice for flexibility within a strong academic program can develop into an ideal match for the student and school:

> I came to the OHS seeking a rigorous academic education that was flexible to allow me to continue to pursue dance at my local public arts high school. I found that environment, certainly, at the OHS, but in it I found so much more. This is my third year as a full-time student at the OHS. Every day I am amazed by the community that has developed around this school, from Skype groups to in-person meetups and even events such as barbeques and prom during graduation weekend. I had no understanding entering the OHS that I had stumbled

> upon a thriving community complete with our own student government, newspaper (the !), and radio show. I am exceedingly thankful for the opportunities provided for me here at the OHS.

To be sure, students in this situation can require coaching, best practices, and clear guidelines in adjudicating the demands of the school and their outside pursuits. But as these guidelines and additional support have emerged, and with careful admissions review, there have been few problems in these cases.

2.3 Change and Informative Trends

Growth in school enrollment has been gradual (See Figure 2.3). It has taken seven years to surpass the halfway mark toward the eventual enrollment target. The school itself has intentionally pursued a strategy focused on growth that is manageable without compromise to the academic program and emerging balances in the student and staff community. A network of factors including graduation, single-course enrollment, attrition, and growth mean that for many years nearly half of the students in a given year were new to the school, and larger growth surely would have overtaxed administrative processes and stretched the community's ability to retain and propagate a consistent school culture. In addition, there are simply only so many students who have the requisite combination of resources, need, talent, and sense of social and academic adventure. But the school has also had to prove itself in a variety of regards: is an intensive curriculum in an online community manageable and rewarding for students; can independent-school student support be delivered online; is a model of low-cost independent school education and personalized instruction financially sustainable; can students accomplish their academic goals in the context of a rigorous curriculum; do colleges recognize and value the rigor of the program? The message of the school's experience, and of this book, is an optimistic 'yes' to each of these questions. But it is further possible that as the school's identity and culture have settled around the answers to some of these questions, the composition and motives of the school's student body have shifted somewhat, reflective of this identity.

One significant development in the student population is intimated in one of the student comments quoted above, which is essentially the story of a limited experimental enrollment at the school that was designed to solve a logistical problem but became an encompassing full-time solution for the student. Quantitatively, the trend appears (See Figure 2.3) as an increasing bifurcation in enrollment-level: students are increasingly either single-course enrollments or full-time students. More specifically, while single-course enrollments have remained rela-

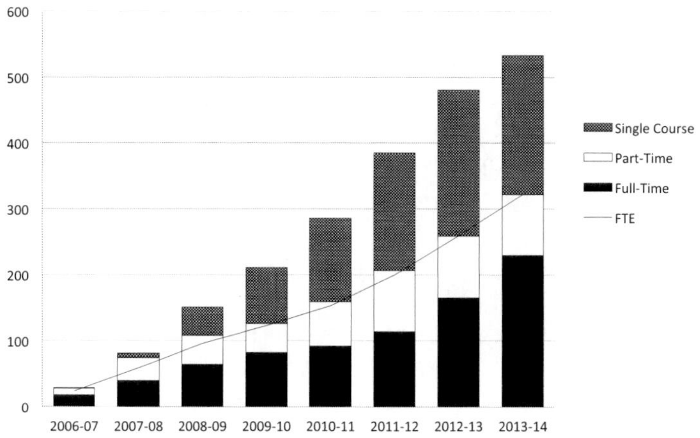

FIGURE 2.3 Enrollment by enrollment-type headcount and by full-time equivalence, by year

tively stable at 35–42% of the population, the percentage of part-time students has declined to 18% from a high of 26%, while full-time enrollments have grown to 44%. In assessing the significance in the classroom of mixed enrollment types, it is important to consider that schoolwide percentages of students at each enrollment type grossly misstates the enrollment-type composition of any given class. Because full-time and part-time students take so many more courses than their single-course peers, they make up far more of each class than not. Schoolwide, an average of 71% of students in each class are enrolled full-time at the school, while part-time students constitute 16% of class enrollments to the 14% who are single-course students, despite being greatly outnumbered in the school population. In the classroom, then, the school is bound to feel more like a school of 300 than one with more than 500 students.

These trends admit of a number of speculative explanations. Expanded residency requirements—a requirement that graduating student be enrolled full-time at the school in the junior and senior year—or more prospective academic planning efforts may have inclined fence-sitting students into full-time enrollment or down to single-course enrollment or out of the school entirely. A strengthened community may have encouraged other part-time students to let go of the security of brick-and-mortar enrollment. An expanded academic program, now including Spanish, more computer science and history, and more advanced courses, may have undercut the need for supplementary external enrollments. Similarly, greater availability of course sections throughout the day and into the evening, which comes with a larger student body and more sections of each course, may have resolved persistent scheduling difficulties for certain groups of students. Routinely strong college acceptance results may have inspired the necessary confidence to abandon hybrid enrollments. Meanwhile, interest in single courses seems to have remained at relatively consistent levels, perhaps indicative of a distinct demand for supplementary courses that is not (at present) sensitive to factors that encourage deeper enrollment among part-time students. The future trajectory of these trends, as well as their causes, are of course topics that bear further investigation.

Shifts in enrollment type are significant for the school in respects that extend beyond budget and staffing questions. Composition of the student body by enrollment type bears directly both on the nature of the school community and on the dynamics and diversity of the classroom. Nor are the implications or prescriptions for composition intuitive. One might assume, for instance, that given the importance of community in the school, there might be a clear preference for a population that approaches universal full-time enrollment, with the greater investment in school life that full-time students bring. However, there is a clear consensus at the school that single-course students make unique and important contributions to the school in a range of contexts. Most prominent is the diversity they represent in the classroom. Students who have been driven to find one particular course outside their local schools are simply more likely to possess an encompassing passion for the subject that may translate into a vivid engagement with the issues of the course. They may also be in a position to devote somewhat more time and attention to the material, enabling them to contribute extensively in class discussion. Individually, single-course students bring fresh ideas and perspectives to the school without unduly compromising the efficacy or unity of the class. Indeed, teachers frequently attest that they cannot always tell, simply on the basis of course engagement, which students among those taking their course are single-course students. Outside the class, these students are not inactive in the life of the school, sometimes participating in clubs, events, or on academic teams. Single-course students, then, even if they are not experimenting at the school with an eye toward eventual full-time enrollment, play a special role in supporting the vibrant experience students have at the school.

Consonant with the increase in full-time enrollment is a somewhat more anecdotal transition in the circumstances of the students who are drawn to the school. In the early years of the school, new and untested as it was, it was expected that the students who did make the rather bold leap to an entirely online high school would have powerful and pressing reasons to do so. Students who had endured long frustration with conventional arrangements, or who had dramatic deficits in their local opportunities would be the most likely to hazard the uncertainty and logistical struggles of the new kind of school the SOHS represented. Students reasonably well served by local options, we anticipated, would be slower to take on those uncertainties and challenges. In the relatively high-stakes world of college preparation for elite high school students, few with workable, if not ideal, solutions, would make the choice to move to an unproven school in a different format. And indeed, this was often the case among our first classes: students had compelling reasons to move to the SOHS, were unusually adventuresome and committed to a challenging education, or were moving from other less-conventional arrangements like homeschooling, such that the relative risk was lower. As the school has matured, developing a record on its questions about social environment, technology, and college results, the choice of the educational experience the school offers is somewhat less frequently catalyzed by a need for the flexibility of the medium.

One way to access the nature of students' decisions to come to SOHS is to consider applicant data. Among students applying to the school in the most recent cycle, for instance, 44% list a public school as their current school of record, 41% are at private schools, and 15% are homeschooled. While the homeschool number is high in the context of a standard independent school or the general population, neither is it in line with the model of a school that is primarily a solution for students who have already found conventional schooling arrangements to be deeply unsatisfactory. The 41% of students applying from private schools, meanwhile, indicates that many of the students considering the SOHS have at least one other non-public schooling option; indeed, more than 40% of them had already availed themselves of that option. Here, the geographic distribution of current students can also be informative. Nearly half of current students (257 or 48%) are from the five most populous states: California, Texas, New York, Florida, and Illinois. In California, further, these students are clearly concentrated in smaller areas in northern and southern California, while in Texas they are concentrated in the Dallas, Houston, and Austin areas. These students have an array of options available to them, including, in many cases, outstanding public schools, independent and parochial schools, and community colleges. To be sure, there are students who live in rural areas in Idaho and Colorado, or who have limited options in an international setting. But where students are looking to the SOHS to meet pressing needs, they are generally choosing from a range of other reasonable options.

Individual stories illustrate some of the spectrum of choices students and families make in coming to the school. For every student whose family faced a decision about relocating to support a student at a gifted program or in early matriculation to college, there are students who chose the school in the face of viable local options. For one family in the San Francisco Bay Area, it was a matter of moving students out of a strong local school dominated by an affluent school culture in order to focus on academics. Another student came to the SOHS from a private school with significant cultural advantages, but which for this student did not foster the sheer joy of intellectual endeavor she sought and found at SOHS. For students making such choices early in the school's life—choosing SOHS in preference to well-established and high-performing options—some insensitivity to traditional metrics of success was requisite. The subsequent success of those students and growth of the school have in large part removed these obstacles and helped to reshape the school from a specialized option for an already select group of students to a real choice for more of those very talented and motivated students.

The composition and development of the SOHS student body provide the first concrete telling of a message we will repeat in a variety of contexts in this book. Rather than being itself the attraction and the defining feature of the school, the online medium is primarily the enabling mechanism for a school that is special for independent reasons. The technology has enabled us to assemble a uniquely talented, diverse, and passionate student body that, in conjunction with the curriculum and staff, is a foundation for the appeal of the school as more than a last alternative. Continued growth, expansion of full-time enrollment, student support for cohorts over independent learning, and shifts toward student populations with other available solutions, together paint a picture of a school that meets unique needs, but that also offers a 'real' and compelling community in which these students can thrive.

3 Teachers

The mention of an online high school, particularly in the age of MOOCs, not infrequently elicits concern about efforts to replace teachers with computers. In the case of the SOHS, at least, nothing could be further from the aim and the lesson of the school in its first eight years. It is true, of course, that any scalable technology in a pedagogical context offers at least some prospect of diminishing the role or requisite qualifications of a teacher. Indeed, some of the early thinking about MOOCs was that they presented the prospect of content creation by a limited pool of superstar professors, to be supported, perhaps, in local college contexts by less qualified ancillary faculty. This model is a conceptual possibility in any flipped classroom: reusable, asynchronous content can be centrally and cheaply produced at scale, erasing a degree of pedagogical expertise in content presentation in the job description of any teacher. To the extent that the SOHS clearly divides the lecture and discussion time in the classic college tradition, it offers a natural framework for the flipped model and therefore more reason to think that the role of the teacher might somehow be transformed in this context. And of course, if the focus of the academic program truly were individual acceleration and flexibility of schedules, there might be further incentive to rely on asynchronous and scalable tools as the basis of instruction, in preference to teacher-driven learning. But as we will describe throughout, the development of curriculum, instruction, and learning in community at SOHS has moved in an entirely different direction. Self-paced courses drawing on clever instructional technologies that were developed when technical talent was abundant in the university setting were immediately dispreferred by students exposed to dynamic, live seminar-based courses. The teachers who led those seminars were far from instructional aides; their expertise in the content, and their expertise-based passion for the material was exactly what enabled them to challenge and motivate talented students. Far from minimizing the role of well-qualified teachers, the model of the Stanford Online High School makes the case that expert instruction (and instructors who are experts) has at least as central a role as enhanced curriculum in better meeting the needs of talented students.

It is somewhat facile to claim that no SOHS teacher ever planned to teach at an online high school. But it is only slightly less secure a pronouncement that few SOHS teachers planned to teach high school at all. The facts about our teachers that explain why this is so go some way to characterizing their unique backgrounds and the role those backgrounds have in shaping the school. In particular, our teaching staff's credentials in academic research, their underlying passion for professional work in their disciplines, and their characteristic trajectories to a home at the school contribute powerfully to the supportive intellectual environment of the school. But it is also a critical truth that one does not have to have long envisioned a particular career to do it with enthusiasm, professionalism, and absolute commitment.

Teachers at the SOHS are not dilettantes in secondary education, pining for a chance at a university job. They are teachers with university-level backgrounds who have found a place crafting a preparation in their disciplines for students who will go on to critically consume or even professionally shape the progress of those disciplines. In the school's eighth year, all full-time teachers hold academic masters degrees or higher, including twenty-seven of forty-one teachers (66%) who hold PhDs in their fields. But, importantly, they are not just passing through. Even with significant and consistent growth from a very small start eight years ago (the size of the faculty has more than doubled since 2009-10), the average length of service among existing staff is 3.7 years. Six of the original eight teachers remain at the school, along with three more who joined in the second year. The connection between SOHS teachers and students is the 'secret sauce' of the school; accordingly, recruiting, developing, and retaining the best teachers for our student demographic and academic program is a priority of the highest rank.

Now, it is absolutely certain that advanced degrees and university backgrounds do not immediately confer potential or the possession of excellent teaching skills. Indeed, there is a considerable shift in mentality regarding proactive student support that must accompany teaching at a student-centered independent school. Such support, along with other training tailored to teachers from an academic and research background, is a project in which the school has been developing best practices. But even teachers with academic backgrounds who are devoted to, and trained in, high-school teaching do not universally fit the models of teaching that have proven particularly powerful at the SOHS. In particular, a professorial 'sage on the stage' style of lecture and commentary does not fit with the priorities of active student engagement and leadership in discussion and a general emphasis on open-ended inquiry.

In the context of the right profile, however, backgrounds in advanced academic work can be a critical asset in driving achievement among talented high-school students. At the most general level, teachers who spent years in graduate school in a given field typically have a deep and visible passion for that discipline. They have a love for both the details and nuances that can grip like-minded students, and the general, aesthetic, and practical features of their subject that can be useful avenues of approach for students less inclined to the material. It is often the best teachers at the school who have given as much thought to what their disciplines can do for non-specialists and a general education as they have to how to recruit and train acolytes in their fields. In the context of course design, such teachers bring a depth of background to bear in shaping course-long narratives that frame familiar material and transform perspectives; they design courses that reflect their own engagement with the field and the questions, themes, and arguments that motivate their scholarship; they envision course objectives that prepare students for the real work of practitioners in the field, and they craft from their own training the assignments, prompts, and projects that develop those skills; and they adapt and adjust the course as they go, tailoring those assignments and discussions to the strengths and weaknesses and idiosyncratic experiences of their students and sections. In the classroom itself, particularly in the discussion seminar, these teachers have the broader knowledge of the field to coax a student comment toward a productive discussion or problem, to draw connections to current issues and research, and to challenge bright students with further questions.

What, then, is the right profile, among teachers with the requisite academic background? With respect to a fit with the students, the essentials are a passion for a discipline and a love for teaching smart students. In practice, this means an embrace of grading and extensive feedback as mechanisms for shaping student improvement. It means finding it natural to have in-depth, contemplative seminar interactions with students on a day-to-day basis, even if the prospect of lecturing everyday to large audiences might seem burdensome and unattractive. And it might mean exhibiting a certain degree of nerdy humor and (controlled) passion for tangents and details. Indeed, with teachers who hail from colleges and graduate schools like Stanford, Harvard, Berkeley, MIT, CalTech, Carleton, Dartmouth, UCLA, Penn, and Cornell, there is some degree of connection with students that stems from knowing what it is like to be a bright and curious student who is exhilarated by inquiry, gripped by certain ideas, and wants desperately to find guidance for further serious study in a discipline. For many SOHS instructors, this is the high school, and these are the peers, that they wish they had had as students. Knowing how to motivate and inspire the students whom the school attracts, then, flows as much from personal experience and reflection as it does from formal training. That said, the ability of instructors to teach these students deepens with their experience in the school in ways that emerge naturally as they learn from the students in the process of the students learning from them.

While pairing well with the students is the most basic measure of fit with the school, other characteristics can be critical as well. Teachers who prize the physical energy of a classroom, or who respond to the feel of a school building and its campus of students, for instance, may struggle to find the SOHS a satisfying environment. To be sure, there are analogues to physical energy, and SOHS has its own very rich staff and student community, as we will discuss. But the energy of a good SOHS discussion, and the nature of the connections that our students and staff develop are exciting and fulfilling in other ways, perhaps to do a little more with the substance of the interactions. As is true with respect to the logistics and curriculum of the school for students, the school is not the right thing for every teacher at every time. Among those with the right combination of academic background and commitment to teaching bright high school students, there are certain preferences and trajectories that seem to make the school a good structural fit. While there are some teachers at the school who envisioned teaching in their disciplines at the high school level and have found SOHS—with its unique students and curriculum—a good place to pursue their careers, a considerable group of others find the school to be a uniquely good fit. For some, the university environment—working at the University with its wealth of academic and intellectual resources, along with its regard for research and academic pursuits—is a special attraction. When combined with talented students often capable of working at the university level at some point in their high-school careers, the university setting can feel importantly like home to teachers with a typical SOHS background.

In many ways, the situation is even more desirable than a conventional university setting: in SOHS students, one has the opportunity to teach young scholars who have self-selected by an almost restless commitment to learning, and who in contrast to college students are still wholly forming their intellectual tools and interests. A college professor might be interested in working with the very best students, who have come trained and equipped to pursue a college-style academic program in her discipline. For those teachers whose academic preparation has led them to an interest in reenvisioning that training, SOHS offers the right students in the right environment at the right time in their academic development. Of course, this is the allure of high school to many with such interests. At SOHS, though, teachers can be part of an academic program shaped to do just this; their efforts in their own classrooms and in their own course development are part of a schoolwide mission to challenge talented students. Such a project is a natural interest for teachers drawn to SOHS. It is not an irrational reaction to the process of writing a dissertation, mired for years in the minutiae that matter to relatively few, to look to share the broader import of one's passion for a subject with talented students who will use those lessons in their general intellectual outlook, rather than solely in their own specialized engagement with that discipline. Teachers engaged in this sort of thinking about how to shape a better preparation for their discipline, for future practitioners as well as for students who will simply think critically about work in those disciplines, will find colleagues and an academic program at SOHS systematically working on this project.

More generally, SOHS attracts and rewards scholarly teachers who prize the opportunity to share their ongoing academic work and interests with their colleagues and students in the research setting of a university. While it is a challenge to pursue concrete academic research alongside the daily routine of teaching at an independent school, such a collection of backgrounds as the school requires for its academic program has a natural momentum toward various kinds of collegial collaboration. Whether it is conversations about the details of a topic in team-taught courses, planning for themed interdisciplinary courses in summer session, or sharing of pedagogical best practices in grading or teaching a particular skill, the everyday work of the school calls for collaboration that is enriched by the unique backgrounds of one's fellow teachers. More formally, though, teachers hold colloquia to present their professional academic work to faculty and students and form reading groups to pursue shared academic interests in greater depth. And school-supported professional development can involve academic work as well as the more standard pedagogical training. Perhaps most significant, though, is the opportunity to pursue serious academic interests that is built into the curriculum itself. In offering courses that go beyond the typical high-school fare, whether in depth, focus, or ultimately level of content, teachers are able to explore topics, narratives, or materials that engage their ongoing academic thinking as well as the interests of the students. The rotating 'advanced topics' courses are the most direct application of a teacher's academic research and specialization: these advanced or 'post-AP' courses change topic by semester or by year and represent a coordination of teachers' academic focus and student interest. More broadly, SOHS courses are typically not conventional surveys of standard material; where it makes sense, teachers or divisions can design or revise courses to develop the desired skills through material that challenges students and teachers alike. The opportunity to develop experimental, college-style courses in the core high-school curriculum is a test—but a welcome one—for serious scholars.

Whatever the recent uptick in notoriety regarding the considerable mismatch between academic jobs at the university level and PhDs to fill them,[5] SOHS draws on a somewhat distinct pool of academic and teaching talent. SOHS teachers are, perhaps, unexpectedly teaching high school, but they are neither haphazardly nor reluctantly doing so.

[5]See, for example, D. Cyranoski, N. Gilbert, H. Ledford, A. Nayar, and M. Yahia, 'The PhD Factory', *Nature* 472 (2011): 276-279, doi:10.1038/472276a.

There are many superlative teachers in academia who are passionate about their disciplines who would love to share their disciplines and even transform high-school training in those disciplines. Perhaps they are reluctant to abandon their research interests, the academic richness of a university, or the prospect of advanced and eager students. Perhaps they are hesitant to embark on a distinct credentialing process after years invested in a doctorate. Or they would love nothing more than to engage in detailed discussion with students around a seminar table but do not relish standing in front of a class, or lecturing over the same material, day-in and day-out, whether in college or high school. SOHS represents an alternative to these and other hurdles, in virtue of the academic program, the medium, and the quality of the students. In turn, our students are able to get precisely what they need: subject-experts who are devoted to teaching these students and can model and guide them to advanced inquiry in the disciplines.

4 Where is the School?

Having seen the students and the teachers, one can imagine the reader asking 'where is the school?' Such a reader would be in a position similar to that of a novice sports fan, who after seeing the players and all their actions, wonders where to find the famous 'esprit de corps': so much of the school is the students and the teachers and their interaction.[6]

As a school, then, the SOHS is mainly an activity—richly structured, to be sure—of the students and teachers who compose it. There are no impressive buildings, traditions are strong but only nascent, and it is hard to imagine that any student or teacher has ever come to the school solely because the technology was so compelling. And yet there is much about the growth of the student population and teacher population that is almost gravitational. As people see the school going on, as they encounter the people of the school and what they are doing, they wind up getting sucked in.

We have talked about the kind of students who get sucked into this; earlier we have made the point that the students are coming not because it is the last resort, or because they are hiding from the world. Rather, they are drawn to a school where they can pursue their passions with fellow students. And in spite of the technology, the result is one of engagement, satisfaction, and a willingness to accept that their best friends are people they have never met face to face. Once they touch the SOHS, they find it difficult to leave.

---

[6] G. Ryle, *The Concept of Mind* (Chicago: University of Chicago Press, 1949.), 17.

For those susceptible to the pedagogical impulse, teaching these kids in this environment gets to the heart of the matter. For dabblers or experimenters, the school becomes an unexpected destination. One teacher started at the school as a job in graduate school, later to turn down a tenure-track professorship to stay. A former professor who stopped out to raise her kids became engaged in their education and saw the school as a way to unify those interests with her academic background. Another veteran of asynchronous teaching, who sought a doctorate in counseling to enhance human connections, realized that he could have that sort of impact on students in the synchronous environment. Again and again we see that for a particular character passionate about education and impact on students, it is impossible to walk past Socrates at the Agora and not want to join in.

3

Curriculum

1 Individualization Online

SOCRATES: Look then how he [a slave boy of his friend Meno] will come out of his perplexity while searching along with me. I shall do nothing more than ask questions and not teach him. Watch whether you find me reaching and explaining things to him instead of asking for his opinion.

SOCRATES: You tell me, is this not a four-foot figure? You understand? –I do.

SOCRATES: We add to it this figure which is equal to it? –Yes.

SOCRATES: And we add this third figure equal to each of them? –Yes.

SOCRATES: Could we then fill in the space in the corner? –Certainly.

SOCRATES: So we have these four equal figures? –Yes.

SOCRATES: Well then, how many times is the whole figure larger than this one? –Four times.

SOCRATES: But we should have had one that was twice as large, or do you not remember? –I certainly do.

SOCRATES: Does not this line from one corner to the other cut each of these figures in two?[1] –Yes.

[1] Socrates now draws the diagonals of the four inside squares, namely, FH, HE, EG, and GF, which together form the square GFHE.

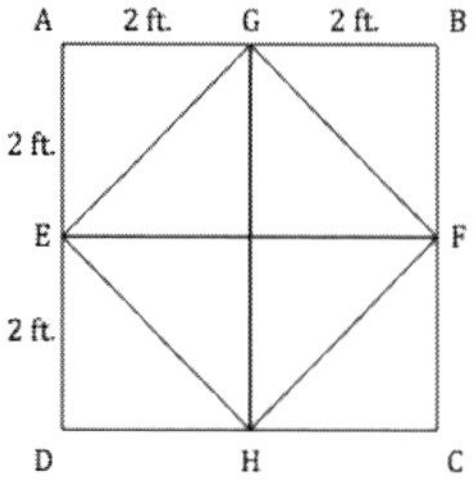

SOCRATES: Consider now: how large is the figure? –I do not understand.

SOCRATES: Within these four figures, each line cuts off half of each, does it not? –Yes.

SOCRATES: How many of this size are there in this figure? –Four.

SOCRATES: How many in this? –Two.

SOCRATES: What is the relation of four to two? –Double.

SOCRATES: How many feet in this? –Eight.

SOCRATES: Based on what line? –This one.

SOCRATES: That is, on the line that stretches from corner to corner of the four-foot figure? –Yes. –Clever men call this the diagonal, so that if diagonal is its name, you say that the double figure would be that based on the diagonal? –Most certainly, Socrates.

SOCRATES: What do you think, Meno? Has he, in his answers, expressed any opinion that was not his own?

MENO: No, they were all his own.

SOCRATES: And yet, as we said a short time ago, he did not know? –That is true.[2]

In this dialogue, the *Meno*, Plato lays out a beautiful and powerful idealization of learning. Of course, his larger contention advances an idiosyncratic argument for a sometimes marginalized model of learning—a version of the 'rationalist' view, according to which knowledge is innate in us and simply needs to be *drawn out* by experience or a skilled teacher. But the accompanying vision of a masterful tutor in dialogue with an individual student, leading him to knowledge through questions calibrated to the student's precisely gauged current state of understanding, remains a compelling ideal today.

In the context of a school, and in the classroom, the ideal of education tailored and responsive to each student's learning emerges in ideas about individualization, tracking, differentiation, and personalization. In the modern setting in which education has been adapted to an industrial scale, these terms all refer to strategies for meeting the needs of individual students by sorting them into categories and addressing the needs of students of each type. Among the powerful motivations for differentiation is the classic vision of kids bored in class, or those left behind to struggle on their way to social promotion.[3] But

[2]Plato, *Complete Works*, ed. John M. Cooper (Indianapolis, IN: Hackett, 1997), 884-885.

[3]For one recent discussion, see D. Sousa and C. A. Tomlinson, *Differentiation and the Brain: How Neuroscience Supports the Learner-Friendly Classroom* (Bloomington, IL: Solution Tree Press, 2011).

debates about pedagogy quickly dissolve into political debates about very real side effects of such grouping—demotivation, stereotyping, and socioeconomic traps. Fights over resources, values, and priorities also ensue: should money and attention be devoted to high-performing kids, to remediation, or to the majority at the expense of other individual students. Behind these legitimate political and ethical considerations, though, remains a basic pedagogical intuition that no single strategy, lesson plan, or program, presented to age-grouped children, is going to equally produce competence and inspiration in each child.

The new embodiment of hope for the Platonic dream is the computer. Some promise a digital tutor—an electronic Aristotle—for every student: adaptive systems that are sensitive to individual differences and deploy strategies tailored to each student type. The 'big data' movement proposes the instrument for assessing the understanding of each student and connecting the student to appropriate training and resources. And the self-paced nature of automated courses, wherein students move from topic to topic at the moment of mastery, removes student learning from the forced-march context of age-grouped classrooms, allowing students to spend time precisely where they need to, pausing for remediation or racing ahead along the most efficient path to individual attainment.

There is little to fault in these aspirations. The long tradition of differentiation in the classroom exhorts teachers to identify the readiness, interests, learning styles, and intelligence types of each student as preliminaries to constructing curricula that give as many as possible the best chance to succeed. Yet it is clear that this is an inexact science, and perhaps an impossible ideal, in classrooms of twenty and thirty students, or in courseloads of 150 students. Surely computers that are measuring students' answers and tendencies and analyzing them in real time against thousands and millions of data points are ideally positioned to mold curricula within the established framework of data and learning theories.

Similarly, the image of the bored and talented student, or the ill-prepared student left behind for want of assumed proficiencies, is a powerful specter of wasted time, opportunity, and potential. For both situations, self-paced instruction offers the prospect of a solution. Students in need of remediation can receive detailed diagnosis of deficiencies and targeted work that can proceed at the level of ability—there needs to be no confusion of lack of readiness and lack of ability. And in the gifted community, accelerated study through automated practice has long been seen as the ticket out of unnecessary repetition, into a cycle of challenge-driven motivation and acceleration.

Efforts to address these needs through computer-based learning are in the DNA of the SOHS. For more than twenty years, programs at Stanford offered individual online learning courses for gifted students in mathematics, physics, and writing, deploying adaptive techniques to move students through material at the optimal pace. For almost ten years, these programs were in place in districts nationwide, where the same adaptive technologies can provide individualized remediation to students working below grade level. Indeed, the Stanford Online High School opened in 2006 with an array of the same self-paced math and physics courses, offered in a school context and supported more closely by instructors. The premise, of course, was that talented, motivated students could accelerate through material at their own pace in an individualized context, not tied to the progress of a class cohort of other students nor limited by availability of instruction.

The only problem with the model of a school in which students sped through adaptive automated math and science curricula, seeking guidance from teachers when needed, was that it was not what the students wanted. And eventually, the school decided that it was not what worked best, either. Exposed to lively interactive discussion seminars in the humanities and in science courses outside of physics, students would throw much of their effort into those courses, while their progress in math and science generally followed the required schedule for getting through the material for a course in roughly an academic year. Students clamored for more interaction with teachers and peers, and teachers advocated for a model of math instruction to which the collaborative work of the class was essential. Despite the trade-off of more required class time, a more regimented schedule, and less potential for rapid individual advancement, students eagerly subscribed to the new seminar model for math, computer science, and physics. Enrollment in math courses doubled in the first year of the transition to seminar-style instruction, while enrollment across the school continued at its regular pace of 20% growth. Student satisfaction increased, incidents of students falling behind decreased, and teachers averred that students were entering new courses with stronger foundations in the material. The program in mathematics, initially envisioned as the strength of the school due to its college-level depth of offerings and built-in flexibility, had suddenly returned from its relative disfavor to become the most heavily enrolled division in the school, and one of the most dynamic areas of student involvement and achievement.[4]

[4]Some of the activities included extensive participation in mathematics contests, such as the High School Mathematical Contest in Modeling (HiMCM), Purple Comet, and Mathematics Olympiad. A 'Problem of the Week' program open to students, teachers, and families, has also fostered community involvement in the mathematics program.

The dream of recruiting computers to maximally personalize the learning of each student—an electronic Aristotle for every student—is a worthy one. It ought to be refined and enriched where additional resources are not available. The experience of the SOHS, in mathematics and throughout our curriculum, however, suggests that the individualized model leaves out a valuable component of learning: the importance of the social setting. Whether fully automated, online, or in a traditional physical setting, individual tutoring abstracts learning away from a social environment in which peers collaborate and enrich one another's experience. Our own experience with online education for talented students substantiates more generally applicable and time-tested traditions in college and independent-school seminars, venerable theories about learning from Aristotle to Dewey, and even early lessons from the move toward massive online courses at the university level.[5] Even talented, independent learners learn best and most eagerly in the collaborative, lively company of their peers. Accordingly, learning in community is a foundational value of the SOHS.

What a focus on seminar-style, discussion-based coursework offers in depth and vitality is weighed against a loss in several of the great promises of online education—scalability and flexibility for individualization. While potential efficiencies of mass delivery do not touch on the mission of the SOHS, individualization and flexibility certainly do. Indeed, these qualities are key to providing challenging education to talented students; if they are not best achieved in the private, automated tutoring of each student, they must be accomplished by other features of the school's design and implementation. It should also be noted that by not adhering to a rigid machine-based program of instruction, we escape the trap of curricular choices made by limitations inherent in the delivery method or the means of assessment. Instead, curricular choices can be shaped by what has proven effective and compelling with students on the ground.

SOHS's approach to individualization spans all areas of the program, informing pedagogy and student feedback, academic advising and student support, and cocurricular offerings. But the key element in the SOHS's balance between structured learning in a seminar environment and private training in course content is the curriculum. In a school context in which uniquely able students are concentrated from diverse locations, the curriculum is already finely tailored to a narrowed set of needs and interests. All courses can be challenging, and many can

[5] T. Lewin, 'U.S. Teams Up With Operator of Online Courses to Plan a Global Network', *New York Times*, November 1, 2013, http://nyti.ms/16PRd4P.

engage material beyond the AP or even at a university level. Careful systems of placement, prerequisites, and student support further ensure appropriate fit among students in a course. And within this narrowed context, a comprehensive curriculum focuses on skills and habits of mind in a manner that challenges every student, particularly in the collegial seminar setting. Whether in the Philosophy Core program that was designed to cultivate a capacity for critical thinking, or in each discipline's focus on the norms and strategies of professional practice in that field, the curriculum finds challenge and reward for students not just in efficient delivery of advanced material, but in the training that comes in *how* that material is taught through the SOHS curriculum.

2 Building a Challenging Curriculum—Material

It is the mission of the Stanford Online High School to provide for gifted students everywhere 'an education ideally suited to their needs', drawing on technology and the resources of the University to do so. As we have seen so far, though, the online medium is not the mechanism for realizing this mission. Providing talented students with endless and automated content, through which they can speed, privately, at the rate of mastery as assessed by a computer, is not the marriage of technology and education that the school envisions for talented students. Whatever role there is for such learning at an earlier level in producing what philosopher Hubert Dreyfus calls 'competence',[6] its benefits, we have found, are surpassed by the opportunities afforded to talented students gathered together in a robust seminar environment. The mission of challenging, training, and inspiring these students, then, falls not to the mechanism for delivering the content, but to the content itself, as engaged in classrooms of other talented students, led by the right sort of teacher. Here we look at what the curriculum can do to meet this foundational goal of the school.

While the SOHS shies away from a model of education for talented students that relies primarily on rapid, individualized acceleration, talented students will inevitably need material that goes beyond the standard high-school curriculum. The SOHS offers such for an array of reasons. To be sure, the gifted community has some traditions of sending particularly precocious students to college at an early age, solving in one stroke the similarly common search for challenging courses for high-school-aged students.[7] While the SOHS does not expressly oppose

---

[6] H. Dreyfus, *On the Internet*, 2nd ed. (New York: Routledge, 2009), 30.

[7] M. Gross, 'Small Poppies: Highly Gifted Children in the Early Years', *Roeper Review* 21, no. 3 (1999): 207-214.

this practice, our aim is to provide an alternative in light of the considerable challenges of early college matriculation. SOHS students can take college-level courses without leaving their parents' homes, without forgoing athletic and social opportunities, and without limiting college choices to schools willing to take younger students. But far more common than the young student who is entirely prepared for college academically, is the student who is advanced to the university level in one or several disciplines, but not all. Whether a ninth-grader who has completed AP Calculus, an eleventh-grader who excels in writing and has passed both English APs, a computer programmer far beyond introductory Java, or a budding scientist who wants to build beyond AP work in physics and biology, students are not always in the position to matriculate to college to find challenges in a subset of major fields. Nor are community or other local colleges always a good match for these students, whether in challenge and audience or in more logistical features.[8] But perhaps most distinctively, SOHS courses covering advanced material are taught in the environment of an independent school, where the material is embedded in structures of student support, pedagogy focused on talented and passionate students, and the familiar social setting of the students' high school. Students go to these advanced classes with friends and teachers they know (and who know them), work within systems and routines in which they are comfortable, and draw upon support resources appropriate to their age. In such a setting, talented students can be confident in stretching their abilities in certain disciplines, with all the accompanying academic excitement, while continuing their high-school academic programs and development.

The most traditional demand for courses dealing with material beyond the standard high-school curriculum is in mathematics and physics. Stanford has been offering online courses, funded by the A.P. Sloan foundation, in these areas to high-school students since the

[8]That advanced placement, extension, and online courses are poor substitutes for students to complete advanced coursework is borne out both in the sizeable reduction in the number of universities accepting advanced placement courses for credit and in the elaborate rules concerning limitations on and applicability of such courses towards degrees. Stanford University limits the number of units non-transfer students can earn outside of Stanford to forty-five (one year's worth of coursework) and those departments that recognize the AP often require students to take accelerated introductory courses in which they can reteach the material students should have learned to make sure that they actually did. See, for example, Office of the University Registrar of Stanford University, *Stanford Bulletin*, updated August 1, 2013, http://exploredegrees.stanford.edu/undergraduatedegreesandprograms/#transferworktext.

early 1990s. That this was a natural place to develop such courses stems in part from the nature of the material. Mathematics has long been an area in which students have attained substantial acceleration, especially through the standard secondary-school curriculum. Moreover, disciplines in which concepts build upon each other in a cumulative fashion according to standard conceptual sequences and curricula both limit the extent and utility of differentiation, and are amenable to individualized or private acceleration. It is at once the case that advanced students visibly *need* access to more advanced material, and that it is relatively straightforward to provide it to them in a manner that admits of clear standards of mastery and established trajectories to the next level. SOHS has been offering university-level courses in mathematics and physics since the start of the school, including (in mathematics) Linear Algebra, Multivariable Differential Calculus, Multivariable Integral Calculus, Differential Equations, Complex Analysis, Modern Algebra, Real Analysis, Partial Differential Equations, Number Theory, Logic, and (in physics) Light and Heat, Modern Physics, and Intermediate Mechanics and Quantum Mechanics.[9]

In other fields, conditions are less conducive to acceleration to the college level, and for this reason, fewer such courses have been developed. Laboratory sciences, for instance, involve experiments and work whose implementation in a self-paced, private program is not as straightforward as in mathematics or other theoretical fields. For similar reasons, they are not as amenable to systematic self-study. And in addition, science is typically taught in a cumulative curriculum that is inflexible in its breadth: typically students study physics, chemistry, and biology in yearlong courses, leaving little room for advancement beyond the AP level when an expected course of study allows room for only one science course a year. At the same time, it is manifestly clear that an excellent AP Biology course can inspire or cement a passion for advanced work in the discipline that should not be put off until the sophomore year in college (when majors or premed students will have completed the prerequisite college courses in chemistry). At SOHS, our efforts to address such situations emerged in response to exactly such passion among students: in 2010, nine students finishing AP Biology created a petition asking for a course for further study in biology. Mindful of the place of such courses in the school's mission, the science division set about designing a course that would give students who had completed AP Biology a deeper grounding in the principles

[9]A full listing of courses is available with ancillary materials at http://www.bricksandmortarbook.com.

of serious scientific research. The next year, eleven students were enrolled in the new course, Research Topics in Biology. Conceived as a seminar course driven by student interests, the class now meets on a weekly basis for an extended period. Each week, discussions focus on a seminal or cutting-edge research article selected to coincide with the interests and projects of course members, and the work is presented by a student. Subsequent iterations made room for interested students to develop literature reviews on a selected topic over the course of a semester. This course has attracted a steady enrollment, despite its advanced prerequisites, and marries particularly well with independent research students might be doing in labs outside the school.

Among disciplines in which college-level material is uncommon in high school, computer science faces obstacles that are the converse of those in lab sciences: whereas lab sciences are not amenable to private study, computer science exactly *is* amenable to such study, and perhaps accordingly is seldom taught in a school setting at a level appropriate to the most advanced students. Any budding programmer with a developed interest in the field will breeze through an AP Computer Science course, only to find subsequent offerings largely absent in a formal school context. While asynchronous resources, from MIT's Scratch to online training at Codecademy to college-level MOOCs, increasingly provide interested students with structured instruction and introduction, classroom instruction is benighted, perhaps exactly for the reason that advanced students find their own way outside the classroom, and are not sitting in unchallenging but required classes, as they might in an analogous situation in math. But with its mix of theory and fundamentals, lessons about strategy and advanced mathematical topics as much as syntax, and personalized attention and collaborative opportunities with peers, classroom instruction still has a role to play for advanced students. While SOHS has long offered a two-year sequence in computer science, initially built on self-paced asynchronous courses but now implemented in a seminar setting, the school began offering material beyond the AP level in 2012. Data Structures and Algorithms in Java focuses on object-oriented programming topics that assume competence in AP material, such as advanced data structures, algorithms for organizing and manipulating data, and the time-complexity of algorithms. Further development and courses may hinge on enrollment factors shaped by the discipline's status as an 'elective'.

The need for advanced material in the humanities is in some ways more ambiguous than in math and science. While students may be superlative readers, sophisticated writers and stylists, or careful and critical thinkers about patterns and causes, much of these individual differences can be at least modestly addressed through differentiation and individualization. Good courses in the humanities engage with rich and original source materials with layers of meaning and connections that commonly repay repeated study throughout an academic career and throughout a lifetime. In conjunction with quality instruction that provides sufficient expectations and feedback to advanced students, this depth of material is sufficient for at least a measure of challenge and opportunity for improvement to advanced students. (Maintaining an appropriate balance of difficulty and accessibility in discussion, however, can be more difficult in a class of students who vary significantly in preparation.) And indeed, real advancement in the humanities can require cognitive maturity and a maturity of perspective that is challenging to rush. But while this formula may be adequate in the humanities when it would not suffice in mathematics, it is by no means optimal. To truly challenge advanced students, to inspire them in ways they would not be just as well on their own, and to prepare them to thrive at the most demanding colleges, specially tailored opportunities are essential.

Over the course of the school's development, we have moved to a model for offering post-AP and university-level material that trains students in college-style methodologies and questions in disciplines across the humanities. The initial university-level offerings in the humanities comprised two semester-long English courses modeled on sophomore literature courses at Stanford. In Making *Moby-Dick* and 20th Century Genre Theory and Practice, students approach classic texts in a manner distinctive of advanced study of literature. The course on *Moby-Dick* guides students through an analysis of the novel in a series of different contexts—literary, historical, genre-specific, and biographical, in the process equipping students with critical skills for literary analysis and interpretation. Genre Theory similarly introduces university-level analytical strategies in asking students to compare and consider together the different media of literature and photography. While the texts at issue in these courses are admittedly quite sophisticated, it is the skills of analysis introduced and expected of students that constitute the unique challenge of the courses.

Outside of the context of the intensive university-level courses, which approximate college-level work and expectations, a range of courses in the humanities offer college-like study of material with additional focus on the transition between high-school and college-level expectations. These courses are considered to exceed the standards of AP courses in their objectives, but also in their approach to the material of a discipline. In particular, they give students exposure to college-level thematic focus and disciplinary modes of analysis. To do so, these courses have open or alternating topics, varying by instructor and student interests much on the model of college or graduate 'special topics' courses. The History Research Seminar, for instance, has focused in its first two years on the European Enlightenment and then Topics in Contemporary History (since 1950). Students undertake individually developed major research projects, including studies of interpretations of the Fourth Amendment in modern America, the controversy over oral education in the Deaf community, and the rise of domestic surveillance in the Cold War, while examining exemplary papers from working historians to draw lessons about the practice of historical research, such as how to muster evidence to develop and support one's claims. Advanced Topics in Literature, which alternates topics on a semester basis, has so far seen courses in Imagining Nations, Medieval and Modern; Xtopias; The Idea of History in Literature (and Art); and The Ode. Much as in the history seminar, students learn critical methodologies rarely taught at the precollegiate level, while developing experience in scholarly research. The success of these courses in moving beyond high-school skills while attending to the transition to collegiate work has fed back to the mathematics program, informing a course on Advanced Problem Solving and Proof Techniques that hones strategies requisite to university study that are rarely present in AP Calculus courses. Indeed, it is in these courses that the SOHS is in relatively uncharted curricular space; but it is also here where the opportunities to challenge and better prepare talented students seem particularly impactful.

3 Building a Challenging Curriculum—Skills

While advanced opportunities at the upper end of the curriculum are an important part of ensuring that talented students will be challenged throughout their high school careers, it is, again, not the exclusive focus of individualization for SOHS students. Rather than achieving challenge by speeding students individually through the curriculum, the SOHS academic program creates challenge in each course, requiring meaningful engagement of material and peers in a manner that supports a degree of differentiation for appropriately placed students. The key to the curriculum, then, is the design and execution of courses capable of accomplishing this tall order. Our approach in creating such courses draws on a combination of know-how, novel curricular elements, and curriculum-wide focus on particular skills. SOHS courses are designed by teachers who are intimately familiar with study in their disciplines at the highest level. Their courses focus on real skills, methods, and habits of mind that this perspective and experience suggest are essential training for such study at the high-school level. And these skills are reinforced and elaborated systematically in a four-year Core sequence that offers a unique emphasis on skills of critical thinking and argumentation across the disciplines.

3.1 Critical Thinking and the Philosophy Core

Whenever the topic of education reform strays from testing and accountability to engage momentarily the central questions of what is taught in classes and how, 'critical thinking' is often a focus of discourse. The new Common Core State Standards take critical thinking as a key objective of curriculum,[10] planned revisions to the SAT target critical-reasoning skills,[11] and myriad independent programs and books advertise training in critical thinking. The term is similarly ubiquitous in independent-school literature, leading to quips that critical thinking or reasoning has become the fourth 'r' of education. But despite the explosion in interest and concern for instruction in critical thinking, there is little concrete consensus on the meaning of the term and what abilities and competencies it entails. This ambiguity has clear implications for the development of effective critical-thinking curricula, as well as for reliable measures of students' proficiency in the desired skills, and accordingly, for measurements of individual programs' efficacy in engendering this proficiency. In the estimation of commentator John McPeck, early theories and programs in critical thinking amounted to the analog of a baseball coach telling his struggling pitcher to 'throw strikes'—the question is really how to do, and teach, what everyone agrees is the goal.[12]

Philosophy is frequently presented as an arbiter and exemplar of good reasoning in the context of the pedagogy of critical thinking, whether in its authority on formal logic and informal argumentation, or its fluency in fallacies and valid argumentative forms. But in reality, philosophy's tools and resources for shaping careful, sophisticated, and rigorous thinkers is far deeper and more nuanced than any rough-and-ready curriculum of fallacies and basic logic can approximate. Familiarity with the philosophical cannon was long a tool in the repertoire of well-educated students, and not simply for its cultural currency. In this spirit, study of those texts and debates was commonly included

[10] 'English Language Arts Standards', Common Core State Standards, http://www.corestandards.org/ELA-Literacy/.

[11] 'Redesigned SAT', College Board, https://www.collegeboard.org/delivering-opportunity/sat/redesign#source.

[12] J. McPeck, *Teaching Critical Thinking* (Routledge: New York, 1990), 14.

in the introductory surveys in the humanities taught at elite colleges and informed by the 'great books' tradition. These courses engendered a fluency in the concepts, skills, and strategies of classic philosophical traditions as part of a common intellectual framework shared by all students as they entered into their disparate studies. Both of these functions are central to the mission of the SOHS: in their disparate academic programs shaped by diverse interests and advancement, SOHS students are in need of a common set of intellectual experiences and understandings to organize their studies; and to deal effectively and creatively with the advanced content of their studies and professions, they need that framework to consist in a robust mastery of norms and tools of careful thinking. To prescribe to busy high-school students a four-year course of study in these skills through the methods and cannon of philosophy, however, incurs a serious responsibility to make this often abstract and theoretical discipline concrete in its relevance and contribution to a general education. The SOHS Core sequence represents, in practice, a philosophically-informed curriculum for critical thinking and argumentation.

The Philosophy Core sequence, which is required of each student planning to graduate from the school in each year at the high-school level, is not a four-year sequence in the texts and arguments of the philosophical cannon. Rather, Core courses take the subject matters of science, history of science, political theory, and philosophy proper as a forum for developing a range of analytical and philosophical skills that can be applied broadly in both academic and public reasoning. While the design of the Core sequence does not represent a principled stake in the debate about whether critical thinking skills are 'discipline specific' or general-purpose and broadly 'transferable' across various domains of knowledge,[13] it does reflect a strategy of learning to engage foundational issues in a discipline from within the practice of that discipline itself. As will be clear in the description of the individual courses below, such philosophical querying of a discipline is not tantamount to a 'philosophy-of' that discipline. While the intellectual framework that Core provides is characterized by an ability to ask conceptual and foundational questions in particular disciplines, it is also a preparation to think critically about work and discourse in these disciplines, and to master the norms of rigorous and logically informed reasoning therein.

[13]For the outline of this debate, see J. McPeck, 'Stalking Beasts, but Swatting Flies: The Teaching of Critical Thinking', *Canadian Journal of Education* 9, no. 1 (1984): 28-44, and R. Ennis, 'Critical Thinking and Subject Specificity: Clarification and Needed Research', *Educational Researcher* 18, no. 4 (1988): 4-10, doi:10.3102/0013189X018003004.

Working from the premise that 'you have to know something to do philosophy' or critical thinking, Core courses teach students these skills in the context of a good deal of study of material in the discipline.[14]

The disciplinary focus of the individual Core courses, then, is first a formula for engendering, in combination, an ability to work critically in central disciplines through familiarity with foundational practices and norms in those disciplines. In sequence, progressing from courses in scientific methodology and the historical development of scientific practices on to normative questions in political theory and classic questions in philosophy, this disciplinary focus permits a gradual introduction of increasingly abstract and open-ended issues and discussions. This progression is sensitive to, and in addition, drives, the cognitive development of students in their careers at the school.

In the first, ninth-grade course, Methodology of Science—Biology, then, students spend considerable attention to mastery of technical statistical skills and foundational biological concepts in preparation to appreciate the nature of strong statistical and biological evidence, and to assess and employ such evidence. Whether in the studies they review or in designing their own data collection and statistical analysis in a culminating project, students become intimately acquainted with the messiness of raw data and the interpretative but standard-intensive process by which those data are mustered to support scientific claims. They not only know enough to be thoughtful about appeals to data in public and scientific discourse, but are equipped to evaluate the soundness of those appeals. They know not only how to regard claims supported by data—how to incorporate these claims into their own thinking—but also how to adjudicate claims based on separate and sometimes conflicting studies. And they know how to ask questions that will yield rich and usable data, and how to query that data in various and appropriate ways. Such an understanding, of course, is not just the basis of critical thinking in a given discipline and in more popular discourse, but is also a source of discovery and creativity.

The second course in the sequence, History of Science: Great Ideas, Observations, and Experiments, further builds students' understanding of scientific knowledge and the implications of its formation. Through exposure to exemplary cases in the development of scientific inquiry—

[14]This approach shares much with McPeck's proposal that standard coursework include instruction in the 'epistemology of the discipline', though the foundational reflection is not limited to epistemology and pervades all aspects of the course, nor is the subject-area content constrained in the way it would be in the context of an ordinary course in that discipline. See McPeck, *Teaching Critical Thinking*, 17.

from observation to modern experimentation—students confront the circumstances under which scientific theory formation occurs, and learn to analyze the argumentative structure which grounds theories in evidence. With such an appreciation of the relationship between theory and evidence, students know what it means, and does not mean, to be a theory. They are not powerless to contest false equivalencies among scientific theories and ideologies, while they are similarly uncowed by entrenched theories. This is because they know what goes into a theory, and are also mindful of the assumptions (methodological and otherwise) that are part of any theory.

By the third, junior-year course, students are more thoroughly prepared to engage the increasing ambiguity and conflicts of values that characterize normative political theory. Democracy, Freedom, and the Rule of Law maintains the Core's focus on foundational concepts and methods of central disciplines in its study of changing conceptions of how a state is and should be organized. In particular, the course charts different treatments of the interwoven concepts of democracy, freedom, and the rule of law, while exploring the role of these concepts in strategies of governance and political justification. Philosophical tools of conceptual and argument analysis prove powerful in this project, equipping students to participate constructively in the discourse that draws on these conceptions of the state. By distinguishing differing conceptions of freedom, equality, or the role of government, for instance, students can better appreciate the basis of opposing positions in contemporary debates about taxes, health care, terrorism, and privacy. And here, the creative potential of critical thinking is apparent: students who can discern the sources of policy disputes in differing conceptions of fundamental values, and who can draw upon an understanding of evolving political values, are not only able to defend their own views, but have the resources to formulate alternative policies that address the shared and divergent elements of opposing ideologies.

The Core program's sequence-long function of building skills of argumentation analysis and development through philosophy's traditional practice of these tasks receives systematic attention in the final course of the sequence, Critical Reading and Argumentation. This course helps students develop these resources through a careful analysis of exemplary pieces of philosophical argument and literature. While its material is that of college-level introductory surveys in philosophy, the focus of the course is on more broadly applicable intellectual tools and habits of mind, engendered by an engagement with the material. Among these tools are the ability to extract arguments (sometimes formalized) from text, to identify and assess key premises and inferences, to identify the argumentative strategy and tailor responses to the strategy, and to develop and defend one's own views against potential criticisms. Students accordingly know a slippery slope argument when they see one, and can determine the severity of the threat and where they might dig in their heels. They know the virtues of thought experiments and argument by analogy, but also how to find counterexamples and disanalogies to probe the worth of those arguments. And, perhaps most powerfully, they acquire an ability to chart the geography of an issue, understanding the objectives of opposing positions and how those objectives shape the positions, and thereby to spot open space in the dialogue that might be productively developed to meet some of the objectives of the participants.

Perhaps the best testament to the efficacy of the Core program is the common refrain from parents that they now really enjoy talking to their students about a great range of issues relevant to their Core courses, but that their students have become very difficult to argue with. Students do emerge from the program formidable interlocutors. They have honed their abilities in years of discussions in which they engage texts, instructors, and classmates, while dissecting, critiquing, and defending. In these writing-intensive classes, they have learned by practice how to construct sophisticated and sustained arguments in papers, and they have learned enough about the disciplines themselves, in their basic concepts, methods, and questions, to navigate novel future encounters in that discipline (whether professional or public) in discerning and constructive fashion. This is an intellectual framework they share with their fellow SOHS graduates, which they practice together across the curriculum, and which marks them and informs all of their future work.

3.2 Course Design throughout the Curriculum

While the Core sequence constitutes an innovative curriculum that supplements instruction in traditional fields, the curricular goals of the SOHS below the post-AP and university levels are not satisfied simply by additional courses. Rather, the SOHS approach to challenging coursework at all levels is characterized by a focus on the skills foundational to advanced thinking in a discipline. Beyond the school's explicit emphasis on such an approach, several other features of the school serve to promote a rigorous training that extends the Core's lessons into each stage of the curriculum. Foremost among these features is the unique concentration of teachers who bring to their course design and instruction the appreciation of foundational disciplinary skills gleaned from advanced degrees in the field. And in support of the work of such teachers is an openness and appreciation for courses that pursue distinctive strategies for instruction in those disciplines, challenging conventional survey models like those set forth by the advanced placement system.

Given the ongoing environment in which AP courses are seen by students and families as requisite marks of accomplishment, despite the trend among elite colleges away from granting meaningful credit or degree progress for AP results,[15] innovation in curriculum design is, for the moment, freest at the earlier and later ends of the curriculum. Among the courses exemplifying the focus of the early curriculum on skill building through college-style course design is the introductory high-school course Revolutions and Rebellions. Designed with the flexibility to shift its historical focus to different periods from one year to the next, the course currently involves a study of the American, French, and Haitian revolutions, spanning 1765 to 1804. One of the key goals in the design of such courses is to provide students with the opportunity to look closely and at length at historical events from multiple perspectives. To that end, this course focuses on the causes and consequences of a small number of interconnected revolutions. In contrast to the forced march through centuries prevalent in AP and survey courses, so constrained a focus permits an attention to multiple sources and types of evidence that helps students begin to think about historical change as complex in nature, focusing on the complexity of historical causation and the diversity of perspectives on historical events. Here, the academic historical perspective of the instructor is essential in setting the stage for a full appreciation of this complexity. By setting in a common context historical developments like early feminism, abolitionism, and the revolutionary culture of the 1790s, for instance, this course prompts students to make meaningful historical connections between seemingly distant events. These rich connections, in turn, foster a mastery of historical content through the development of an understanding of the significance of events, rather than through the memorization of details. Similar methods and strategies, employed in other courses and disciplines, will be explored in greater depth in the second volume.

4 Supports for Making Advanced Curriculum Work

The SOHS's approach to challenging talented students is therefore not based on a strategy of speeding students through the curriculum. Rather, as any student from the middle school to the graduating class

[15] T. Lewin, 'Dartmouth Stops Credits for Excelling on A.P. Test', *New York Times*, January 17, 2013, http://www.nytimes.com/2013/01/18/education/dartmouth-stops-credits-for-excelling-on-ap-test.html.

can attest, the curriculum is challenging all the way through. And this, as we have seen, is not just because the courses cover material above grade level—we teach algebra, introductory sciences, and composition just as a typical school. Nor, again, do the courses challenge merely by going fast or assigning a lot of work; while both are perhaps the case, again, students do not necessarily advance above grade level in the course of a year. As we have suggested, the challenge comes from what students are asked to do—the questions they are trained to ask, the depth in which they are led to engage material, the connections they are positioned to make among topics and from their work to the world they live in, and the exchanges they routinely make with their peers.

In such courses, where students will be pressed at each step, working in a group format, and without much in-class differentiation for variation in preparation or ability, it is essential to be in the right class. Whether one is able and eager to move ahead in the material and is unchallenged by the contributions of her peers, or lacks assumed skills such that seminars are inaccessible and the contributions of fellow students inscrutable, inappropriate placement into a course undermines the SOHS strategy for challenging students through curriculum and the seminar model, rather than private learning. And in fact, placement is not simply more *important* at the SOHS; it is also more *difficult.*

Numerous factors complicate the project of assigning students accurately to courses; in many ways, student placement at SOHS more closely resembles the dynamics of a community college than those of a local middle school or high school. To start, the traditional activity of taking in a new student, establishing an ability and readiness level, and reconciling that course assignment with an academic graduation plan, is not simply a task limited to students entering the school at one or two primary entry points. Due to the nature of the school—it is often a school discovered only midway through middle school or even high school, or it is a 'solution' to a felt need that arises in the normal course of a middle-school or high-school career—students just as regularly enter in tenth grade as they do in ninth or seventh. And in a dynamic independent boarding schools are perhaps more familiar with, those students do not hail from a small set of known feeders, whose academic program and correspondences to the school's own curriculum are well established. Rather, new SOHS students have learned prerequisite material for SOHS coursework from sources of variable approaches, intensity, and quality. Even beyond difference across schools and districts, nonstandard backgrounds like homeschool or mixtures of other online programs are common. The full story of students' preparation, then, is not easily established from objectively interpretable markers. Indeed, since SOHS courses are often more rigorous or demanding than standard fare, students will often encounter a gap or hurdle as they enter a discipline at SOHS from elsewhere, making the quality of the previous program of even greater import—a substandard preparation will sometimes put the student in significant peril at the opening of a career at SOHS. Placement of students, then, is a perpetual process that is not limited to a single cohort of students each year, involves disparate and relatively unknowable backgrounds, and must anticipate the significance of a leap in intensity at the start of work at SOHS.

For all of these reasons, SOHS has developed an elaborate system for evaluating students' appropriate entry points into the curriculum. Wedded as we are to serving students at their level of readiness and ability, rather than age, the school seldom places students in a course by grade level. The school instead requires that each student be placed in each new discipline according to a proctored placement test. It is not uncommon for a student to test down a level, particularly in the early years of high school—to an earlier-than-expected year of foreign language, math, or English—and such unexpected measures are typically borne out. Moderate exceptions in this placement approach include history courses, which (currently) do not directly assess students' competence in historical skills, but do index prerequisites to English placement results, and the Core sequence, which due to its role as a common, cohort-specific experience and its uniqueness beyond the SOHS, does not provide for acceleration through placement. While the placement process is extensive and somewhat cumbersome, it has proven essential in identifying differences in readiness and in avoiding painful struggles.

Requisite as such a placement system is to a unique and advanced curriculum, it risks stifling the potential for advancement as a student's readiness for advanced material improves and as passions and talents are discovered. A placement test does not identify a student's ability for a four- to six-year period, nor should it prevent a student from working assiduously toward a particular objective in the curriculum. Accordingly, as the need for—and success of—an encompassing placement process became more evident during the school's first several years, and as we simultaneously moved further from individual acceleration through self-paced course materials and intensified summer courses, we also began to introduce measures to provide students flexibility for individualized acceleration from year to year that they might not have in the context of a given course in a given subject during the year.

A central strategy for providing this critical flexibility is the advantageous use of 'inflection points' in the curriculum of a discipline. Particularly in English, where students do sometimes place lower than would be indicated by external coursework, and where students have numerous options at the upper end of the curriculum, the curriculum has been designed to accommodate the skipping of certain courses. In practice, particularly able students sometimes skip over the second middle-school course and AP English Language and Composition, making at least one year's worth of space for a post-AP-level course. A student who has, by contrast, placed into a course that did not provide for completion of both AP courses by senior year might be able to meet that standard by accelerating back to the standard sequence. Similar mechanisms are available in the history sequence, though they are somewhat less standardized, as students are not required to take a history course in each year at the high-school level. In any case, students with constrained schedules may nonetheless be able to reach the post-AP History Research Seminar by passing over AP World History while completing Revolutions and AP United States History.

In the sciences, the diversity and flexibility of the curriculum generally allows talented students to reach advanced coursework (particularly in Advanced Research Topics in Biology or university-level physics) through judicious course selection. However, students who enter high school having not yet taken a high-school-level physics course would need to take more than four years of science to reach the highest high-school-level courses in each subfield. Here, the most notable mechanism for acceleration consists in the 'bootcamps' offered over the summer in chemistry and physics. These roughly six-week, asynchronous mini-courses, available during the summer, offer students an introduction to fundamental concepts and principles, such that they might be sufficiently prepared to achieve placement into the AP version of the science course. Bootcamps are in this sense a different sort of mechanism for accommodating differences in students' initial preparation: as the AP courses assume some previous work in these areas, students without that training would otherwise have to spend two years in a subfield to complete the AP sequence. By completing a bootcamp and passing into the AP course, students who have the ability to manage the AP material and want only for basic background, are able to gain AP-level mastery of the material and to move on to more advanced coursework.

For either of these mechanisms—bootcamps and inflection points—to represent viable pathways for acceleration, it must be the case that disciplinary sequences at SOHS have significant 'layering' at key points in the curriculum. In the sciences, for instance, even the most gifted student could not absorb a year's worth of material and practice in a six-week asynchronous bootcamp; these only make sense if the 'honors' and AP courses cover some common core of material, differing in depth and scope in a way that makes the two-year sequence profitable for many students, but manageable for the particularly proficient in a single AP course. In the English program, this layering of courses is particularly powerful in appropriately meeting the needs of all students. The existence of two very challenging courses early in the English sequence—the second year in the middle-school program and the standard first-year course in high school—not infrequently left students in need of appropriate alternative courses if they were to take English at the SOHS. Some initial experimentation and reflection convinced us that 'tracking' of students into more- and less-challenging, parallel sequences was in tension with the program's goals for individual students, and with the school's emphasis on a high standard for all students, independent of differences in preparation. Often, students were simply in need of some initial preparation in a more scaffolded environment, or simply further cognitive maturation, before jumping to the abstractions of the central courses in the curriculum. These goals could be addressed in an intermediate course that feeds back into the main sequence without repetition; similar layering surrounding the AP English courses enables thriving students to skip a given course without entirely missing essential skills and emphases. The clear alternative, on this model, to harnessing adaptive technology to privately accelerate students through *all* the material in a sequence, is to interlace emphases and focuses over several stages in the curriculum, such that students for whom acceleration is appropriate can make their way to university-level work with enough in-class exposure to core skills and content.

5 Challenges in an Advanced Curriculum

The development of an advanced curriculum at SOHS has not been without challenges. Indeed, we have and continue to grapple with a host of issues that flow from the novelty and difficulty of the academic program as well as the seminar, school-based format in which it is accomplished. A curriculum designed by teachers and staff with serious academic backgrounds to challenge talented and passionate students is unlikely to skirt the challenges of a strenuous workload, particularly among students who strive for perfection in their academic work as well as in their extracurricular engagements. Preserving students' flexibility in pursuing all of their academic interests to their fullest extent is also a unique challenge in the SOHS program. When the curriculum has the means to challenge each student in each subject, and distinctive courses do not map easily onto formulaic college expectations for high-school coursework, students have less room to maneuver in meeting requirements while pursuing their own interests. And in the context of the school's enrollment model, these same pressures on student flexibility can constrain development of the innovative and challenging courses that make the SOHS curriculum a distinctive fit for our students.

5.1 Workload

As soon as the school opened its doors, students and parents had questions and concerns about the workload in individual courses and on the whole. And it has been both a topic of discussion and a focus of work by staff ever since, at the level of individual students and throughout the curriculum. Our most recent systematic efforts to mitigate what is clearly a taxing workload have been informed by a 2012-13 survey of students in which 11% of respondents characterized the workload at SOHS as 'overwhelming' and 41% called it 'a little too much/unreasonable' (only one bold student called the workload 'light'). In the same survey, 63% of respondents were 'very concerned' or 'concerned' that the SOHS workload significantly prevents them from pursuing other things, while 41% 'agreed' or 'strongly agreed' that the workload at SOHS is in need of adjustment.[16] While these numbers are somewhat lower than expected given the tenor of the open discussions regarding workload, and while workload is certainly not an issue unique to SOHS, the staff did take these findings, in the context of other considerations, to justify systematic efforts to address academic expectations for student work in a manner consistent with the school's pedagogical goals.

Despite the extent of discussions, there is little concern that the strain of the workload stems from busywork. Rather, the situation is largely a result of carefully designed courses modeled on college-style treatment of challenging material. Whether reading from original texts, diving into secondary literature, conducting home experiments and crafting lab reports, or tackling challenging mathematical exercises, students have a lot to do because this kind of deep engagement in the

[16]Notably, the 41% interested in change is a lower figure than those expressing concern. Indeed, 22% of students disagreed that change should be made. Free responses in the survey expressed some sentiment that students saw the workload as an anticipated feature of the school that was an important part of the education they were seeking in choosing the school.

curriculum is fundamentally an intensive process. Guidelines advertised to potential students and to teachers alike entail eight to ten hours of work, in and out of class, per course per week at the high-school level, and six hours or less at the middle-school level. Difficulties can magnify when students struggle significantly with a given assignment or course or feel compelled to work on projects more than indicated, or when major projects in different courses coalesce around a small window of time. And in this context, individual academic plans calling for five or even six courses (a full-time student takes four to five yearlong courses) in a given year present serious challenges.

In working to address concerns about workload, both on the part of families and among staff, the school has adopted an 'all of the above' approach, working on an assortment of projects to streamline work where possible and to mitigate the effect of necessary work on students. Regarding the extent of work assigned, itself, the staff has shared best practices in both division and faculty-wide settings, and in the current academic year, instructors are each working to implement at least one approach to streamlining work. These initiatives include trimming lectures, scaffolding lengthier assignments into several parts, paring down routine assignments such as science lab reports, and ensuring that exams and tests are only as long and frequent as necessary. There is a lot of room for fine-tuning ambitious courses in ways that do not compromise rigor. But beyond these adjustments, the most powerful steps, endorsed by students, may be the measures to coordinate assignment times across classes and against external exams, like the various SAT exams. As at any school, the logic of the school calendar frequently manifests itself across courses, such that students will end up with several major projects, essays, or exams due at a few critical points in the semester or school year. Particularly in advanced classes, where research papers and concluding projects are common end-of-semester work, a reasonable workload in the context of a single course can become unmanageable in the context of a full course of study. In addressing this sort of issue, the school has been hamstrung by the same realities that make alignment of curriculum difficult across disciplines: there really is no such thing as a 'standard course of study' for particular grade levels at SOHS that would be the basis for straightforward coordination of assignment timing for a group of students. Even so, the imperfect approach adopted—periodic check-ins among instructors in patches of the curriculum often taken together, sometimes supplemented by reports from students, and framed against a staff-wide calendar of midterms and external testing dates—has produced improvements noticeable to students.

5.2 Requirements

SOHS's approach to building a challenging curriculum for gifted students encounters further tensions in conventional models of acceleration and individualized learning. Most visibly, the SOHS academic program modifies a conventional program's constraints on students' academic plans in two ways: (1) it increases the difficulty of each course, often thereby *decreasing* the number of courses a student can realistically take at a given time, and (2) it *increases* the numbered of required courses, most saliently in the requirement that each graduating student take a Core course in each year at the high-school level. For both of these reasons, students cannot easily achieve their curricular goals simply by taking on more courses—taking, for instance, two science or English courses in a year in order to reach university-level work, or adding 'electives' like computer science, economics, or additional history or advanced language courses to a standard schedule. And this dilemma affects a range of students: students with strong academic identities who want to take multiple courses in a certain area of the curriculum, students with a particular passion for an elective discipline like history, foreign language, or computer science, and students who do not pursue a specialty, but rather want to pursue each major field to its fullest extent.[17]

We are confident that the depth of the SOHS curriculum and the challenge of its courses provides talented students a special opportunity for meaningful academic preparation. But within this framework, we have also explored a spectrum of practices and programs to accommodate some students' needs for greater breadth in their courses of study. One strategy for giving students more options in shaping their schedules involves recognizing relevant Core courses as satisfying requirements in the discipline treated: Democracy, Freedom, and the Rule of Law clearly covers material in the social sciences in its treatment of political theory and history, and is also recognized in the University of California 'a-g' subject requirement system as doing so; History of Science can also be counted as a social science course in its extensive treatment of the historical context of the scientific process; and Methodology of Science—Biology can be considered a non-laboratory science. Given the exposure gained in these courses to the content and skills of the relevant disciplines, students with serious interests elsewhere in the curriculum win some space for those interests. However, our administration and the students themselves are mindful of prospective colleges' interpretation of the academic plans that result from these strategies;

---

[17]Some sample courses of study are provided at http://bricksandmortarbook.com.

it is critical that colleges are in a position to appreciate the depth of students' preparation in all fields, even if it does not include courses that have the traditional trappings of coursework in those areas.

While students can acquire appropriate preparation in the standard fields by drawing on cross-listings such as those in the Core program, it is not always ideal to rely on these mechanisms to help students focus on particular aspects of the curriculum. Most poignant are the cases of students who would dearly love to take advanced courses in many disciplines, but who find this increasingly difficult later in the curriculum. It is, for instance, difficult to maintain a foreign language for four years, while also pursuing several non-required courses in a discipline like history. The school's most promising strategy for addressing situations of this sort consists in the design of the Advanced Topics courses. These courses occupy a critical place in the curriculum, geared as they are to providing students real exposure to college-style pedagogy and study in a discipline. And this is exactly the kind of preparation students can miss if they truncate their study in a given subject due to constraints on their time. Our approach, then, was to find a way to make these courses more widely available to students with already strenuous academic plans, without overloading them. What emerged was a model sometimes used in college or in graduate programs, on which students could select to attend and participate in class, do the weekly preparation and work, and then opt into or out of the major semester-long research project required for full credit. Students wanting the full experience of the course receive the unique benefits of engaging in extended, college-style research, paper writing, or literature reviews, while those looking for exposure to advanced treatment of material can fit the class in for half-credit and essentially half of the commitment of time and resources.

6 Looking Forward

Computer-based education has long appeared as the ideal tool for common modes of gifted education, particularly with the potential for extreme individualization, solving classic problems in differentiation, resources, and lack of challenge. Online education in the manner of the SOHS, however, presents a new possibility that allows us to consider whether such individualization is indeed the best option for talented students, or is instead the adventitious product of logistics. The natural distribution of intellectual abilities entails that the population of students ready for serious advancement and challenge beyond what local schools can provide will be small, and inadequate to support rich classroom curriculum. Models for meeting these needs, from individual study to enrichment to self-paced computerized instruction are necessarily designed for private implementation. Even early matriculation is often a matter of access to advanced curriculum, and occurs *in spite of* an adverse social environment. SOHS, on the other hand, uses technology to aggregate abilities and interests on a scale that not only makes tailored curriculum possible, but makes it possible in a school environment in which students work together in a live, shared setting.

One parent expresses a sentiment common among students and families at the SOHS in describing her extremely talented son's enthusiasm for a particular course: 'He's at his happiest and best when he's talking about things in a group of other smart kids.' The premise of the school's model, eight years on, is that the best, most vibrant learning environment for talented students is in the company of others. And since gifted kids are more like one another than like undergraduates, the aggregation of such students that the technology makes possible is technology's most promising contribution to a challenging education for particularly talented high-school students.

With the focus of curriculum development clearly fixed on challenging students in a class setting through the nature, not the rapidity, of the content, the SOHS is well begun in the task of reworking a classical curriculum to challenge gifted students in the context of contemporary expectations. With the exception of the Core sequence and some of the post-AP-level courses, this project has been accomplished at the level of individual courses, without inordinately upsetting standard sequences in English, history, languages, science, or mathematics. Such an approach is appropriate for a new school that is innovative already in so many ways; it has been important for the school to offer popular AP courses, suitably enriched, and to adhere to disciplinary boundaries and requirements. However, in assessing the limitations that these standard progressions place on our students' development in terms of both skills and advanced content, and in seeing the results of courses designed to facilitate the development of critical skills within a discipline and more broadly, the next steps for the school's curriculum are apparent. As the school earns more discretion to innovate at a curriculum-wide level, from our families and from colleges, we look to create course offerings, sequences, and disciplinary requirements that expand on the strategy of developing targeted skills in the appropriate context of material and focus. With more flexibility to craft alternatives to survey courses, to pursue particular skills in the disciplines most appropriate for students, and to layer in skills of character development and creativity throughout the curriculum, the academic program can more systematically build the dynamic and flexible thinkers our students have the unique potential to become.

4

Pedagogy Online

1 Introduction

Teachers are quick to resort to metaphors to describe what it is that they do. Socrates' account of teaching, cited in the previous chapter, imagines the teacher as guide, coaxing out from the student the knowledge he already innately possesses. An image with roots in Plato gets modern expression in Dewey, for whom teachers are gardeners who prepare the proper environment in which a student unfolds like a seed.[1] Dickens's Gradgrind filled 'little pitchers' with facts, albeit satirically,[2] calling to mind Plutarch's admonition that the mind is not such a vessel, but wood to be kindled.[3] Skinner advises that children be trained through selective reinforcement of desired behavior, like other animals.[4] And then there are teachers as coaches: coaches of basketball, drilling their students in skills, practicing elaborate plays and defenses, and orchestrating the result; thoroughbred trainers teach their students to run (in a direction of their choosing?) and set them on their way. What sort of teaching is possible online? We have seen now who the students and teachers are and what they are studying. But does the technology transform the methods, strategies, and interactions that define the discipline?

But it is not just the technology that might shape the modes of instruction in an online environment. The proliferation of online programs brings with it a diversity of rationales for online instruction, each suggesting its own instructional model. Some programs, particularly some

[1] J. Dewey, *Democracy and Education*, (New York: Macmillan, 1916), chap. 8.

[2] C. Dickens, *Hard Times*, Illustrated edition, (London: Heritage Illustrated Publishing, 2014).

[3] Plutarch, *Plutarch: Moralia, Volume I*, trans. Frank Cole Babbitt (Loeb Classical Library, 1927).

[4] B. F. Skinner, 'How to Teach Animals', *Scientific American* 185 (1951): 26-29.

of the original MOOCs, are trying to solve issues of access, costs for users, and scale, making instruction in college-level topics available to more students, sometimes outside of the usual venues in higher education. Small colleges and independent schools are addressing institutional costs and expertise, exploring ways to maintain or expand the scope of their offerings without the traditional staffing requirements. Remediation and acceleration are perennial desiderata at most levels, as, perhaps, is the newer potential for flipped instruction. And nearly every kind of institution is examining possibilities for blended learning in at least some limited contexts, from snow days to summer vacations. In each context, success in the educational project depends on more than the technology and curriculum. Success in online programs, both in terms of learning and retention of students, hinges on whether and how the technology can be used to provide the resources and opportunities to do what the pedagogy appropriate to the rationale demands.

Critical observers of online education rightly make distinctions in their assessments of the adequacy of online technologies to the mode of instruction that might be ideal for particular subjects or stages of learning. On one view,

> As far as education is concerned, the Net is useful in supplying the facts and rules as well as the drill and practice required by a beginner. It seems, however, that the involvement and risk that come from making interpretations that can be mistaken and learning from one's mistakes are necessary if one is to acquire expertise...Only in a classroom where the teacher and learner sense that they are taking risks in each other's presence, and each can count on criticism from the other, are the conditions present that promote acquiring proficiency, and only by acting in the real world can one acquire expertise.[5]

While we argue in Chapter 6 that it is a mistake to define an interactive classroom too narrowly—to the exclusion of the right kind of online synchronous environment—the experience of the Stanford Online High School affirms the transformative role of live instruction, and in this way we often find ourselves ironically agreeing with skeptics of online learning. Particularly as the educational goal moves beyond foundational mastery of basic concepts to an emphasis on developing an ability to engage in a time-extended process of critical reflection, real-time feedback and interaction is essential, as is the opportunity for students to demonstrate in its totality the thing that we are trying to teach them. Returning to our earlier example of online golf training, the advantage afforded by the coach was the attending not to the out-

[5]Dreyfus, *On the Internet*, 122.

comes (where the ball was landing) but to the underlying process (the swing). Current technologies have scant means to monitor a student's thinking in process. One could imagine developing better and better approximations of such coaching, eliciting a student's reasoning asynchronously in an electronic 'blue book' or via podcasts of explanation and providing swift analysis. But much better, of course, to get the suggestions from a coach who knows you, who is watching your swing as you make it, correcting your corrections, and modeling the target process. And better still to do it in discussion with peers, where at least to some extent, the shots count.

Classes at the Stanford Online High School do indeed occur in an online setting, and pedagogy at the school is shaped by and makes use of this technology and format. However, the format of instruction at the school and of the underlying technological infrastructure is sufficiently flexible and robust that it supports the pedagogy characteristic of a college-style seminar course; the technology is enough to make possible the live, interactive experimentation that we have found to work best for our students in our curriculum. That courses and teaching are online, then, is of significance primarily in the adjustments and benefits that it entails. Indeed, the success of the seminar format, in conjunction with the founding mission of the school, prescribed a rebalancing of the school's early format to expand the scope of seminar courses.[6] In examining the pedagogical strategies of the SOHS in its online context, then, we will suggest that the methods are largely those of a traditional seminar course, focused on what those in the independent school world might term a 'virtual Harkness table', where creative use of the technology realizes those traditions in relatively transparent ways. Accordingly, SOHS students are positioned to benefit from the distinctive expertise of their instructors, the unique diversity and talents of their peers, and the occasional innovation to the classroom or course-material format afforded by the technology.

2 The SOHS Seminar and its Development

While the asynchronous courses at Stanford from which the SOHS emerged were conceived to allow students to accelerate in a discipline without leaving their normal school environment, many considerations pointed to the distinct utility of advanced coursework offered in a rich school setting. And so the Stanford Online High School was founded with the following mission:

[6] See the discussion in Chapters 1 and 3 of the transition to a seminar format, particularly in mathematics classes.

> Through advanced technology, rigorous courses, and the resources of Stanford University, the Online High School affords gifted students everywhere an education ideally suited to their needs: one which sets high expectations and challenges them to reach their potential; one which cultivates creativity, fosters analytical reason, and refines argumentative skills; one in which students pursue intellectual passions, and engage in philosophical reflection; one which builds the foundation for success in future academic pursuits and in life itself.[7]

The logic of these initial goals for the school, which still guide its development, did not immediately dictate the nature of the instructional setting and the lively school community that emerged and lend the school much of its vitality today. Many of the courses in the first year of the school adopted an asynchronous, individualized approach that would allow students to proceed at their own pace through a standardized course of study. And for reasons already discussed in the first chapter, this proved to be neither what students wanted nor what they needed, which was opportunities for real-time interaction. The story of the development of the school has been very much the story of the increasing centrality of synchronous, immersive class meetings. Much of our experience with an exploration of online classroom facilities and other technologies in support of community have therefore been in the service of furthering our mandate to provide rigorous and individualized instruction for talented students, precisely through a classroom setting in which students from around the world explore material together with teachers who are experts in their fields.

With a few remaining exceptions in the upper end of the university-level physics curriculum, all courses at the SOHS meet at least biweekly for sixty to ninety minutes a session in a video-conferencing environment that also features a shared whiteboard, text-chat facility, and various other capacities. Teachers and students are able to draw on the essential features of a classroom environment in order to facilitate rich discussions evocative of small seminars at the college level. The excerpt below offers an illustrative description of a sample discussion section from the perspective of an observer:

> As class begins, students log on and see a list, running down the left side of their screens, of everyone present. As Scarborough starts the class, his face pops up on a small video screen in the upper left-hand corner. The bulk of the screen is a virtual whiteboard, on which Scarborough presents the points of the lesson, changing them to reflect the discussion as the class unfolds.

---

[7] R. Ravaglia, 'Founding Proposal for Online High School' (unpublished submission to the Malone Family Foundation, August 2005).

And the discussion—today, it's about John Dewey's *Liberalism and Social Action* and F.A. Hayek's *The Constitution of Liberty*—is lively. As Scarborough speaks, little hand icons pop up next to student's names, meaning they have their hands raised to talk. As he calls on students, their video images replace his. The talk is quick and sharp, ranging over the meaning of liberty, the ancillary meaning of freedom and the question of whether political liberty is naturally occurring.

It is heady stuff, a lot to absorb. But that's not all that's going on. On top of reading Scarborough's notes on the screen and listening to him and their classmates speaking, the students maintain a running conversation of instant messages, which pop up near the bottom of the screen. It's like students passing notes in class, except that this is sanctioned—mostly. Occasionally, when the messages spin off into nonstop puns or other forms of nonacademic amusement, Scarborough has to issue a warning to focus on the class material.

Mostly, though, these are 21st century students who seem capable of doing five things at once.[8]

The description above of an SOHS class highlights some of the main features of the classroom experience and offers a glimpse of the extent to which the online technology shapes or facilitates that experience. A more detailed account of these features and their pedagogical impact will help to situate the discussion of how the SOHS has and will continue looking to develop the online classroom to more fully achieve its aims.

These synchronous class sessions occur in the context of a robust network of additional work and support, including recorded lectures, reading, problem sets, exercises in increasingly third-party software, papers, projects, live office hours, and Skype study groups. In all of these other aspects, instruction at the SOHS leverages technology to establish flexibility in student schedules and to enable students to focus on what is most important for their studies, consistent with the goals of the school in serving talented and motivated students. That is, the work required of students is distributed across asynchronous tasks to the extent that pedagogy for advanced students in a given subject commends, such that students are able to accomplish those tasks at an individualized pace and at times of the day that prove both efficient and perhaps carve out time for independent cocurricular activities such as research at local labs. In broad conception, this allocation of student time resembles the approach of a college schedule, where class meetings are

[8] M. Landsberg, 'More Clicks than Cliques: Love of Learning Propels Students from Around the World at Stanford's Online High School', *Los Angeles Times*, June 17, 2007, http://articles.latimes.com/2007/jun/17/local/me-online17.

spread across the day, and in which these impactful and highly focused meetings at once set the stage and also make room for a considerable body of self-directed activities including research, exercises, labs, and preparation for class.

In addition to the college-like schedule of discussion seminars, classes at the SOHS are, in the current terminology, 'flipped' with respect to both conventional classroom activities and even university-level pedagogy.[9] That is, the online classroom technology makes very natural the segregation into a student's asynchronous preparation the traditional lecturing component of live classroom instruction. At its simplest, producing a lecture might entail no more than recording a classroom session, complete with visual aids, video, and presentation, but in the absence of students. An important lesson we have learned repeatedly over the years is that our students are much more sophisticated consumers of media than we are producers. They are endlessly accommodating when presented with authentic efforts rooted in substantive treatment of content. But if one tries to get sophisticated and professional in the production, they are relentless and unforgiving in their criticism if things fall short. In other words, being primitive is not a sin, but being hokey is.

Students are therefore able to work through the lectures at times that make sense in their own preparation, for instance before doing the reading, after the reading, or shortly before class, as most appropriate to learning style and the particular subject or material. And as students are free to replay difficult or critical passages, teachers can calibrate the density and pacing of the lecture in a manner that sets a high bar for students and also aids in differentiation, particularly in a talented population of students. With respect to the content of the lectures itself, the asynchronous context makes it possible for the duration and frequency of lectures to follow the contours of the material rather than the logistical factors that conventionally shape a school day, resulting in a spectrum of practices across the school, including grade levels and discipline, and even from topic to topic within a course.

In this context of asynchronous tasks, designed to expose students to content and afford practice and reflection in a format that can be calibrated to individual needs and styles, the guiding mandate of synchronous meeting time is that it take maximal advantage of the relatively precious and unique resources afforded by a live (if remote)

---

[9] A recent discussion of flipped pedagogy for brick-and-mortar contexts is J. Bergmann and A. Sams, *Flip Your Classroom: Reach Every Student in Every Class Every Day* (Washington, DC: International Society for Technology in Education, 2012).

gathering of talented instructors and a student population scattered across the country and around the world, all of whom share an often rare preparation and passion for the material. In the absence of lectures that would be largely a poor use of the potential for interaction, and with students' preparation already largely accomplished by reading and lecture, and further shaped and perhaps verified by appropriate exercises, the primary function of the discussion seminar is then to engage students in the material in a variety of ways that deepen understanding, develop skills of criticism and argument, and enliven the topics. In the humanities, this can mean, as above, delving into an analysis of the views at issue by, for instance, working collaboratively to extract the logical structure of an argument and then submitting it to criticism, electing competing views from students who must then defend those views against the probing of teachers and fellow students, and both illustrating and evaluating the implications of classical positions by applying them to contemporary circumstances. In math and sciences, discussion can leverage the diverse training and style of students to demonstrate different approaches to solutions of problems, while similarly offering students and teachers the opportunity to explore creative applications of concepts to new technologies, discoveries, and everyday phenomena. In English, meanwhile, the potential in all fields for constructive group work in the online classroom can be appreciated in writers' workshops, in which students gather in small groups ('breakout rooms', in the current video-conferencing parlance) to critique one another's work. In all of these activities, and in the many other synchronous methods possible online and familiar from brick-and-mortar seminar settings, the SOHS emphasizes the opportunity that the live interaction provides for teachers to model, and to elicit from students, the standards and practices of serious academic inquiry. Anecdotal but compelling experience suggests that students learn these norms—these habits of careful thinking in a discipline—most decisively not from private study, but in the collaborative engagement with teachers who know these standards from their professional academic work, and with peers who are similarly exploring the material.

It is important to note, in the context of a discussion of the ways in which an online seminar can accomplish goals familiar to the best traditions of a physical classroom while also increasing the focus and time dedicated to those goals, that the online setting can also add an unparalleled diversity that tangibly shapes the content of the sessions and the experiences of students. The SOHS has from its start featured a strong international representation, paired with considerable geographic distribution across the United States. And so it has been clear from the outset that not only does the online character of the school succeed in concentrating scattered populations of uniquely qualified and passionate students, but it also, particularly in the live, interactive setting, brings directly into contact students who embody the different experiences and perspectives that teachers often struggle to illustrate (or even themselves consider) for their homogeneous students. Nor is the full extent of this effect mimicked by brick-and-mortar schools and universities with global reach: in virtue of the online classroom, discussions at SOHS occur among students who do not just come from different places and backgrounds, but rather *are in* different places, bringing their locally-shaped experiences of international developments, or their first-hand experience of a regional phenomenon, into the common classroom. From a teacher's point of view, there is no quicker way to undermine assumptions and highlight the conceptual choices at stake in, for instance, democratic government in the Madisonian style, than to field the question from a student living in a parliamentary tradition in Europe, or an entirely different system in Asia. Indeed, much smaller differences in expertise, training, and opinion color SOHS seminars every day and across the curriculum.

3 In-class Tools

The focus in a seminar on dialogue among students and teacher calls for a minimal technical apparatus when transferred online. The technology does not need to transform pedagogy in any way. Rather, what is needed are the tools of a classroom: students and teachers with the means to interact in real time, and a means for sharing content. To be sure, there are better and worse instances of such a system, with features that vary in their suitability for classroom exchanges. And while reliability is perhaps the most precious commodity of an online classroom, there are also some possibilities that the medium affords that are not possible in a brick-and-mortar setting.

3.1 Video-conferencing

Participation in SOHS discussion seminars requires use of a webcam. While video capacities in the virtual classroom system we have used since the start of the school have historically been minimal—a small, single-point video image that can be passed to the speaker along with the microphone—the function of even minimal video engagement is significant, to a degree that creates an imperative for further development of video capabilities. Speaking broadly, video lends a presence and focal point for immersion in the event. It is the video stream that effectively signals to students (and teachers) that there is someone on the other side of their screens, actively engaging them, to the exclusion of other tasks and events occurring in both the local and electronic environment. The visible intentionality of the speaker—the directness of her speech and body language toward an interlocutor who might in turn take the microphone and video to reply—helps to distinguish the synchronous classroom from other passive activities students might engage in. Video also plays more subtle and less clearly academic roles in the school community, but these can be explored separately, as we do in Chapter 6.

Certainly, video conferencing has far more potential than is realized in the limited, if important, role that it has played at the SOHS to this point. Indeed, the absence of persistent visual access to each student is perhaps the most significant pedagogical disparity between a conventional and an online classroom. Without the strong visual cues of student comprehension, engagement, and interest, teachers must work hard and with concerted appeal to a variety of strategies in order to coordinate their management of the class with the dynamics of the class as a whole and with the needs of individual students. While such efforts are imperfect and demanding, and while they have unavoidable logistical implications for the school (such as limits on the size of an effective class), SOHS instructors have developed a spectrum of strategies, norms, and best practices to accomplish these important pedagogical tasks. Several tools built into the school's classroom environment have emerged in the SOHS culture to serve in place of the traditional visual dynamic between student and teacher. Green checkmarks and red Xs signal, depending on context, agreement or discord, the truth or falsity of a proposition relative to individual students, or simple casual tracking or comprehension of an unfolding comment or point. Clapping and laughing emoticons, meanwhile, convey obvious meaning, but also function as implicit signals of attention and interest. (Whenever students participate in another video-conferencing environment, they are quick to create analogous conventions—lamenting the lack of a diverse range—to these communicative functions.) For their own part, it is incumbent upon teachers to make skillful and attentive use of these cues, to elicit periodic responsiveness among students, to track individual students' views and engagement over the course of a class and year, and also to gauge, in conjunction with other cues and information, when a reticent student might be 'on the edge of her seat' and open to being drawn into discussion. Indeed, the art of calling on students is even more complex without persistent video. But teachers must engage in those practices as well, taking care to prevent students from slipping easily into the background, where averted glances by struggling students are not discernible from irritation and boredom on the one hand, or competent tracking, on the other. Thorough work outside the classroom is still more critical in this regard. Speaking with students and parents about a student's interests in a course and more broadly can help detect problems that might normally be visible in body language, and can also reveal quiet students open to engagement on topics of special interest. Similar information is available in written work for incorporation in discussion. And while many of these are classic strategies, they take on particular importance in the online classroom.

3.2 Whiteboard

Every class needs a chalkboard, whiteboard, or some other visual tool for tracking the flow of conversation, capturing vital elements of an equation or problem, or displaying text or graphics for consideration. Somewhat strikingly, though perhaps not surprisingly, many videoconferencing systems designed for enterprise use do not feature robust tools for content sharing, particularly with support for easy markup. But the virtual whiteboard has pride of place in SOHS classrooms, displaying images, documents, PowerPoints, and available real estate for subsequent marking up as the class moves through material. Teachers use the space in the myriad ways any teacher does: cataloging and organizing student comments, working problems or asking students to do so, marking up text, and drawing graphs and quirky illustrations.

The parallels to physical whiteboards predominate in a comparison, particularly in the main lines of traditional use. But a well-designed virtual whiteboard shares much of the potential of electronic whiteboards, and additional benefits still, which give teachers and students some flexibility in stretching its traditional pedagogical function. To be sure, electronic whiteboards generally feature added efficiency and richness: complicated and striking content can be drawn from a variety of sources in advance, be displayed on demand, and reused in subsequent iterations. The complexity of the material that can be displayed is of some pedagogical significance—how does the ready display of a passage, rather than the mere reading, benefit learners of different stripes, for instance—though it is not without the 'traditional' analogue of classroom display media. In a similar vein, the electronic ability to save material on the board, routinely exercised at SOHS, can facilitate later review or discussion for individual students and the class as a whole. Student notes can be supplemented with the markup from class and quick reference for paper-writing and exam preparation.

More striking, though, are the modest structural transformations to student participation afforded by a virtual whiteboard that is accessible to students in the manner of SOHS classrooms. This accessibility has two key features: writing on the whiteboard is easy, and it can be anonymous. Easy access—any student can write directly on the board with the teacher's authorization—is a boon to collective tasks like brainstorming or simultaneous board work, and generally lowers the bar, or even invites, casual student contributions to the record on the board. Students can be asked to distill a point just made in audio-visual discussion for reference, recruited to illustrate a concept, or allowed to post relevant citations from the text, all casually and without impeding the progress of the discussion. Creative teachers have also drawn on the anonymity of an unclaimed whiteboard markup to elicit participation from reticent students or honest feedback from the class as a whole. One strategy (approximated by clickers or other polling mechanisms in brick-and-mortar classes) calls for students to adopt avatars—from simple drawings to a unique pen color—with which they symbolize their affiliation with a possible answer, solve a problem, or represent their level of comfort with a concept. While the confidence to claim one's work is an important quality to develop, teachers are generally glad to have an array of tools with which to spur participation and ease the initial steps toward that confidence.

3.3 Text Chat

If limited visual cues are an impoverishment of the current online classroom, the text-chat capacity is a tremendous and nuanced resource that is unavailable in traditional contexts. The texting system in the SOHS classroom and in similar systems can be configured to allow texting visible to all participants in the class, as well as private texts between the instructor and individual students. In this form, texting opens an additional line of communication in the classroom that provides a degree of pedagogical flexibility and efficiency, and with appropriate management, lends a unique dynamism to the classroom.

As an additional tool in the classroom, text chat provides students and teacher a direct line of communication simultaneous with the ongoing audio-visual discussion. Students can ask brief questions of clarification as a teacher speaks, enabling her to modulate her comments dynamically to communicate the desired point or to direct those comments toward the avenue that is resonating most successfully with students. A teacher can also 'bank' questions and comments from students submitted in text chat, using them selectively to transition to the next phase of the discussion or to further illustrate a previous point. For students, text provides a mechanism for a quick response to a teacher's question or a comment from a fellow student. It can be a way to register a longer comment for which there was not time in the main audio-visual discussion. Or it can be a recourse when the conversation has gotten away or is assuming a concept that remains unclear. Sometimes fellow students can answer before the teacher has to adjust the flow of the conversation to respond. Texting also addresses several conundrums of a traditional classroom. It supports strategies for eliciting participation from reticent students, with private text permitting teacher or student to communicate in a low-stakes environment to strategize about good places for the student to interject, while the public text discussion affords a less intimidating forum in which a student can practice participation, sometimes giving the teacher an opportunity to work the substance of the exchange into the audio-visual discussion. And for the loquacious student, or for comments that begin to stray from a key point, private text is a gentle correction.

Partly as a function of these possibilities, text chat can serve to enhance the excitement characteristic of the best discussion seminars. To the extent that text helps to break down the strong linearity of a discussion, especially one occurring online with a single video stream, and also minimizes excessive declamation by a teacher or student, it fosters a fast-paced and collegial conversation in which students can have their say and get feedback from several sources, without monopolizing the conversation. To be sure, a conversation of this sort requires careful and practiced management, respect for norms of topicality and deference, and consideration of the limits of attention. But with proper execution, it can be thoroughly productive, exhilarating, and intellectually immersive.

As this discussion of the role of video in the classroom suggests, the primary point of continued development of the online classroom is the potential for more immersive video capabilities, particularly the capacity for high-definition multi-point video. In the past several years, we have taken significant steps toward understanding the technical underpinnings of such capabilities, as well as their pedagogical implications and significance. Working with several other schools, we have piloted courses taught in video-intensive platforms making use of a variety of hardware at the various locations. Several trials in selected courses at SOHS are also in progress. Beyond the challenge of orchestrating the technical interoperability across locations and systems, and in addition to the exercise of cobbling together the elements of an online classroom detailed above to pair with the high-definition multi-point video, as well as thinking through instructional norms appropriate to this new environment, the payoff in the classroom experience is as one would expect. It is precisely the ability to see all of the members of the seminar, and to see them in expressive detail, that elevates the online classroom to a still more collegial seminar discussion. In this environment, it is easy to tell when students have energy to pursue a line of discussion further, when a topic strikes a chord with a particular student, when a transition is appropriate, or whether a student is expressing confusion or is pondering a possibility. Among advanced and experienced students, the conversation regulates itself: students themselves can see if another is about to speak, and can time their own contribution to the discussion, while the instructor can curtail his own comment to allow an eager student to seize on a point. As discussed above, there are rhythms to a class that can be reconstructed with care in a classroom with minimal visual context; however, the addition of familiar and robust visual cues makes the process considerably easier and perhaps more enjoyable. The full implementation of this or similar technology in the online classroom will take us much closer to the realization of a goal of both intellectual and social presence in a unique classroom setting that spans continents—one which to many of our students, already feels very much like home.

3.4 Other Tools

SOHS instructors employ a variety of additional tools and strategies to realize the desired classroom activity. Some possibilities are expressly built into the SOHS classroom software, others are adapted from third-party sources, and many are simply improvised from available tools and media by resourceful teachers and students.

In any classroom, but particularly in those predicated on active student involvement, the entreaty to 'turn to your neighbor' or 'get into groups' is a common refrain. No less at the SOHS: small-group work is a staple of classes across the curriculum, useful for facilitating one-on-one practice, generating a range of responses, eliciting participation from all or different students, atomizing a larger task, deemphasizing the role of the teacher and promoting student leadership, and varying activities during class time. Creating a setting for this universal activity, while wholly natural in physical space, is hardly easy online, where the minimal task of a video-conferencing forum is to connect all the members of a particular meeting. Video-conferencing systems, including that used by SOHS, standardly feature a built-in tool for this task—the 'breakout room'. The tool creates individual mini-classrooms for groups of the specified size and randomly assigns students and a 'leader' to each room (though teachers can do this manually or tweak the assignments to foster desired dynamics). Teachers can then move among the rooms, observing or assisting as students work on the assigned task in their private version of the regular classroom environment. Reporting-back or other follow-up activities flow naturally from this context. Breakout rooms are a familiar and efficient tool at the SOHS, to such an extent that various norms, jokes, and practices have and continue to emerge at the schoolwide, course, and class-section levels. This is one context in which a properly implemented tool accomplishes the traditional pedagogical function without much notable variation. A superlative tool, perhaps, might move to support teachers in better addressing the traditional difficulties and frustrations of group work.

Similarly foundational to common classroom techniques is the use of external or supplementary materials. That the classroom occurs in a digital medium clearly calls for different strategies and tools than does a physical setting. But here again, the difference consists mainly in accommodating the technical requirements of the medium and relevant classroom systems, as opposed to reenvisioning or replacing traditional classroom dynamics and techniques. Rather than posters, slides, transparencies, or photocopies, SOHS instructors rely on .jpgs, .gifs, .pdfs, and PowerPoints on a virtual whiteboard; similarly, rather than snippets of a tape or film played in class, they queue up an excerpt from YouTube or a privately-digitized file. In some cases, a little ingenuity and a hacker mentality is required to muscle the desired content into the proper format. But as brick-and-mortar instructional technology increasingly embraces the expansion of digital content, even the gymnastics of dealing with digital content are proliferating more significantly in the physical classroom. Indeed, while the bells and whistles of a well-appointed digital 'recording studio' or seminar room are quite conceivable and worth exploring, SOHS instructors can draw on the wealth of digital content using some very simple file-management techniques; there is little use and little demand for electronic chalkboards, projectors, and one-to-one laptops in the classroom. Paradoxically, most of the flashy booths at educational technology conferences have little to offer to the SOHS. In our experience, this is only partly because the relevant technology is already built-in to an electronic classroom. More tellingly, it speaks to the thesis that when it comes to instruction in the SOHS classroom, technology is primarily a tool used to re-create, and occasionally enhance, a traditional seminar setting among teachers and students who are simply not in the same place.

To say that technology use at the SOHS is primarily in the service of traditional seminar dynamics is not to suggest that there is no experimentation or even broad use of emerging electronic tools. On the contrary, instructors judiciously pilot a variety of external tools; however, it is typically the case that these tools generally represent mechanisms for facilitating student participation and interaction, and are of interest exactly in virtue of their potential to further the goals of the seminar setting. So, for instance, teachers in the chemistry course and middle-school science courses first piloted, and then made more widespread use of the Learning Catalytics program. This system allows the teacher to send out questions to all students, cataloging their responses, and then prescribes that students work with partners to solve the same problem, submitting a revised answer on the basis of that discussion. In accordance with both time-worn anecdote and more contemporary research, the collaborative arrangement tends to yield significantly higher accuracy and comprehension. In addition, it proves effective in the SOHS project of connecting students in a collaborative work situation, and in fostering habits of participation and collaborative inquiry in the class setting.

4 Asynchronous Instruction

The SOHS has, for most purposes, been using a flipped style of instruction since its inception. As the technology-driven movement to use video and other automation to move lecture and drilling outside of class time has grown in popularity, the SOHS in this sense finds itself at the forefront of an emerging trend in educational technology. To be sure, eight years of exploring pedagogy in this model has yielded a wealth of experience that might be applied to other flipped initiatives. However, it is significant to the school's strategies for addressing the questions that arise regarding asynchronous learning that our own move to the flipped classroom's division of labor was not driven directly by the availability of asynchronous technology, as has been the norm. Rather, SOHS started with the model of a college-style seminar, and college-style pedagogy more generally, where lectures are often relegated to dedicated mass sessions and much of the most impactful engagement with the material occurs in small, active discussion sections. The trick to realizing this model in the online context of SOHS was simply to put the lecture material into an asynchronous format, reserving the rare and precious time when teachers and students could gather together for the more compelling interaction of the seminar. In this sense, the flipped model, and much of its pedagogy, is quite old; it is simply the venue for the lecturing that has changed in the online setting. For the teachers at SOHS, themselves often veterans of the university model, the question is not so much what to do in newly-free class time, nor, necessarily, what to segment into lecture—these are well-rehearsed skills of their traditional training. The exploration of the past eight years concerning the interplay of in-class and out-of-class activities has focused on refinements of this classic model that are appropriate to the private viewing of asynchronous lectures (compared to the largely passive reception in lecture halls), or to the implementation of this model in the high-school and middle-school setting, or in disciplines such as languages where lectures are less instrumental or have declined in common practice. Implementation of the flipped classroom at SOHS, and its treatment of asynchronous learning, is therefore a mixture of traditional practices and the modern adjustments appropriate to the online realization of some of these traditional components.

4.1 Lectures

Despite the basic academic equivalence of lectures conducted in a class setting and those recorded for asynchronous viewing, the transition from the former to the latter raises a host of considerations stemming primarily from the fact that at SOHS, these lectures are not delivered in a live class setting. One implication, which also prescribes a challenge for asynchronous materials, is the deficit of community context for online lectures. In a traditional setting, lecture can run the range from formal to informal, and from participatory to performance. Lectures can be interspersed with other classroom activities (less common at the university level or when a focus is on seminars) and also tuned to a particular cohort's progress and interests. Delivered real time in front of a physically present audience, lectures can also be calibrated to the apparent comprehension and engagement of the students on a given day and topic. Asynchronously produced and viewed lectures are far more constrained in many of these dimensions. Such lectures can, of course, be revised on the basis of experience and feedback. Indeed, the medium offers the possibility of automated data-collection, though this has not been a focus of revision in the SOHS, which has to this point relied mainly on more direct student feedback and the judgment of academic staff. However, the intensity of lecture-production and the cascade of changes necessitated by a slight shift in, for instance, the amount of material covered in a given lecture, make it good practice to record lectures in a relatively self-contained fashion, such that well-executed lectures can be reused for a number of years. In many ways, asynchronous lectures assume the character of course-specific textbooks, written by the teacher.[10] And with this status comes all the traditional pedagogical

[10]The intent at the start of the school was that lectures would function very much like textbooks, and in that sense, should be designed for use by any number

baggage of textbooks: measuring engagement, tracking comprehension and completion, and integrating the lecture material into class interactions.

If lectures come to be seen by students to function as a kind of audio-visual textbook, it is essential that, like readings for the course, the lectures have a clear function in the course, and one that is both clearly understood, and also distinct from the function of other course activities. This clarity of purpose is, of course, essential for the efficiency and effectiveness of instruction, but also bears on the shaping of student behavior. To be sure, students attending a live lecture can pay more or less attention, but they have little choice in being exposed to the material in class. In an asynchronous context, students have more discretion to do their own triage, much as they do with assigned reading, creating a similar dynamic of incentivizing and assessing to motivate completion. In a recent end-of-year survey given to students in each course, for instance, students indicated that when pressed for time, they would quickly opt to complete fewer than all the lectures in much the same way that students at university will often stop showing up for class when hunkering down to complete end-of-term papers. Independent of efforts to track and ensure completion, perceived importance is critical. In anecdotal feedback, students frequently attest that they did or did not watch all the lectures for a course as a function of their perceived utility. Lectures that were summarized in class, reiterated readings, or dealt in material that was not transparently assessed or tied to success in the class were cited as shaping completion decisions. Both anecdotal comments and quantitative survey data indicate that lecture-viewing varies by course, as we would expect if students' decisions are driven by perceptions of relevance that are sensitive to differences across courses.[11]

---

of teachers responsible for classroom instruction. The happy development of a close-knit student-instructor community in the early years of the school and the trend toward a model of instruction in which every teacher is a scholar of the relevant course material did complicate that model. Reliance on materials from a departed instructor by a new 'owner' of the course accordingly stands as something of an incongruity. In practice, the departure of a course designer or primary teacher from the school or from active involvement in the course has sometimes proven an opportune time for revision of the course, and with it, some, if not all, of the lectures. However, the school continues to address these issues on a case-by-case basis, sensitive to the particulars of the case.

[11] An advantage that an online school affords is that all of the lectures are recorded, and as such, more senior instructors can work with more junior instructors, whose lectures might not be serving their intended goals, to drive forward a process of continual improvement.

The school began with an admittedly provisional model of lecturing informed by twin considerations: first, that lectures should be used to communicate that which does not require interaction between students and the teacher, in order to maximize the impact of the limited time together; and second, that lectures might be considered to fill out (in conjunction with synchronous class time) rough expectations regarding total instructional time. Instructors set out to pair two to three hours of in-class time each week with another sixty to ninety minutes of lecture, divided into segments of twenty to thirty minutes each and subdivided into logical units of three to five minutes. In many cases, this prescription proved to be too much—for instructors, for students, and for the discussions—and additionally was not sufficiently sensitive to the needs and norms in different disciplines. In some disciplines, such as math, philosophy, and history, the pace and role of lectures fit rather closely to this initial model, while in others, like foreign language and to some extent, English, the function of frequent lectures was less obvious. Exercises that might be engaging and instructive to undertake with students in a live setting sometimes could be translated into asynchronous presentations, but reviews of a translation or modeling of a grammatical form did not necessarily make for gripping asynchronous viewing. Nor, indeed, did it ultimately seem like a judicious use of student time: the sixty or ninety minutes a student might be required to spend in watching lectures could be more productively employed in language *practice*. SOHS language teachers compensated initially by emphasizing the use of office hours, setting up individual or small-group practice sessions, and doing whatever was necessary to get students the repetition needed. Eventually, however, the school acted in the fourth year on a clearly articulated need for more class time, scheduling language courses for four days per week of live meetings, one of which was designated for less-structured activities.[12] Despite the complications of scheduling, and accordingly, some limitation on the number of students who are able to participate in the SOHS language program, lectures no longer play a significant role in language study at the school. As the school reflects on its experience at the middle-school level, similar considerations have been broached.

What emerged, then, from the early years' experience with asynchronous lectures, was an approach specific to individual disciplines, courses, and grade levels. Lacking clear pedagogical motivation for lectures, courses in foreign languages, some English courses, and courses at

[12]A similar trend has occurred with Stanford undergraduate instruction in languages, where most courses now meet four or five times a week.

the middle-school and also at the post-AP level do not have prominent lectures. That time has been replaced with more class time or different modes of instruction and interaction. However, asynchronous lectures continue to figure prominently in a range of disciplines where an express and unique role for the lecture format has been established. In math and science, a clear tradition persists in relying on lectures to provide students with a first look at material and concepts, including online exercises, major result derivations, and modeling of different styles of approach to a problem. In some contexts in the sciences, the format allows the teacher to rehearse the exposition of a concept or experiment in a manner that highlights the approach of a working scientist. A broadened version of this function drives lectures in other disciplines as well, particularly in the humanities, where instructors seek to model scholarship in their exposition and analysis of texts, arguments, works of art, and events. In the Philosophy Core program, for instance, a lecture might model an approach to dissecting and reconstructing an argument, offer illustrations or test cases of the point at issue, situate the significance of the argument in a larger terrain of positions, and, importantly, probe the argument with counterexamples or other types of critique. While these are skills that students are expected to practice themselves in class discussions, the consistent demonstration of this style of thinking provides students a wealth of strategies and examples by which to hone and expand their own intellectual habits. Lectures also afford SOHS teachers an opportunity to flesh out the unique features of their approach to the material in the course at hand. Course themes or narratives can be articulated and traced out in the context of the lecture's topic, as can be particular methods, questions, or findings that situate the course in the sequence of courses in a given discipline or in the broader academic program of the school. And while asynchronous lectures should not be tied too tightly to a particular year's lesson plan or schedule, they can frame activities for discussion in seminar in a more generic manner, highlighting concepts, problems, or issues that are most germane to a course or unit from among the many possible topics of further discussion.

Most SOHS courses chart their use of lectures along these lines, making use of lectures to accomplish course- and subject-specific goals, or minimizing the role of lectures to further emphasize seminar-focused activities. However, in some courses and subjects, SOHS instructors have encountered the same questions emerging nationally at the university level with the proliferation of online courses and course materials, particularly MOOCs. At their best, MOOCs, featuring material produced by professors at prominent universities, present faculty and administration at other schools across the country with the nearly existential question of what they can contribute to the elaborate materials on offer, typically for free, from their famed colleagues. Indeed, some recent models for incorporating these materials into state and public colleges envision the local faculty doing less of their own lecturing and dedicating more of their time to individual interaction with students, following a version of the flipped approach, though it might not translate so clearly into the traditional responsibilities and role of the college professor. Less existential, though just as important, is the related question that online content poses to teachers at the secondary level: with videos, simulations, lesson plans, assignments, and all manner of supplementary material available online, curated or created by staff of nonprofits like Gooru or the Khan Academy, or produced by NSF-supported projects like PhET at the university level, what is the focus of the teacher's own contribution?

At the SOHS, these questions are most pointed in courses covering a standard repertoire of concepts, particularly when clear traditions of exposition have emerged which can be helpfully illustrated by production-intensive materials. The physics simulations at PhET, lectures bundled with math textbooks, or demonstrations of basic musical concepts are all useful, well produced, and often grounded in significant pedagogical research. In some courses, these materials are clearly supplemental: a National Geographic episode on Troy might offer much that an in-house lecture will not, but also calls for framing by the instructor (in lecture or in class) to integrate the material into the context of the course, including the questions and narratives that drive it. The mathematics division has similarly determined that bundled lectures should be referenced as additional resources for students in need of another perspective on a topic, but are subordinate to the lectures crafted by SOHS instructors, with the methodology and personalities characteristic of the program. In physics, an area where available resources appear to be notably strong and widely adopted, and where interest in the creation of more interactive in-house materials percolates, the issue is in greater flux. But throughout the school, instructors and division heads are challenged to approach the place of SOHS-created lectures and the use of external material with particular attention to the unique contribution—of approach, calibration to SOHS students, personality, unifying narrative and themes, and alignment—that our own asynchronous lectures make to students' experiences in their courses.

Constructing lectures with a unique and transparent function in the course has proven one of the most concrete mechanisms for ensuring that students watch the lectures assigned. Direct, automated mechanisms have in the past been unreliable, though tools for in-lecture quizzes are becoming increasingly common. More effective, then, are measures that reinforce the message of the unique functional value of lectures. Avoiding the temptation to relecture in class helps to drive students to the actual lectures, provided they are of consistent use. Lecture-based quizzes or written questions, exam questions, or discussion questions helpfully illustrate to students that lectures have a distinct and valuable role in the course. In-class references to more detailed or alternative treatments of material in lectures also helps to encourage and direct purposeful viewing. Ultimately, SOHS students are responsive to the culture of a class; if a critical mass of students engage the lectures in discussion in and out of class, and if those points are not recapitulated for those who have not watched the lectures, non-participation quickly and visibly marginalizes a student's prospects in a course. In this sense too, lectures that have a well-articulated function in a course are much like the readings for a course, and are consumed or not in response to the same pressures and incentives as this very traditional medium of instruction.

4.2 Other Asynchronous Tools

Despite some differences in intensity of usage stemming from the online nature of the school, SOHS instructors approach the use of other asynchronous materials—learning management systems (LMS), chat or discussion boards, email, supplementary resources—with the same goals as teachers in a conventional setting: to extend learning, particularly in the context of the class community, outside of class time. To be sure, the lack of a physical classroom creates slightly more dependence on the LMS for transactions, as there is no 'handing out', 'turning in', or 'handing back' that can happen in a non-electronic medium. In addition, SOHS students are more habituated to and perhaps are more comfortable conducting all aspects of their coursework online. Because students are accordingly more invested in the asynchronous system, and also more accustomed to it, teachers may face less of a hurdle in extending their engagement into online asynchronous forums than they might with students for whom online forums are dramatically different and distinct from their 'normal' class interactions. The low threshold for student engagement with asynchronous tools is fortunate, as the organization that can be conveyed through these tools is of magnified importance in the online setting and rigorous academic context of the SOHS.

The SOHS has come some ways in the sophistication of its LMS and the use of that system. From the first year's instructor-maintained html course pages, emailed assignments and work returns, and home-grown gradebook, to experimental adoption of Stanford's in-house Coursework system, to the adoption of the current third-party model, the transition has been to more comprehensive systems targeted to the needs of a conventional school. Some collaboration with the development team of OpenEdX in their platform, targeted more directly to MOOCs, holds prospects for more sophisticated capacities specific to flipped-classroom environments. However, the most important development in asynchronous learning management tools at SOHS has been in their use. Consistent organization of course pages across the school has been a point of emphasis, such that students can easily determine where to look for standard course documents, assignments, returned work, and supplementary materials. Among these course documents is an idiosyncratic 'course schedule', whose basic format is also standardized across the school. Our course schedules detail by day or by week which activities students need to accomplish to be prepared for class, including readings, problem sets, and lectures. Increasingly, these documents link out to external online materials or class lectures. The importance of such a degree of detail, articulated at the beginning of each semester, became apparent in the first few years of the school, as even well-prepared students struggled somewhat to understand the patterns of preparation common in a college-like setting, and to move consistently across the array of platforms and materials involved in each course. While detail of this sort is rarely available in the college or high-school setting, the combination of intense academics and self-directed work involved in an online implementation of college-style courses makes exacting organization a necessity. Other programs adopting flipped and online instruction appear to be moving toward similar norms.[13]

Despite the investment that students have in the LMS course pages, it remains difficult to generate a natural, casual class community in a forum that students visit only for work purposes. While students can be relied upon to participate in required threaded forums or in other assigned activities, spontaneous exchange and exploration is rare in these arenas, where instructors would have the most ability to shape

[13]Self-assessments and accreditation processes for online courses and programs commonly stress the organization of asynchronous materials. See, for example, International Association for K-12 Online Learning (iNACOL), 'National Standards for Quality Online Courses', version 2 (Vienna, VA: iNACOL, 2011), http://www.inacol.org/cms/wp-content/uploads/2013/02/iNACOL_CourseStandards_2011.pdf.

and assess it. Some instructors have for these reasons begun experimentation with further systems that mimic the kinds of interactions students have with one another on a daily basis. However, proliferation and fragmentation of systems are themselves concerns in an online school. It is important that any system that aims to foster incipient dialogue about course material be readily accessible to students, and, ideally, integrated into the forums (such as Skype or Facebook) where they have their own communities.

5 Assignments and Assessments

Online instruction creates a great temptation to automate the assignment and assessment process. The technology affords possibilities of automatic and even adaptive exams and quizzes, impressive and informative analytics, and immediate scoring and feedback for students. There is much to recommend these possibilities from a pedagogical perspective. Differentiation on assessments is a prized goal, and computers are equipped to do it with precision and systematicity, assuming the software is built around well-founded pedagogy. Detailed performance data for individual students and across classes poses opportunities for refining exams (e.g. eliminating or refining poorly functioning questions), identifying class-level weaknesses, retooling lessons and emphasis, and tracking individual student progress, to say nothing of furnishing data for comparisons across larger populations. And common sense and research alike suggest that timely feedback, appropriately considered, positively shapes student learning from assessments.[14] Further, purely logistical considerations agitate for the proliferation of automated assessments. Automated exams can be administered to students on a schedule tailored to the individual student, both facilitating self-paced advancement through the material, and accommodating varying student schedules throughout the course of a day or week. And, to be sure, automated assessments that can be scored by a machine make for more manageable teacher loads, removing barriers to a routine of assessment dictated by pedagogical concerns alone.

With such considerations to its credit, it might be difficult to account for the infrequency with which automated assessment makes any substantial appearance at the SOHS. But outside of routine and low-level quizzes and the feedback available through practice software from book publishers (in both cases, some of the benefits of automated assessment just mentioned are decisive), such assessment has no real presence at the school. This trend, based in the emergent practices of the school's

[14] Sousa and Tomlinson, *Differentiation and the Brain.*

teachers, fits informatively with the main themes of this discussion of online pedagogy. Most fundamentally, it is the school's view and experience that while automated training may indeed have a role in the acquisition of foundational skills and concepts, the unique role of this school, its curriculum, and its teachers, lies in engendering a mastery of critical, creative, and problem-solving thinking skills. As Dreyfus suggests in the opening passage, these more meaningful skills are best developed in engagement—the engagement of the student with her peers, of an instructor with a particular student's work, and of a community of students and teachers with a problem or topic. The SOHS emphasis on seminar-based learning constitutes a recognition of these same views, providing for a collaborative environment where an atomized, self-paced setting would be infinitely more convenient.

And so, students at SOHS write (and revise) a lot of papers and lab reports, they do a lot of discursive problems sets, they make presentations, work on projects, and conduct research and experiments. There is no good automated approximation of these activities, nor are there automated assessments of the skills involved in the process of completing these tasks. And teachers grade students' work, painstakingly, obsessively, by hand. Students receive volumes of feedback (even if it is sometimes slow in coming), from extensive comments on a paper or report, to individual conferences regarding participation or project ideas, to thorough commentary even on a math exam. Style, creativity, originality, methods, and ambition matter, in addition to outcome. This feedback is often the foundation of a teacher's relationship with individual students, and is the mechanism by which many teachers feel they are most able to shape the performance of each student. There is no economy of scale and it consumes great energy and time from teachers. But repeatedly and consistently, students and teachers identify this aspect of the school to be a centerpiece of its mission; it is among the very last things they would give up.

6 Conclusion

A great deal of pedagogical thinking goes on at the SOHS that has little reference at all to technology, from broad questions about how to challenge and motivate talented students in class and in the curriculum, to more intricate daily strategies for improving a particular student's selection of evidence. But this is common fodder for many schools. In focusing on the intersection of pedagogy and online technology, we have stressed that at SOHS, the technology that enables the daily operation of the school is, with respect to pedagogy and curriculum, simply a tool that makes it broadly possible to implement the desired academic program among the right population of students. While the practices of instruction that have emerged overlap informatively with more recent trends toward flipped classrooms, the underlying goal is facilitating a far more traditional model of seminar-style coursework common at universities and some independent schools. In the accumulated experience of the school in effecting a seminar-based curriculum online, the translation of traditional practices into relatively straightforward technology is often smooth and sometimes even brings benefits, such as the natural role for flipped content and the added dimension of text chat in class. However, the school has also resolved to cleave to more conventional practices where an aggressive use of available technology might confer some advantages that come at the expense of the educational experience that is the aim of the school. Possibilities for more individualized self-pacing, greater flexibility in attending synchronous seminars only as desired, and increasingly automated and analyzable assessments are all novel conveniences with some pedagogical merit; however, they have proven not to be part of the model of dynamic learning in an engaged community which our students and teachers alike have identified as the great strength and pleasure of the school.

5

Schoolness and Student Support

1 'Schoolness'

What does a school do when there is no school parking lot for parents to chat in? When there is no front office door a stymied parent can break down? When a parent cannot corner his child's teacher before or after school? How do teachers detect and connect with struggling students when students are only visible on camera, one at a time, twice a week? How do they follow up on missing work when students are just a click away from leaving the 'room' at the end of class? And when student issues get passed to administration, how can all of the relevant information and affected parties be assembled in a sufficiently timely fashion? But the biggest questions may be for students themselves. How do they adjust to significant changes in so many aspects of their school experience: harder work, college-style class schedule, self-directed working environment, and participation-intensive class discussions? How do the online environment, challenging work, and challenging peers impact the social and emotional transitions of high school? How does all this business of a school get done, without compromising student learning, when every step of it is more complicated than students, parents, teachers, and administrators have ever experienced before?

In distinguishing students' experiences in the Stanford Online High School from those of students studying a subject in some other online context, the notion of 'schoolness' refers in many ways to the role of the SOHS community, both within classes and more generally. But in considering how the school functions, how it supports its students, and how it more broadly sets the stage for learning in and out of the classroom, the notion of schoolness refers to the dynamic product of people and processes that hold the school and its students together. At the Stanford Online High School, answering these questions with a robust, creative, and proactive school apparatus—its schoolness—

has proven to be a critical feature of the school's support for talented students doing challenging work online.

If one were to approach the SOHS as a technological endeavor, from a perspective outside of the school world, one might legitimately wonder how central an administrative apparatus might be. After all, this is a school for talented kids, who have demonstrated their academic prowess and passion before their arrival; students and families are attentive and proactive in charting students' academic paths, having found their way to the SOHS to begin with; and there are not any sports teams or physical interactions to navigate, with their attendant logistics and social and emotional implications. It is true: SOHS students are unusually passionate and proven learners; families have quite often come to the school having developed clear educational objectives, after long trials elsewhere; and it has so far been the rare exception when an SOHS student sees another in person more than a few times in a year. But every facile inference from these premises is misguided. Even talented students will encounter difficulties in an environment that is sufficiently challenging for it to be worthwhile. The academic choices faced by students and families, similarly, become more complex the more they stray from the prescribed and familiar path that these families were seeking to improve upon. And the connections that SOHS students form, and the endeavors they engage in together, are real enough to necessitate all the careful thinking and creative planning that parents and educators can manage.

Indeed, once we recognize that it is a real school we are dealing with, and not some shadow approximation, it turns out to be the case that almost everything that happens at a school is more complicated in the online version. At every turn, one is reinventing processes and policies that have been long settled (if not well) in the brick-and-mortar context. Nor is this simply a process of translating standard practices into a new medium or a new venue. In many cases, the realities of online interactions and attitudes call for a rethinking or adjustment of the educational routine. Still, such challenges are for the best; there is little room to rest content with received paradigms that might not work, as the necessity of re-creation and the acid testing-ground of an online independent school will lay bare the dysfunction and show the need for something new.

The school's experience in its first eight years chronicled several critical lessons, some of them common to schools and growing organizations generally, and some particular to online instances of schools and growing communities. Consistent with its independent-school mission, the

SOHS has from the start emphasized individualized attention to the circumstances and experience of each student and family. As the school has grown, though, we have had to develop the practices that make such a degree of attention and consideration scalable to a full independent-school population. The transition of creating departments, specialists, and processes to deepen and expand upon the service of singular personalities making case-by-case adjustments has been an important but complicated one for our staff and our community. Among the critical services made possible by a more specialized staff and accompanying formal practices are the proactive and richer programs the school has developed to detect, address, and even prevent types of struggles that students in our environment commonly encounter. These difficulties and their remedies are shaped by both the online environment and the dynamic of talented students in a rigorous academic program. Intertwined in the changes that have accompanied the growth of the school and the expansion of student support is the emergence of an imperative to communication tailored to the peculiar nature of the SOHS and its community. Robust, carefully considered communication in a mixture of forums has proven, repeatedly, to be an essential basis of trust in our online community, as well as a necessity for everyday functioning in a complex and novel program.

That best practices and approaches to particularly hard problems are still in development testifies to the complexity and novelty of these questions about how to be a school online, particularly *outside* of the classroom. But even this prescription for holding a school together online—personalized attention, rich student support, and abundant communication—is incomplete. The changing complexion of online education nationwide and internationally also bears implications for the coherence of the SOHS as a school. While SOHS seeks to foster connections, community, and behaviors characteristic of a school, an explosion of *à la carte* online options popularizes a piecemeal, atomized approach to education online. In the midst of these developments, SOHS sees independent, pedagogical, and curricular reasons to craft policies that move counter to these emerging tendencies. Encouraging more full-time and part-time enrollment, and its concomitant investment in the school community and academic program, are seen as important to the prospect of a school experience online. But at the same time, SOHS must balance these imperatives with the flexibility of an online program to meet the particular needs of our students. This is a balance that confronts the school system more generally as it considers how to integrate online options into the core mission of schools.

2 Student Support for the Academically Talented

It is tempting to assume that academically talented students, who have gone through an admissions process attentive to motivation and past performance, will transition seamlessly into a challenging high school and encounter none of the academic, motivational, social and emotional, or study-habit problems common at every other school. Why would a school for talented students need student-support systems? Even those alert to the utopian air of that hope may not anticipate precisely the difficulties that talented students do encounter in the environment of the SOHS. While students do generally thrive at the school, almost all undergo some academic adjustment, quite often to the difficulty and volume of work. But it is not uncommon for students to experience more significant challenges. For some, the adjustment to the material, both in content and expected work-product, stems from the preparation offered at a previous school, leaving the student in need of work in writing or concepts and skills for a particular course. Such students will sometimes fall behind in their work and then struggle mightily to catch up—a difficult feat when staying afloat in the courses normally requires a serious, disciplined effort. The structure of the school and the nature of the students also introduce possibilities for struggle: talented students are apt to be overscheduled already, and are inclined to seek an overload of classes and activities both in and outside the SOHS. While many students at SOHS do continue to manage significant pursuits outside the classroom during their time at the school, most, and even these students, require careful balancing of their activities and development of time-management skills.

Part of the challenge of SOHS for these students consists in developing those skills, focusing their intellectual curiosity, learning how to study systematically, and planning in advance to manage multiple engaging projects. When things do start to go poorly, for these or other reasons, the online environment can sometimes hamper the detection and resolution of difficulties. However engaging a classroom discussion is, it affords some cover for students who are struggling—staying off the camera in a couple classes, letting emails pile up, or accumulating a little incomplete work can buy a student enough time to really get in a hole that parents and teachers might not ordinarily anticipate for so successful and talented a student. Over the years, SOHS has come to terms with the nature of the challenges that talented students can face in our environment. Through work in individual cases, we have developed a range of policies and practices to anticipate these difficulties and help students recover. Challenges and fundamental difficulties, though, do persist, and the systems themselves continue to evolve as we grow. To be sure, the task of supporting students academically is not smaller by virtue of the academic gifts of our student body.

2.1 Academic Preparation and Identity

Most college students encounter, in the first months of freshman year, a degree of shock and adjustment at the standards of their courses and the abilities of their peers. Especially for students at highly selective colleges, whose acceptance to such a school was the capstone to a necessarily successful high-school career, the transition into a bigger pool with a more homogeneous grouping of student abilities can be a difficult one. As at many independent schools, at SOHS, this transition happens in high school or middle school. (Indeed, as we will discuss later, our alumni commonly report smooth, and even easy, transitions into college, however elite.) And for students who have long experienced academic success, this experience can be particularly difficult to navigate, especially when it involves a more substantial academic obstacle.

SOHS students come to the school from every type of educational background, from excellent schools and districts, to weaker ones, from structured environments that stress idiosyncratic skills and neglect others to unstructured environments that prioritize student autonomy. Additionally, only a minority of students start at the school in ninth grade or earlier, though this number is and has been growing. With students regularly enrolling at all levels in the school, from a fundamentally fragmented set of backgrounds, there is no level of preparation that can be assumed as the basis of the curriculum. And preparation matters, even for talented students, and especially when the pace and challenge of courses is extreme—there is little room to catch up on the side while keeping pace with the class. These points, though, are sometimes hard to impress upon incoming families. For students who have coasted through classes and have had even to fight for access to more challenging material, the notion of a 'normal' or grade-level class that might be too advanced is difficult to credit, and may seem like more of the same underestimation and bureaucratic obstructionism that drove them to the SOHS in the first place. Accordingly, it has always been a distinctive project of the school to balance its mission of flexibility and challenge, and the precepts of age-independent groupings, with the underlying responsibility to do what is best for students.

In the early days of the school, when patterns of success and preparation for classes had not been thoroughly established, placement tests were largely diagnostic tools administered in the absence of clear information. Students would take placement tests, particularly in math or English, when they had not been involved in a standard math or science sequence prior to coming to the school. Even then, with a small school and a focus on individualization, a measured weakness in English might, for instance, simply be registered with the teacher as a basis for close attention and support. But experience has shown that this form of individualization is not beneficial to students with any regularity. Students placed above their placement scores would commonly struggle, fall behind, and suffer across their full range of courses due to the frustration or extra time required to stay afloat and pursue additional help. While the school was designed and able to provide additional attention, extensions, or tutoring, these solutions did not always fit in a student's schedule, required draining schedules for completion over the summer, and proved difficult emotionally. And perhaps most decisively, the students were unlikely to extract all from the course that they would were they to come in well prepared.

Placement tests are now required of students for every discipline they begin at SOHS. While the school will certainly discuss unexpected results with families, we now have a powerful message of experience, in addition to testimony from veteran families who can underline the reality of the challenge SOHS can pose. And so students who come in having completed an algebra sequence elsewhere may find themselves profitably engaged with a second year of algebra; a junior might be deemed not yet ready for an AP English course; or Latin II might be the prescription for a student who has already taken two years of the language. In some ways, such situations are the other side of true ability-grouping at the school; if students really are going to accelerate and be challenged in a course through the normal pace of the course and in virtue of the abilities of their peers, they need to be in the right course, even if it represents a nominal step backwards. Avoiding such measures, and being able to accelerate to advanced courses through proper placement and coursework in the normal progression, is another reason why students are best served getting to the school as early as possible, rather than waiting and trying to make do with imperfect solutions. Imperfect solutions often serve mainly to waste time and ultimately to hamper progress.

In Chapter 3, we discussed how curricular design affords students possibilities for acceleration through techniques such as layering and use of inflection points. Viewed as part of the school's system of supports for talented students, these same techniques are harnessed to mitigate the impact of gaps in experience or preparation that some students may encounter. Of primary importance is the availability of a meaningful and worthwhile learning experience to all students, especially those who might be working at a level below their expectations. In this regard, the focus on skills over prescribed content is important, since indeed, it is usually skills—such as sentence- or paragraph-level writing skills—that incoming students struggle with. Accordingly, students do not find themselves repeating material they have seen before; rather, they are cultivating skills that have not necessarily received thorough attention at previous points in their careers. Still, however, it can often be an extreme remedy to move a student back an entire year on the basis of some gaps in his or her preparation. At points in the school's development, this would have meant that an incoming ninth-grader would have to take a middle-school course, or that an incoming seventh-grader simply had no available options for English or math at the school, and therefore was not eligible to enroll at the school on a full-time basis. These were difficult decisions and conversations, and indeed, were not good for the student or school. Particularly in disciplines where preparation varied substantially, then, we have focused on expanding the curriculum at early levels. The strategy has not been to create courses that 'track' students to a less challenging sequence, but rather to offer a diversity of courses at critical junctures, in order to have available an appropriate, finely-tuned fit for each student. These courses, again, are designed not around content coverage—the overlap of content generated would be considerable—but on skills as practiced in appropriate content. Thus an additional middle-school course in English might provide students training in more sophisticated paper-writing skills while they develop the cognitive readiness for the abstract thinking that is the mainstay of subsequent courses. An early high-school course in history allows students to develop foundational historical skills in the context of a narrower thematic focus before they are expected to absorb and analyze the broad trends and developments covered in the canonical survey courses. And in math, which does involve more content-mastery, the school has added a full seminar-style course in prealgebra. Possibilities in foreign language courses also present themselves, as interested middle-schoolers are not always ready for entry into the formal language sequence; similarly, a middle-school Core course would be compelling both in itself, and as an option for students interested in Core who do not yet have the writing skills or other readiness. This model of curricular flexibility, finally, also plays an important role in the school's ability to provide appropriate starting-points for students in every discipline, and not simply in their strengths; not every student is equally talented in every discipline.

For some students, then, the transition into the SOHS consists in finding and thriving in courses that target skills appropriate to their preparation. For others whose preparation may not create obstacles to their expectations, the challenge may lie in adjusting to the demands of their courses and the abilities of their peers: the pace and depth of discussion, complexity of the material, and expectations for their work and participation in class. Here the adjustments are varied, and can involve both academic and psychological accommodation. Many students start at SOHS never having faced real academic challenges. Indeed, that is often why they have come to the school: to learn something harder, to receive criticism, and to be with others who are similarly engaged and advanced. But in practice, encountering challenges, whether for the first time, or to such an extent, can be jarring. Academically, responding to challenge entails practice, systematic study, openness to critique, and an ability to digest and respond to critique. It means navigating ambiguity and uncertainty, considering the views of others, being creative, looking outside the text, reflecting on a problem or question that cannot be solved in a moment, understanding when you just do not know something yet, and learning how to ask the questions that will get you closer to an answer. And it requires students to come to terms with weaknesses that were obscured in less demanding environments by their other strengths. Psychologically, challenge can pose threats to identities constructed around being the smartest kid in the room. Perhaps it is always great fun to practice shooting for hours and spend the rest of the day in the gym if you're Kobe Bryant or Lebron James, but for students who have always been stars, the sudden appearance of peers and limits can deter the enthusiasm and passion that are necessary to pushing those limits.

As a school, we have developed an array of programs and practices to assist students and families with the considerations, pitfalls, and habits involved in adjusting to the academic life of SOHS. But in many ways the most critical aspect of this adjustment consists in being part of the school and the school community. There is no better remedy to the disillusionment of encountering peers whose abilities match or exceed one's own than the thrill and satisfaction of working with them, learning from them, and contributing to shared projects and conversations. Similarly, discovering the potential for improvement—and making those improvements—is more than enough compensation for bumping up against one's limits. Two vignettes illustrate these points, respectively. In an episode now famous at the school, one enthusiastic student, after contributing to a particularly vibrant discussion, celebrated by jumping up and down and shouting 'That was awesome!' for a minute or so before realizing that her microphone, and video, were still on for the class to witness. The class understood the sentiment. Another is a story recounted by an alumnus, four years later: a supremely capable student, he was frustrated with the A he had received on a lengthy research paper, and rewrote the paper (against the teacher's recommendation) to see if he could get an A+. While the revised paper was indeed improved, he did not get the higher grade. As he recounts it, the teacher's comments about what such an achievement would require occasioned a pivotal recognition of where and how he could improve that has helped him challenge himself in his subsequent academic career. This recognition does not often occur in the space between an A and A+ at SOHS, though the moral of the story is a common one at the school: criticism and higher standards can require difficult adjustments, but in the right sort of environment, few talented students fail to embrace the opportunity and direction to improve. Such experiences facilitate two major realizations necessary for the success of these students. The first is that they are not the best in their chosen fields. The second, and equally important, realization is that they can perform on par with those who are among the best, and that the only way they can get better is to expose themselves to learning and to the failure that is inherent in the process. It is important for talented students to understand this from early on, and it is certainly better for them to learn these sometimes painful lessons when they are in high school, rather than deep into college.

2.2 Study Skills

Talented students do not always have study skills commensurate with their academic abilities. In part, this discrepancy is unsurprising: students who have not been thoroughly challenged can often succeed in virtue of facile memorization, quick apprehension, intellectual intuitions, and other tools, without being compelled to develop habits of study, repetition, and completion of assigned reading. The most talented of students sometimes share the plight of a virtuoso musician, who has never had to formally learn to play her instrument, but who must track back at some point to do so, before she can move to the next level. In many ways this can be a harder task, or at least a more frustrating one, than that faced by the novice learning formally at the outset, due to the clear sense of regression.

Additional factors can contribute to this phenomenon in more subtle ways. After years of mundane busywork, many students and families have, perhaps understandably, adopted practices of not completing assigned work, relying on performance on exams to demonstrate comprehension and using the spare time to pursue other enrichment. Indeed, some centers for gifted education encourage students and parents to embrace this approach in the belief that the courses were designed for average students and as such are not going to be appropriate or necessary for a gifted child. Talented students, additionally, develop intellectual tendencies that in the right context and to the right degree are fruitful and, indeed, are traditional markers of giftedness. These students frequently harbor an intellectual curiosity that can incline them to intensive and absorbing study of intriguing topics, sometimes at the expense of focus on assigned tasks and their completion. Additionally, talented students commonly set high standards for themselves, ranging to perfectionism, that can make it difficult for these students to begin and complete work, or to prioritize time and effort in ways appropriate to the work at hand. In the context of the intentionally designed, self-directed, and intensive workload of the SOHS, these tendencies can quickly imperil a student's academic wellbeing, to such an extent that a variety of measures is still evolving in response.

A student taking five courses at the SOHS will, in the course of an average week, spend as much as forty-five hours on schoolwork. Of that time, only ten to twelve hours are passed in the classroom. The college-style format of intensive but relatively brief periods of direct instruction and interaction, framed by considerable independently navigated work and study, leaves a tremendous amount of a student's course of study in her own hands. Students must organize, plan, and motivate their efforts across long stretches of time, and in the context of a lot of difficult work. The work that takes up the rest of the time is extensive: activities outside class can include office hours, lectures, readings, problem sets and exercises, labs, essays, presentations, memorization, translation, and study groups, among other tasks. And that work is indeed difficult; students routinely report initial struggles with coursework and workload without expressing concerns about busywork. All of this must occur in the online setting, where assignments, tools, and resources reside in various places and systems, and where the teacher and classroom are not fixed, daily presences that in a traditional school ground students' management of their work.

For those students who have been identified, or have identified themselves as grappling with some of these issues, a series of courses on study skills and life skills has been developed. Over seven to nine weeks, students in these courses acquire skills, tools, and experience in organization, goal setting, time management and scheduling, note taking, test preparation, communication, and finding a balance between one's studies and other activities. These courses are taught by the SOHS advising and counseling staff, which has grown over the course of the school's life from a single staff member to six, in order to meet these needs. The staff has both professional expertise in these areas, as well as the rich experience accumulated through a number of years of dealing with cases in which students grappling with these topics have stumbled at the school. We have learned that almost every full-time student at SOHS needs or makes use of a calendaring system of some sort. Indeed, students have, unsurprisingly, learned to make sophisticated use of an array of available tools. And one student has gone so far as to develop and publish an app tailored to organization and productivity in a school environment. As the mantra of organization among SOHS students suggests, passionate and engaged students are characteristically eager to improve their learning strategies, especially in a demanding environment. But in addition to general tips on pervasive topics like organization or test-preparation, students commonly need strategies for transforming their more idiosyncratic habits and practices. Lessons in goal setting provide students methods for taking on changes to their tendencies—like improving their planning and organization—that are both focused and pervasive in nature, from tracking assignments to speaking more in class. In many cases, these goals involve plans for addressing more deeply ingrained mindsets, like perfectionism. Strategies on this front involve helping students develop habits that reinforce the notion of work that is 'good enough'. It is a consequence of the mission of the school—to challenge the very best students—that perfection is neither very likely nor the real goal. And it is part of the practice of the school, given the quantity of work, that striving for perfection in every task is unsustainable. (As G.K. Chesterton famously wrote, 'Anything worth doing is worth doing badly.') The study skills courses reinforce these realities with strategies for assessing the importance and goals of individual assignments and creating habits of turning things in, and turning to other work.[1]

The study skills courses now available were first offered in 2010, made possible with the expansion of the advising and counseling program. Now they are available to interested students, as well as to students

[1] In our new Academic Skills for Life middle-school study-skills course, we focus on Dweck's notion of 'mindset' as usefully relevant to SOHS students. Many of our students might be seen as entering the school with a 'fixed mindset' developed over a long string of academic successes. In this mindset, initial challenges and struggles lead them to believe that they then must be 'not smart' or 'not smart enough to belong at the SOHS'. We discuss these issues with the aim of helping them to develop attitudes consonant with what Dweck calls a 'growth mindset'. See C. Dweck, *Mindset: The New Psychology of Success* (New York: Random House, 2006).

who are recommended by teachers, academic advisors, or the admissions office. To be certain, though, general skills of the sort taught in these courses, as well as the imperatives of organization and communication, are critical to all of our incoming students and are accordingly included in a variety of orientation activities. When the school opened its doors in 2006, what passed for orientation involved several hours in an online session with the Headmaster and Director the day before school. Students learned the ropes of the virtual classroom (and thereby were nearly as expert as all of their instructors), shared a slide about their own background and interests, were reminded that the school was a 'grand experiment' and that virtual office doors were always open, and with that, the students were on their way. More substantive academic orientations were delivered on the first day of class; after all, we knew what we would be asking and expecting of them as students. To be fair, what difficulties students might encounter along the way, in virtue of both the novel curriculum and the novel medium for a school were largely unknown, and the best strategy was engaged, responsive, individualized attention. But we all learned quickly. At the first summer session program, a brief presentation offered students some of the collected guidance in anticipation of the coming year. In subsequent years, instructors from different courses and disciplines also participated in the session, sharing discipline-specific study skills and other tricks of the trades, and the online orientation program for all students (not just those who were able to attend summer session) grew to incorporate major points as well.[2]

The pivotal transition in the school's efforts to equip students through orientation with particular study skills and perspectives came, however, with a determination that entry into the school and its culture in and out of the classroom was singular enough in nature to require more proactive preparation. In the summer session of 2012, what had once been a single study-skills course was fleshed out into a dedicated orientation program for incoming students. In this model, students worked through a refreshed introduction to elements of school life, from technology to study habits to school norms and culture. As always, the critical refrain was to attend to organization; to learn to appreciate, rather than compete with, one's peers; and to take advantage of teachers' availability at all times, but especially when it is tough going. Increasingly, the orientation students' other academic courses, as

[2]The forthcoming second volume in this set, *Perspectives from the Disciplines*, will feature discipline-specific discussions of the school's experiences, with respect both to the pedagogy and curriculum for gifted students, and to the peculiarities of implementing such an academic program in the setting of an online school.

well as extracurricular activities during the session have become more overtly tailored to providing an orientation to life at the school. Students who were not able to attend orientation during summer session were required to complete an online orientation course featuring much of the same material. Peer mentoring groups composed of new and veteran students—'Pixel Clusters'—were formed to provide students an on-the-ground perspective of preparation for academic and social elements of school life. These groups are now part of a more robust sequence of preparatory events and meetings scattered throughout late spring and summer that draw on the perspectives and experiences of the school community, including an admit day, new parent 'teas', and opening orientations. From the telling perspective of classroom teachers, the results have legitimated the effort: students more reliably arrive in class ready and able to turn in work, equipped with the right and working technology, and clear on the expectations of participation and attendance. Even in the days of MOOCs and well into the life of SOHS, one still cannot take these things for granted.

2.3 Interventions and Onlineness

The central place of individualization in the mission of the SOHS encourages a particularized approach to the struggles of individual students. Students at the SOHS have uniquely complex schedules and activities, balancing SOHS courses with classes at local schools, with professional or preprofessional activities outside the classroom, with cocurricular academic research or competitions, or simply with other coursework or study. In a school conceived in part to facilitate serious and meaningful pursuits in the context of a rigorous academic program, and in equal part to enable students to pursue an intellectual passion or topic with intense focus, a slavish adherence to schedules and artificial deadlines seems to be in tension with mission. Indeed, in a school with sophisticated students and teachers capable of appreciating students' different roads to mastery of the material, there is an assumption of flexibility in accommodating individual students' choices and needs. And for teachers sensitive to the autonomy and responsibility of a university environment, this flexibility is familiar. Experience at the school, however, has generally pointed us away from some of these preconceptions, for reasons rooted in the school's unique curriculum, the demographics of its students, and some of the peculiarities of the medium. Experience in the struggles that even talented students can encounter in an academic program designed to challenge them is paired with lessons in the difficulty of detecting and addressing those struggles remotely and in a timely fashion. What has emerged, then, is a surprisingly robust and articulated network of requirements and processes for intervention that aims at ensuring awareness of students' current progress among all the parties in a position to guide the student.

For all the theory that can be leveled on questions of late or missing work from talented students, it has been our experience that the question is much simpler in practice. As it turns out, there are relatively few students at the school who fail to turn in work from disinterest or on the basis of judgments that the work is remedial for them. The work is hard enough, and is assigned with sufficient intention to challenge the relatively narrow range of ability and background in given SOHS classes. Far more common are instances of students falling behind due to issues of organization, scheduling, or understanding; missing or late work is a sign that a student is struggling or has not yet mastered the skills that will be important to academic success at the school and beyond. What is more, it turns out that giving students leeway in this work tends to lead to incomplete courses, compounded academic struggle, and sometimes dramatic, postponed collapse. Where struggles completing work in a satisfactory manner are well documented, disincentivized, and addressed by notes and phone calls from teachers, habits change and struggles are more readily identified and resolved before they lead to more serious consequences.

These experience-driven conclusions regarding simple questions of assigned work dovetail with best practices developed for effective detection and communication regarding academic struggles: in both cases, a proactive regime of timely information and dialogue has proven critical in averting serious student problems. At the heart of the SOHS's approach to intervention in students' academic progress is an acknowledgement of the potential for delay, confusion, and surprise in the online environment, particularly in the course of asynchronous communication. To start, the basic pedagogical challenge faced by online teachers—not being able to see all students at all times during class—also makes it difficult to identify struggling students over time. Students who are confused or disengaged are not easily distinguished from students who are quietly tracking a conversation. In the online environment, other indicators of problems including work that is not handed in, work that is substantially incomplete, tardiness, or absence, require careful notation and tracking—they are not apparent in a glance. When difficulties do emerge, following up with a student can be a slow process. Emails must go out and be returned, inadequate answers or further questions must be clarified, fellow teachers or advisors might be consulted, and meetings with administration and parents must be arranged. At its worst, this project can drag on interminably, stalling at any step. Unusual or difficult cases can stimulate extended conversation, or indecipherable technological factors can obscure issues that have to occur repeatedly to reveal true patterns while the student's struggles compound. Much more straightforward models are the classic physical paradigms of pulling aside a distracted or tardy student after class, calling a parent on the phone, chatting with colleagues in the hallway, or hammering out a course of action in an ad hoc meeting of counselors and teachers.

At SOHS, the fundamental challenge posed by the dynamics of a distributed school and staff is to routinize procedures that either replicate the standard approach of conventional schools, or protect against the pitfalls common to asynchronous exchanges. Numerous features of the school make it the case that the foundation for effective intervention at the school is a sharing of relevant information. Students cannot adjust their performance without robust and timely feedback, teachers cannot assist struggling students who do not show the furious paddling beneath the surface, parents cannot aid or redirect their students if they do not have regular indications of progress, and administration and advising staff cannot intervene to diagnose problems and collaborate on solutions without a consistent picture of students' work across classes.

But in an online context, all of these things can fail to occur quite readily. So it is has been a central project of student support at SOHS to avoid surprises—to identify problems reliably and to transmit relevant information to an intentionally prescribed set of relevant parties. At the basis of this effort is consistent and timely posting of student grades in the staff- and parent-accessible student gradebooks. Ensuring this information is sufficiently accurate to yield the right sort of alerts among students, administration, and parents has required more intricate maneuvering than might be expected. For missing work and participation scores to impact the visible grade, for instance, these scores cannot be withheld until the end of the term; on the contrary, we had to institute a school-wide policy of filling in zeros for late work (even if the student might eventually turn in the work and receive at least some credit) so that students who had begun to fall behind would notice visible and immediate signs in their running grades. On the basis of these grades, the advising group sends out monthly notifications to students (and their parents) receiving a C- or below in a course. Parent-teacher conferences in late October provide an additional occasion for notifications surrounding student progress. Attendance at conferences has increased to a schoolwide average of more than 60% through efforts of streamlining and publicity, indicating a growing awareness among families of the importance of achieving a first-hand perspective on student performance. These mechanical checks are supplemented by monthly meetings of instructors and academic advisors to discuss—across courses—struggling students at different grade levels.

Periodic communication regarding grades, though, is only a formal mechanism targeting, primarily, ongoing situations that might require further discussions. Still more important to master are the pressing and ambiguous individual instances of struggling students that require personalized follow-up and more elaborate arrangements. For teachers from a university setting, for an online school with families around the world, involved in their students' studies to varying degrees, and in a new school without timeworn models of communication, a lack of clear pathways for intervention can discourage important steps. Over the years, the administration has worked with instructors to develop a system that articulates clear first steps—emails and phone calls to parents—that quickly move to academic and counseling administration in an attempt to return the teacher to the classroom efficiently when a student's situation reaches beyond specific issues with course content. In the unique environment of the SOHS, where seemingly every case presents a new question or new wrinkle on past incidents, information gathering, reflection, and coordination can quickly absorb the time and attention of affected teachers, such that it has made sense to minimize their roles in non-academic aspects of this process. Instead, the process draws on the subject-level expertise of division heads and the academic perspective of other academic leadership, pairing it with the logistical, counseling, and planning experience of the advising group. More streamlined, consistent, and transparent resolutions have resulted, with emerging best practices benefiting students, in particular.

In some cases, of course, intervention beyond sharing of information regarding student performance is necessary. In this event, the appropriate collection of counselors, advisors, academic leadership, and student and family collaborate to develop a plan to place the student in a more tenable situation. This might involve adjusting academic plans or workload, identifying and addressing incomplete skillsets or background, or considering whether the school is the best fit for the student. The school's flexibility is generally an asset in this process: individualized attention is available where appropriate, asynchronous material can be used for review or catch up, and students can often adjust their schedules at local schools to scale back their enrollment at SOHS for a time. But it is also a particular challenge to ensure that the flexibility of the school does not facilitate plans that are prima facie remedies but do not resolve longer term difficulties. The most difficult cases involve struggles related to the unique aspects of the SOHS, such as workload, organization and self-direction, and general intensity of classes. While cutting down a course out of a heavy schedule for a new student is far from a dramatic maneuver, there must be confidence that the student will develop the skills and strategies to manage a schedule that will allow for on-time graduation. Just as repeated courseload reductions for an individual student may not be in the student's best interest, neither may be a perpetual balance of intensive support, tutoring, and additional material. In both cases, special measures or scaffolding must be such that they can fade away at some juncture if the school is really to be a good fit for the student.

At a school of choice designed to challenge talented students in an independent school environment, determinations regarding the appropriate limits to student support are elusive. It is the premise of both instruction and student support at the school that students who have been admitted for their talent and passion should be capable of succeeding at the school with a level of transitional or periodic support. And indeed, the school has developed the resources to support its admitted students in the face of serious challenges and setbacks, to such an extent that we have struggled at times to identify the point at which a student is better served by success, or some degree of failure or alternate school choices. Inevitably, this general question is one that must be resolved on the basis of the details and circumstances of each student. Two questions characteristically provide useful guidance in these cases: (1) will this student be capable of succeeding in college and professional environments that lack the support mechanisms of an independent school; and (2) are this student's talents (and weaknesses) best developed through a certain degree of support, and at SOHS? Even a student capable of superlative work by SOHS standards, but who can accomplish that work only with an array of exceptions, reminders, and interventions even by the time of graduation, may well fail out of a selective college or a large school without significant support structures. If some failure is necessary along the way in order to instill the requisite skills, even at the expense of some damage to the student's college profile and level of achievement, the school needs to be in a position to carve out a protected space for those experiences. Just as delicate is the balance between our obligation to ensure that all of our students are learning and progressing, and a broader responsibility to help students and families determine when continuing in a certain capacity at SOHS is counterproductive for the student. When individual students have to compromise good health and robust personal development in order to get by at SOHS, when they feel compelled to take academic shortcuts, or when they might be able to participate more actively and profitably in other school environments, the school needs to refrain from facilitating those adverse situations and must succeed in communicating these implications to families. In such nuanced and fraught judgments, the accumulation of experience and best practices in our environment has been essential.

2.4 Social and Emotional Health

The development of a counseling department at the school has proven valuable, of course, in providing experienced and focused attention to individual student issues. In addition to those described above, individual student issues at SOHS, as at any school, have involved incidents of eating-disorders, anxiety, family stress and tragedy, loneliness and friendship struggles, disabilities, and serious challenges of mental health. Counselors work to ensure that students are appropriately connected to local resources, collaborate with teachers to arrange targeted accommodation or individualized support, and strategize with students and parents to articulate plans for building students' social engagement at SOHS. More generally, they seek to help students overcome any obstacles to meeting their academic potential. In some cases, these discussions point students to environments outside of the SOHS that might be better suited to their needs.

But the experience of the school has vividly affirmed the importance of helping to put students in the right social and emotional situation for academic success at the school. Doing so is a task for the school not only at the level of emergent cases, addressed individually, but also in the schoolwide context. In this setting, the Counseling department has developed a repertoire of courses, programs, and trainings, for parents and teachers as well as students. Driving such programs for students has been a focus on strategies and factors particularly salient in the context of our talented demographic and online medium. Some initiatives have focused on challenging the fixed self-conception or 'mindset' talented students often form around their past and present academic achievement. Developing incremental goals, exploring strengths and interests, and challenging themselves to reach out socially, whether in SOHS clubs or beyond the screen, can be productive processes for students in developing the confidence and participation important for academic growth at SOHS. Other elements of these programs stress skills that supplement academic motivation and equip students to take risks, face challenges that are social as well as academic, and deal with setbacks.

Counseling has also undertaken to help equip parents and teachers to better support students in their social and emotional development in the context of a demanding school. In orchestrating professional developments, hosting issue-focused sessions, and facilitating book discussions, counselors continue to raise sensitivity to students' academic tendencies, behavior changes, and important competencies beyond the test and text. The initial successes of these programs have generated interest in collaboration and consultation with outside groups to integrate proactive attention to social and emotional development, whose role in learning has been particularly visible at an online school of high performing students working in an intense and fundamentally social environment.

3 Communication

Some features of a school, we have found, change very little in an online context. For instance, we have argued that a good classroom discussion looks quite similar, whether in a conventional classroom or online. In other areas, best practices may vary considerably in virtue of the medium, addressing different dynamics and different pitfalls. Communication is one such element of school life; while certainly essential in a brick-and-mortar setting, it takes on a singular importance online, simultaneously requiring unique measures and attention. (It is telling that the one administration-wide meeting that happens every week, while often brief, is the communication meeting.) Much of the importance of communication, and its challenge, flows from the complex and often unusual processes that must be conveyed and executed to hold an online school together. Little in the way of process can be left to families' intuitions, common sense, or previous experiences. Nor can informal, 'parking lot' conversations be assumed to fill the gaps of official communication: even when the processes have been long established at the school, these informal conversations will not happen automatically. Rather, informal venues and communications must be considered, planned, and provided for at an online school, just like anything else. But planning and articulating events and processes is not enough. Effective communication at an online school—as in many other online settings—must be carefully tailored for different habits, audiences, and preferences. Messages must be read (and understood) in order to constitute communication, and resources must be organized and easily accessible to be usable. But not all of the challenge and strategy of communication, finally, consists in the dissemination of information and provision of sufficient reference materials. Indeed, many of the school's communication projects, beyond the fundamentals, have focused on building a schoolwide community capable of supporting the rich pathways of communication that help to make an endeavor a school, rather than an education service.

3.1 Why and How

Things just work differently at an online school. Much of this is obvious: students show up to class by logging into a computer system, click a button to raise their hands, hand in and receive their work back online, and travel to get to summer session and graduation. Some of these more apparent differences, while certainly not mean technological or logistical feats, are not inordinately hard to put into place or navigate. Instead of taking care of a building, an online school must manage a more elaborate technological infrastructure. However, the 'building' analogy only goes so far, at least with any real informativeness. More significantly in the context of communication, complexities in school logistics become more nuanced and pervasive outside of the classroom. Among the unorthodox processes parents and students must grapple with are the scheduling of courses, academic planning, proctoring, technical support, use of multiple technical systems, absence reporting, parent-teacher conferences and other meetings, registration and signups of all stripes, collaboration among parents and among students, volunteering and mentoring, and simply interacting with teachers and the administration. A schedule for 500 students around the world, running from six in the morning to ten at night Pacific time, crafted around the availability of students who are deeply engaged in sports, professional activities, and research; who are often enrolled in other schools; and who by age are more and less able to meet for long stretches, or early or late at night, is a study in complexity that demands careful input and planning from families. At SOHS, finding an available administrator to answer questions in real time, meeting with a teacher, participating in school projects, or playing a role in the parent association are not things one can do simply by showing up at a school building. Some of these issues are magnified in importance or complexity due to the unique academic program. Academic planning requires more elaborate discussion with unusual courses, prerequisites, and graduation requirements. Further complexities follow from variable student backgrounds and in the context of student enrollment types that range from full time to single course. In short, the school operates regularly in ways that parents are not in a position to intuit. Breakdowns in communication, whether through omission or ambiguity, are therefore quite likely to lead to problems.

Much of the solution to the unusual complexity of online processes consists in appreciating the problem and its intensity. From there, the work is mainly a matter of identifying critical information about processes, producing a variety of material in a range of different modes of presentation, and organizing these materials for visibility and ease of use. At SOHS, the process of documentation has been one of gradual collaboration with students and parents to determine common points of ambiguity or unclarity. The growth of administrative staff over the past several years has also been essential in this task, particularly in the extent to which it has allowed administrators to take on specialized professional responsibility for a focused set of tasks. This focus enables administrators to gain familiarity with common issues and then to develop best practices before documenting them, as, of course, much of the initial uncertainty among families concerned novel issues where no concrete policies had existed to start with. An early informational request by parents, for instance, led to the creation of division 'flow charts' illustrating typical paths through the courses in a discipline, along with prerequisites. These routes become particularly complex as multiple pathways emerge in a discipline that offers more than a simple serial sequence, to the extent that unconventional and university-level courses do not always involve absolute requirements, and as different progressions may be appropriate for different students. The school was in more uncharted territory still in its policies regarding exam proctors—who an appropriate proctor might be, what conditions were requisite, and what constituted legitimate reasons for rescheduling exams, or even what necessitates that an exam be proctored at all. As in many other areas, best practices emerged in time, and clarity of instruction and communication followed: family friends or employees are not appropriate proctors, proctoring centers are ideal, and unavailability of a given proctor does not entitle a student to a later test date.

Even after processes have been standardized and articulated to a reasonable extent, the answers need to be readily accessible, and the processes themselves must be manageable and supported by accessible and informed staff. None of these steps is easy online. After struggling to include documentation in the school LMS for several years, the expanded documentation catalyzed the creation of a protected school 'gateway' to house the many announcements, documents, forms, and school and student publications flowing from all corners of the school. Maintaining the transparency of this site remains a challenge; in its first year, the number of forms alone created for administrative functions inspired jokes among students and staff that there was a form for just about anything. But at a unique school populated by exceptional students, forms and documentation will not cover all cases. For this purpose, ensuring that a virtual school does not preclude human contact has proven critical: relevant staff and points of contact need to be well known and not buried beneath endless voicemails. Sufficient staff with responsibilities clearly articulated to the community have been the only real answer to this need.

3.2 Engaging Families

The SOHS started off with a clear idea, and even some experience, of how to meet the needs of students who lived around the country without any classrooms or school buildings. The simple formula of small seminars, heavily invested instructors, and growing student-support systems proved a strong foundation for the emergent student community. But when it comes to building an active, informed, and constructive parent community, the school has always been in uncharted territory. In the first several years, with student populations of thirty, eighty, and one-hundred twenty, the prescription was relatively straightforward: a small, ultra-accessible administration dealt with each family individually, addressing questions, concerns, and idiosyncratic academic histories. But even when, after those first few years, the size and structure of the administration preserved the possibility of this sort of interaction, it became clear that individual school-family relationships were neither the only effective, nor the only desired form of connection that SOHS families sought within the school community. Just as students wanted more than an individual relationship with their instructors, parents wanted more than an individual relationship with the administration. In other words, both students and parents wanted a school, and not just to be schooled. Parents who had long struggled on their own to find the right fit for their talented children wanted to compare notes with others who had made the same journey to this new sort of school. Families grappling with the unconventional social environment and intense curriculum were looking to see how others were managing these challenges. And confronted by the same, sometimes byzantine complications of navigating a complex curriculum, remotely, and through systems that were both in their infancy and altogether novel to many parents, they were eager for veteran knowhow and advice.

The school's experiences in building a community that incorporates families in a meaningful way are in many ways generic—they are the challenges of any new school or organization. They are also specific to the online context and to the field of gifted education. But as a whole, they highlight a particular set of dynamics that shape the growth of a substantive community online. Whereas the SOHS student community involves a depth of interaction rarely approached elsewhere on the internet, the parent and family community models issues arising in interactions that are still weighty, but closer to those we are likely to encounter in communities that are slightly less all-encompassing than those of students and teachers in school. These are parents working with other parents, teachers, and administrators at their children's school—planning and advocating for their children, collaborating on the growth of the school, contributing to school initiatives and events, and building community. In emails, discussion boards, phone calls, meetings, and conferences, their interactions are shaped by distance and onlineness in some uniquely challenging ways.

Community among families and the school has at least three central roles in the functioning of SOHS: it supports families in their navigation of the program, facilitates involvement in the initiatives and direction of the school, and potentially is a source of enrichment for both parents and students. In the early years of the school, the first of these functions has perhaps been paramount, due to a convergence of the newness of the school itself, the complexity of the school's academic program, and the online context in which these factors are adjudicated. Like any new school, SOHS has had birth and growing pains. Policies and practices were protean, growing with the size of the school, shifting with the clash of theory and practice, and developing to address the SOHS's unique issues surrounding onlineness, part- and full-time enrollment, and the expanding academic program. Unpredictable growth, a value of excellent instruction, and a mandate to eventual fiscal sustainability dictated heavy investment in teaching staff, at times testing the bandwidth of a smaller administration in implementing these practices. In this context, the school adopted a strategy early on of partnering with parents to support other families navigating the school. As the school has matured and its staff has expanded, the role of families has shifted from filling in informational gaps toward offering a unique perspective and, gradually, more substantive interaction.

Not long after the school began, parents wanted to connect with one another, creating ad hoc online groups to communicate, ask questions, and share experiences. To be sure, this forum created a great deal of practical value for the community, participants, and school alike. Parents compared notes about previous experiences and about navigating the school, passing emerging concerns to the administration (which did not participate in the forum). Through this channel and through individual contact with the Headmaster, many of the initial questions about best practices within the model of the emerging school were raised and addressed, based on the experiences of students. This is just what the 'experiment' metaphor for the school would have prescribed: a vision for the school is implemented, with content experts making decisions about how to realize that vision in practice, and students and parents furnishing feedback by which the fidelity of the implementation to the founding vision and other values is assessed. Resulting changes ranged from fine-tuning of workload and organization of syllabi and course pages to a gradual expansion of the seminar model of instruction. As the school community grew, what became known as the 'Parent Forum' became a mechanism for supporting new families in their adjustment to the school, with its range of logistical, academic, and lifestyle complexities. It also fostered discussions about pedagogy and curriculum, issues and challenges in gifted education, and social and enrichment activities. In light of this central role in supporting school community, as well as the complexity of managing membership in an ever-expanding population, the moderation of the group transitioned to the school's Parent Association, with the school providing the association with confirmation of potential members' affiliation with the school. Within this structure, the online Parent Forum remains a significant element of parent-parent interaction at the school.

While the Parent Forum remains an important component of the school after eight years, it is not immune to some of the dynamics that commonly emerge in other online communities. Certainly, the size of the forum and its lack of anonymity within the community itself go quite a ways toward preventing verbal attacks on others prevalent in massive online forums. However, questions, concerns, or complaints about events at the school can magnify and intensify concerns in a way that is unique to the medium. In the proverbial school parking lot, a conversation is ephemeral and limited in audience; those not connected or directly interested in an event are unlikely to encounter it by the very nature of the discussion, particularly if the issue is quickly addressed, clarified, or resolved. In an online forum, a negative incident or comment can alarm many others long after it has been addressed, or can gain considerable momentum before it reaches the administration. It is further difficult, once an issue has been resolved, to communicate the resolution effectively to all who encountered the original discussion. And, of course, it is natural that concerns—which require attention and time—constitute an outsized proportion of the discourse, given that positive experiences engender less discussion and require no resolution that drives further discussion. These dynamics can transform legitimate and well-intentioned questions and concerns into hurt or negative feelings.

Particularly in light of the centrality of the parent forum to the experience of parents—who are not in class on a daily basis—in the school, the entire community has an interest in a productive discourse in the forum. Parents, as much as administrators, have contributed to ensuring that the forum approaches this goal. One central principle in this effort recommends that activity in the forum conduce, and should not prevent, communication that can result in a resolution of the issue. The school and veteran parents emphasize that questions or concerns about events or trends in a classroom, or particular administrative issues, should be raised first with the relevant teacher, division head, or point of contact in the administration, where the specific issue can be addressed in a timely and informed fashion. When more generic or widespread considerations arise in the forum, members of the parent association can transmit the nature of the issues to administration so that they can, again, be addressed effectively, without frustration or undue alarm. We are particularly sensitive to avoiding the confusion of a well-meaning parent's opinions with school policy itself. A variety of forums for engaging these issues, once raised, has proven important. Parent Association meetings, in particular, provide an opportunity for relevant presentations, clarifications, and discussion in a large, interactive setting. Monthly newsletters host more detailed discussions of an issue or policy, or result of a survey or project. Open office hours with the Director or parent-staff working groups provide standing and more frequent occasions for conversation.

But most critical, perhaps, is the creation and maintenance of trust in the institution, staff, and instructors as effective custodians of students' interests and welfare. This trust is first founded on transparent and effective responsiveness to issues faced by students and families. In many cases, such responsiveness can consist in clarification, discussion, or appropriate adjustments by the school. But not a few of the challenges that emerge in an online school such as the SOHS are formidable and recalcitrant—there are not always easy solutions. In these cases, families need to be included in the processes developed to consider the issue so that they can both see the mechanism in action and contribute to the deliberation in ways that make clear the complications involved. On the perennial topic of student workload, for instance, the school has appealed to numerous surveys to assess critical factors contributing to difficulties students experience surrounding workload and attitudes toward possible measures. Drawing on these results, the administration identified a number of projects to address workload, discussed the survey results and the projects with families, considered feedback, resurveyed a year later, and reported considerable satisfaction with the measures. Interestingly, the measures adopted involved very little reduction in workload—indeed, some students did not want any adjustment to the intense workload, even though they characterized it as heavy—but instead focused on timing of major assignments and coordination of work across commonly paired courses.[3] This more manageable project emerged as a consensus approach in light of open discussion in the community, shaped by data suggesting that the workload was an important feature of the school's mission that called for peripheral management, rather than outright revision. But this is a message that likely would not have been viewed as well founded had it not come in the context of data from across the school. A similarly open dialogue has been appropriate to entrenched concerns that SOHS students are disadvantaged in college applications by difficult courses and rigorous grading at the school. Articulation of the school's efforts to communicate the rigor of the curriculum to colleges, grade distribution data, and graduates' college results, paired with discussion of the rationale for grading practices and the challenges inherent in grading at a rigorous school for accomplished students, have all contributed to an appreciation of the school's ongoing engagement in this complex issue.

These points about the centrality of dialogue, communication, transparency, and trust in the context of the parent forum apply more broadly in the online context in which the parent community unfolds. While students quickly develop close relationships with their peers, teachers, and, ideally, administrators, parents do not benefit from similar close and regular interaction. To be sure, this same dynamic exists in a brick-and-mortar school context, but it has additional significance online. When parents receive adverse news or decisions from administrators or staff they have never met in person, whose investment in their children they have never seen expressed in personal interactions, and whose background or role in the school they do not much know, there is little basis to interpret the exchange charitably. Phone calls are surely more interactive and flexible, providing more cues and opportunities to reach an understanding. But they are not a panacea: we are all much more likely to treat strangers on the phone with more suspicion and less generosity than we would a person before us. When a school has little alternative to communications conducted over distance, the sometimes fraught interactions that characterize school administration and student support can be still more difficult to navigate with the requisite goodwill and trust.

---

[3]See discussion above, in Chapter 3.

In addition, then, to cultivating trust through transparency, engagement, communication, and accessibility, the SOHS is invested simply in building the relationships with parents that are a foundation for navigating more difficult conversations. Expanded in-person meetings are, of course, a great asset. Graduation weekend, dropoff or pickup at summer session, individual visits to Stanford, and fortuitous regional gatherings have been a focus for such meetings with dedicated parent events at those gatherings. In an online setting, longstanding parent association meetings have been supplemented with working groups, open office hours, and parent-focused orientation events. But the strategy that is perhaps most promising in building a usable community between families and the school appeals precisely to the greatest strengths of the school: meaningful intellectual interaction among engaged participants in an online environment. No matter how pivotal an in-person encounter, these encounters will never be prevalent or sustained enough to serve as more than vivid reference points; the substance of relationships even with parents must come in remote interactions. To this end, the school is exploring limited contexts in which parents and members of the school can work together in goal-oriented tasks or discussions. Working groups, such as that focused on middle school, and graduation planning committees have initiated this model of interaction. But also promising are new efforts still closer to the rich interactions students experience at the school, *in their classes.* Over the most recent summer, staff and parents were invited to read *Sticks and Stones*[4] as the basis of a book discussion in the fall. Interest was sufficient to encourage a second iteration, based on Susan Cain's *Quiet*,[5] a topic relevant to many of the adults in a school with more than its share of introverts. In addition to the substance of these discussions, the clear demonstration of shared commitment to questions relevant to students is an important foundation of trust. The closest approximation of class is class itself, and SOHS is exploring this, too. Parents have often admitted to listening in to lectures or the occasional class (after all, these courses unfold in their homes), while others express interest in getting a taste of some of the courses they hear about throughout their students' careers at the school. Accordingly, the school is exploring a model of abbreviated, low-intensity versions of central courses in the curriculum, both to

[4]E. Bazelon, *Sticks and Stones: Defeating the Culture of Bullying and Rediscovering the Power of Character and Empathy* (New York: Random House, 2013).

[5]S. Cain, *Quiet: The Power of Introverts in a World that Can't Stop Talking* (New York: Crown Publishers, 2012).

meet these interests, and to broaden substantive interactions between teachers and parents. This engagement is the sort of 'remote' interaction that will help both parties work together to better support students.

4 Conclusion

Classes at the Stanford Online High School are difficult. That is why students come to the school. Indeed, they are hard enough that even mature, talented, and passionate students typically cannot navigate them without significant adjustment and acquisition of new skills and strategies, without monitoring and mentoring, and without collaborative support from the school and from families. The school's response to these realities is not that of a typical university or provider of supplementary academic programs: our school does not rely entirely on the student, in her talent and incentives, coupled with sheer scale, to ensure that some acceptable number of students persevere to the completion of a course. Nor does the school expect some combination of maturity and academic polish to carry the deserving through a gauntlet of challenge and independence to baseline standards. It is not consistent with the mission of the school to have students dropping out en masse, regularly failing, or drifting through courses without real engagement. Rather, SOHS deploys the tools of a real school—an independent high school—to help students through its unique version of challenges that are common to most any school.

Accomplishing the collaboration across the school community that appropriate student support requires—the SOHS's schoolness—has required an unusual degree of innovation, coordination, and communication. All of the unusual features of the school, from its distributed nature and its curriculum to its growth and different modes of enrollment, magnify the challenges of creating this schoolness. It is a sign that the school is on the right track in this regard that the community has a fierce and wonderful sense of ownership of the school. The community's tangible investment in decisions about the school's name, the structure of summer session, nascent traditions, and course offerings, both greatly benefits the quality of decisions made, and indicates an investment that families have in a school that they simply do not have in vendors of education services.

6

Community

Will my student be alone all day on the computer? Is that healthy? What will happen to my social life if I am not at my local school each day with my friends? How do online interactions and 'friendships' compare to 'real' ones? Will my child manage to develop the social skills she will need in college and in her career? How will he get to know his teacher and fellow students well enough to be interested and successful in class? These serious questions are at the heart of initial concerns many students and families at the Stanford Online High School confront in considering the school, and they are the responsible questions to ask, both of the program and of each student's individual situation. Underlying these questions are more general convictions about online interactions, the role of sociability in education, and the prospects for a salutary marriage of the two.

A spate of recent analyses reflect on proliferating studies about the extent of technology-mediated interactions. A 2010 Kaiser Family Foundation study reported that children ages eight to eighteen averaged 10.75 hours of media use (often simultaneous) over the course of 7.63 hours a day.[1] Debates rage about where that time comes from, whether these changes in our lives make us happy, and whether they undermine meaning in our interactions. Provocatively for an online school, the MIT sociologist Sherry Turkle contends that apparent contentment with technology-mediated interactions reflects not the robustness of those relationships, but rather a diminishment of our expectations of depth in the contemporary, technology-saturated environment.[2] Stanford researchers in psychology and human-computer interaction have

[1] D. F. Roberts, U. G. Foehr, and V. Rideout, *Generation M: Media in the lives of 8-18 year-olds* (Menlo Park, CA: HJKF Foundation, 2010).

[2] S. Turkle, *Alone Together: Why we Expect More from Technology and Less from Each Other* (New York: Basic Books, 2011).

found evidence of deficits in the ability of what they call 'chronic media multitaskers' to filter out irrelevant stimuli and representations.[3] Is an online school contributing to, and operating in, an environment that adversely affects cognitive virtues as well as sociability?

Meanwhile, critics of trends toward online coursework target depersonalization in automated and massive learning environments. Hubert Dreyfus has extended his concerns about technology and sociability into the special case of technology-based education, focusing on the role of community in education and the perils of technologically-mediated communities. His critique of an earlier wave of triumphalism about the prospects of distance education speaks as well to current visions like those of Salman Khan in his 'One World Schoolhouse'[4] and the bolder proponents of MOOCs:

> The vision of a *worldwide* electronic agora precisely misses the Kierkegaardian point that the people talking to each other in the Athenian agora were members of a direct democracy who were directly affected by the issues they were discussing, and, most importantly, the point of the discussion was for them to take the responsibility and risk of voting publicly on the questions they were debating...The Athenian agora is precisely the opposite of the public sphere, where anonymous electronic kibitzers from all over the world, who risk nothing, come together to announce and defend their positions.[5]

In the experience of SOHS, Dreyfus is exactly right in his criteria for a meaningful community, and in identifying such community as essential to education. He simply has not fully anticipated the online contexts in which that community can occur.

The internet is awash with communities: generic communities of acquaintances, professional networks, communities surrounding products and publications and institutions, and interest groups for every movement or passion or struggle or curiosity under the sun. Not all of these groups are massive and depersonalized, and many of them provide intellectual and sometimes emotional sustenance for their members. Still, critics like Turkle and Dreyfus offer weighty concerns about communities that are nothing more than extensions or enhancements to their traditional analogues, that exist only as forums to augment or replace the 'authentic' action and relationships that occur out in the real world. The SOHS community is different in exactly this regard. It is not simply

[3]E. Ophir, C. Nass, and A. Wagner, 'Cognitive Control in Media Multitaskers', *Proceedings of the National Academy of Sciences*, 106 (2009): 15583-15587, doi:10.1073/pnas.0903620106.

[4]S. Khan, *The One World Schoolhouse* (New York: Twelve, 2012).

[5]Dreyfus, *On the Internet*, 139.

an online community that engages students receiving their schooling in a different medium, but rather has grown out of an activity that is already essentially online—the schooling itself. What goes on online at the SOHS is the real life of a school. The members of the school are invested in their actions and those of others; they cannot simply walk away to their real lives when the fancy strikes because what goes on in the school affects and is part of their real lives. And because community is essential to education, members of the SOHS community have every reason to enrich the substance of their community, in and out of the virtual classroom: students learn and are sustained and inspired in a community with their peers and teachers; teachers, administrators, and parents serve students best in a collaborative community; and teachers and school staff challenge and enrich each other in a dynamic working community.

In building a school community that is a strength for the right sort of student or parent or teacher, rather than an unavoidable deficit, SOHS has done more than clear a hurdle to the feasibility of its educational mission. As the meaningful activities in our lives and in the life of our society continue to move online, and in more substantial fashion, it is imperative that we establish strategies and norms for deepening the interactions we have there. The Stanford Online High School has in many ways managed to do this in a context in which community matters most. In its example are visible some of the successful strategies, as well as some of the perpetual challenges, that will inform the growth of online communities in education and in other enterprises.

1 A Real Community

Graduation weekend at SOHS is a remarkable event. For three days, students and families descend on the Stanford campus from across the country (and in some cases, from around the world) to celebrate the accomplishments of SOHS students. But they are not just graduates. Middle-school students, students at the end of their first year at the school, three-year veterans, and even alumni gather to enjoy traditions, ceremonies, celebrations, but mainly, one another's company. The event grows each year in attendance, logistical complexity, technological sophistication, and diversity of activities. Once a two-day gathering with a single attending graduate, assorted other students, and eight teachers, the seventh graduation was attended by twenty-four of twenty-nine graduating seniors, ninety students, thirty-nine teachers, and guest and families totaling over 350. Ninety-five unique viewers from the community tuned in to watch a live stream of the ceremony itself, from

Anchorage to Yorktown Heights in the United States and including China, Taiwan, and Singapore internationally. Social events surrounding the now three-day weekend grew from a four-member gathering of the culinary club in an instructor's kitchen into a barbecue, opening scavenger hunt, awards ceremony, senior-instructor dinner, middle-school party, parent breakfast, prom, alumni reception, graduation and banquet, and senior grad night.

To teachers and staff who, while still amazed by these students on a daily basis, have grown somewhat accustomed to the exceptional, what is most striking about this annual gathering is its ordinariness. What could be ordinary about 90 extraordinary students, who attend class and interact virtually, descending on Stanford from around the country and around the world to meet and celebrate in person? To be sure, there is a momentary pause at the opening event, as students (and instructors!) survey one another, compensating for the distortions of the camera and the disjunction between physical cues of identity and the rich knowledge of each other they have developed online. But then voices, quirks, and mannerisms are identified, friends and teachers are recognized, and a community resumes its life in a different medium, *in media res.*

The SOHS community is not just real, but also compassionate. Remarkably, for so talented and driven a collection of students, the SOHS has developed a culture of mutual support and admiration. Exposed to the reality of others who may be more accomplished than they in certain subjects, SOHS students happily flourish: they are excited to engage these students on difficult issues and material, inspired to demand more of themselves, and moved to share sympathetic assistance with their peers. This ethos pervades the virtual classroom discussions and the general life of the school, and it flows out into the myriad student-initiated contacts and forums that make it possible for the 'first meetings' of the graduation week to be reunions in what may become lifelong friendships.

While the school's founding mission is to provide a uniquely challenging academic program to talented students, and indeed, while students may initially seek out the school largely for this curriculum, the intellectual and social community that has grown up around the curriculum figures at least as prominently in many students' experiences and learning at the school. Two common observations speak to this point. The first, typically offered at university orientations is a promise that ninety percent of what a student will learn at the institution will be learned outside the classroom, in interactions with other students. The second observation that stresses the importance of the impact of being at a school, rather than things learned, is seen in the oft-quoted saw that 'An education is what remains when you have forgotten everything you learned.' Students speak compellingly of the talent and challenge of their peers, the excitement of shared interests and academic commitment, and of the inclusiveness and camaraderie of the student body. Alumni, meanwhile, demonstrate the depth and enduring nature of the friendships they formed with their classmates. And while the next chapter will show that the alumni have been well educated, if only in the above sense, it also shows the depth and persistence of the impact that the school has had on their whole person.

The school's unanticipated but welcome ability to sustain so meaningful a community, and the value students place on that community, have been the focus of continuous schoolwide initiatives. The central role of community in the school's identity motivated a recent revision of its mission to reflect the contribution community makes to students' education and experience. A 2010 accreditation self-study confirmed the observed extent to which the community valued the relationships students form with their classmates, expressing a desire for more contact, virtual and physical. After three years of intensive work on projects to strengthen and expand interactions among all members of the school, 77% of students agree that they 'have adequate opportunities to connect with their SOHS classmates', while 7% disagree, a notable improvement.[6] But in truth, a school only provides the occasion and framework for the community that the SOHS has become. The creative, industrious, and kind students of our pioneering classes deserve the credit for the bonds they formed. And the inheritors of this tradition deserve credit for cherishing it, adopting and enhancing it, and passing it on. To the school staff falls the challenge of facilitating and building on the community that the students themselves have so auspiciously begun. Much of the story of the school's work in its first eight years is the story of identifying and encouraging models of productive citizenship in the community, mustering logistical support, and getting out of the way of a dynamic and colorful student body with a voracious appetite for more connectedness.

The best way to tell the story of the school community is to start with the pieces, the broad assortment of contexts in which SOHS students interact: formal and informal, school-sponsored and student-initiated, asynchronous and live, large-group and small, electronic and physical. While patterns and technologies shift, the various contexts and the more specific forums that populate them meet a variety of needs in the

[6] *SOHS Accreditation Student Survey* (2013).

life of the community. The nature of these components of SOHS life, their development, and the roles they play in the school constitute the school's answer to social critiques of online learning. They simultaneously model, in the example of a school, how real community can grow in a virtual setting.

2 In Class

Discussion sections are where the action is at SOHS, even when it comes to community. Participation in these regular, live seminars, led or managed by instructors, is of course the focus of academic life at SOHS. But given their pivotal place in the academic life of the school, as well as the unique features of the interactions students enjoy in this setting, seminars play a foundational role in creating and defining the SOHS community.

Seminars provide students with an environment for interaction that is unique within the school. Most prominently, perhaps, seminars represent the largest sustained period of live interaction that students experience at the school. At the minimum represented by a single-course student, seminars constitute two hours per week of live interaction in a group setting; a full-time student taking five courses might be in class with teachers and fellow students for ten or more hours (though such students are likely to spend additional time in office hours or other less structured but still academically-focused live interactions). As noted above, this time is not spent in lecture, which is accomplished asynchronously where appropriate, but represents opportunity for active engagement with the material by each member of the seminar. Work in seminars is additionally designed to be collaborative, such that students are not participating serially in discrete exercises, but are working together, whether in small groups or as a class. Thus questions are not primarily factual, requiring individual performance. Individually-worked problems are subjected to group analysis, which might include detecting errors or identifying and evaluating the approach used. Discussions do not focus on sharing of opinions, but rather on articulation of argued positions, criticism, and defense. And where possible, the teacher is not simply an arbiter of correctness, but rather serves as a skilled interlocutor whose questioning can elicit critical observations from students. In this sort of approach, students take themselves to be working with their peers and their teacher to arrive at conclusions, discover strengths and weaknesses, and probe the material. The results of any such seminar discussion depend on the cumulative and particular contributions of the members, and are not the foreordained product of endlessly repeated individual exercises. While students may collaborate in other contexts throughout the school—in planning events or pursuing the work of clubs, their regular, intensive, and foundational exposure to productive collaboration comes in their seminar experiences.

The collaborative setting of the discussion seminar is also where students learn and practice the norms for discourse, both of collaborative work more generally, and of particular disciplines. Here, students are called upon to formulate criticisms of the texts they read or the views of others, trying their hands at strategies for finding weaknesses in arguments. They learn how to constructively disagree with their peers, how to extend points they agree with, and how to defend their own positions, if called into question. More generally, they practice and are reminded of principles of topicality—what counts as germane, and what advances a conversation. They are subject to rules of evidence, learning how to muster texts, examples, and data to their purpose. And they learn how to explore a question and follow a lead together, identifying a useful suggestion and building on it through the contributions of other participants in the conversation. In these experiments in the norms of academic and argumentative discourse, they are held accountable by their instructors, who, themselves practitioners in the field, model these norms in their own treatment of the material or the arguments of students. In this context, students acquire the skills to engage one another in a measured academic manner that extends to interactions outside the classroom, whether in political or religious discussions, maneuverings in student government, or in the many encounters in high school life in which principles and argument can be brought to bear. SOHS students learn and imbibe a common intellectual standard and framework that informs their interactions throughout the community.

In a similar vein, the seminar experience contributes to the formation of community in the course of both establishing tightly knit small-group communities, and imparting skills of working productively in small-group settings. In virtue of their frequency, duration, and collaborative design, seminar sections tend to establish their own identity over the course of the year. This character is shaped by the individual contributions of students, but also their shared jokes, tropes, memories, struggles, and tendencies. Teachers and students frequently attest to the different character of different sections of the same course—a diversity which speaks to the intensity and depth of the interactions common in seminars, and suggests the significance that a shared section holds for student relationships outside of class. There is the class in which the relativist position must always be considered, the class that prefers its thought experiments with zombies, the class that is obsessed with cancer research, and the class that has a special appetite for practice question after practice question. But beyond the particular identity and bond of the students in a given section, seminars also foster skills and habits of collaborative work that manifest themselves throughout the school community. Club and competitive work, service projects, and service to the school and other students commonly depend on the coordinated contributions students are comfortable and skilled in making to collaborative efforts. Surely, these are also skills that will serve students well beyond their time at the SOHS.

In addition to creating shared experiences that provide the foundation for friendships, seminars facilitate a sharing of skills, interests, and perspectives that is particularly dynamic in the context of the SOHS student body. In the essentially collaborative nature of SOHS seminars, where participation is both required and in service of the seminar group's common inquiry, students necessarily demonstrate their strengths, academic and social passions, and unique experiences and perspectives in ways that help to build ties among individual students. SOHS students invariably thrill at the talents and shared but uncommon interests of their peers; collected as they are from around the world in an academic program for passionate and talented students, they are likely to find at SOHS an unprecedented circle of like-minded and similarly-equipped friends. It is in the seminar setting that these interests are clearly on display—where political views, literary or scientific predilections, or artistic enthusiasms find their way into discussions and exchanges. But experiences and backgrounds are similarly evidenced: a student might reference in casual or formal class discussion his responsibilities on a farm, her experiences living in the American South, or her perceptions of American democracy from the parliamentary traditions of her native Sweden. Whether these backgrounds are common or provocatively foreign, they are invitations to deeper interactions outside the classroom that sustain and enrich students in an online school community.

A community that begins in the shared experiences of the classroom, and then animates and flourishes in formal and unstructured interactions outside the classroom, finds its way back into the classroom as an essential feature. The ideal of a discussion seminar, for instance, as a place to think on one's feet, be challenged by the views of others, and to get feedback from others, is predicated on students taking risks and engaging one another in a manner that will not happen without firm trust and respect. You cannot learn about the rule of law in China from a student who is too intimidated to speak, or if you are only waiting to say your own piece. At the same time, two or three hours of discussion in a class per week, no matter how lively and exciting, is a narrow part of the learning that can—and needs to—take place in a school. Were it not for the relationships SOHS students build outside of the classroom and the forums they find to pursue them, the intensity of the program and the virtual medium might not be viable or profitable to students outside of an *à la carte* context. In other words, what makes the SOHS work as a school, beyond being a collection of courses, is everything that the students are doing with each other, both in and out of class.

3 Out of Class

Central as the guided, academically-focused seminars are to the intellectual and community life of the school, it is the far less structured venues of interaction and collaboration, for which the seminar interactions are a foundation, that make the SOHS a true school, and its students classmates. These are the settings in which students pursue acquaintances and friendships, explore their academic and other passions on their own terms, and incorporate their academic work into their daily lives. Accordingly, just as the school has expanded the seminar format in part to capitalize on the social component of classroom learning, it has worked to support and expand forums for less structured interactions among students, both physical and virtual. Indeed, among the programs described below, only orientation, summer session, and clubs were envisioned or in process on the first day of class in 2006, and these only in scarcely recognizable form. But perhaps the most striking developments in community life, unsurprisingly, are the products of the students' own experimentation, vision, and will to find meaningful vehicles for their burgeoning friendships and deeply-valued kinship.

3.1 Before and After Class

The unstructured social venue at SOHS most like class is a simple extension of class—the time shortly before class and immediately after it, during which students chat with one another and with their teachers as they arrive or depart on either side of the (entirely metaphorical) bell. Students immediately began taking advantage of the fifteen-minute presession built into the virtual classroom system to text chat with one another before the start of class. Teachers often arrive in class to see a lengthy exchange chronicled in text chat, with topics ranging from local storms to inside jokes to birthday greetings to scattered commentary on the readings. Time before and after class is, of course, also useful for teachers and students alike to ask about progress on an assignment or seek some other clarification.[7] In the school's third year, the daily schedule formally accommodated this valuable time by extending periods to seventy-five minutes, with many classes running in the first sixty minutes of the period in order to allow students and teachers with consecutive classes to stay late or arrive early to a subsequent class. (Advanced courses often run for seventy minutes, while select others extend for ninety minutes.) It is indicative of the place of this time in school culture that traditions have emerged for its use across the school and in individual courses, ranging from contests to be the first to document one's arrival in class, to the sharing of live banjo or favored opera music.

3.2 Homeroom

The same call for unstructured synchronous venues, mixed with a range of other motives, prompted the introduction of Academic Advisory Periods (now conceived as 'Homeroom') in the school's third year. These biweekly, thirty minute small-group pairings of students with an instructor were designed to address at least four felt needs: (1) improving communication with students; (2) providing a forum for discussion of study skills and other academic tools; (3) providing a chance for students to interact with members of the SOHS community with whom they might not otherwise interact, including students of different ages and in different classes; and (4) drawing on that nonacademic relationship between teachers and a small group of students to provide a personalized point of contact for monitoring academic and other difficulties that individual students might encounter. As the school has adopted other and additional mechanisms of facilitating each of these goals, particularly those involving student support (the second and fourth goals), those functions that foster community have come to predominate in subsequent incarnations of homeroom. Adjustments reflect that focus on building non-academic community: homerooms were quickly expanded to a weekly meeting schedule to increase the sense of a real group; planned or suggested activities came to emphasize getting to know interests and talents of fellow students, drawing on individual experiences at the school (often among older students) to support others, and building a group culture; and homeroom groupings have become increasingly grade-level specific to allow tailoring to the interests and interactions of different groups of students. (While some advan-

[7] Of students responding, 59% (116) list the time before and after class as a tool they employ to connect with their instructors, behind office hours (74%, 147) and email (94%, 187). In *SOHS Accreditation Student Survey* (2013).

tages of mentorship of younger by older students were sought and perceived in earlier years, the growth of the school to include ninth grade and then grades seven and eight exacerbated divergences in interests, priorities, and needs among members of undifferentiated homeroom groups.)

Homerooms have succeeded or faltered with respect to their goals and the general experience of their members, largely on the basis of quirks of composition. The lucky coincidence of interests and character of individual students and teachers in a given homeroom, the presence of strong student leadership and initiative, or a shared level of engagement in the student community, might make for a dynamic and enriching homeroom. In the best of cases, students and teacher would happen upon an exercise or game, or establish an alternating routine of projects (e.g. collaborative short-story writing or reading, or solving weekly math challenge problems). But uninterested, well-established, or overly-taxed students could also find the time wasteful or burdensome. Surveys reflect this picture of mixed results, while supporting recent and planned adjustments. A small majority of students affirms homeroom as an effective setting for making social connections to peers,[8] with middle-school students finding it more valuable and veteran students finding it less useful with each successive year at the school.[9] Splitting students by grade groupings, differentiating the activities, and matching instructors with grade-levels promises flexibility in addressing the differences reflected in these results. The increased ownership of this project by a dedicated Director of Student Life additionally supports the homeroom function.

3.3 Clubs

On February 26th, 2010, a group of six SOHS students gathered at the national final of the Junior Engineering Technical Society (JETS) competition in Washington, D.C. Like the other select teams, they had worked over the course of a year to conceive, design, and implement a tool to meet the parameters of the competition—in this year's competition, a tool to assist a particular disability. Their design

---

[8]Of responding students, 56% (100) report that homerooms provide excellent, very good, or good opportunities to connect socially with their peers, while 23% (43) rank it as 'poor' in this regard. In *SOHS Accreditation Student Survey* (2013).

[9]More experienced SOHS students find homerooms less rewarding, with the excellent, very good, or good rating falling for each year at the school: 63% (57) for first-year students, 53% (25) for second year students, and 44% (12) for third year students (the number returns to 53% (9) for fourth-year students, though only one ranks it 'excellent'). In *SOHS Accreditation Student Survey* (2013).

for a 'Tactile Office Phone (TOP) Adapter'—a glove whose vibrations help visually-disabled receptionists manage multiple telephone lines—had gotten them through the preliminary rounds and past teams from schools around the country, earning them paid trips to the national competition. But even as they might have looked like any other team as they checked over their glove one last time, tweaked components, and rehearsed their presentation, this team was just a little different. Until that day, they had never met in person. Indeed, none of them even lived in the same state. They had worked for months to identify a need and hash out designs in the usual array of online forums. Each member focused on a component of the glove, doing his or her part before shipping it on to the next. And despite the extra rush on that final day to iron out details and presentation strategies most teams had occasion to finalize together days before, the SOHS team collected two of the top national awards at the competition.

Outside the context of the classroom and small academic projects, students look to clubs like the JETS team as forums for sharing interests and working collaboratively on focused projects. At a school whose demographics serve to concentrate unique interests and talents, and to expose students who have often pursued those interests independently to similarly-interested peers, it is not surprising that there are numerous, eclectic, and active clubs driven by passionate students. To best facilitate student interests, clubs are initiated or continued on an annual basis through student initiative and supported by staff sponsors. And while the obligations of students in the classroom and in their activities outside of the school exert a drag on the progress of some of these groups, enough enthusiasm and commitment exist that clubs persist and frequently make tangible impacts on the school and occasionally in the wider community, in addition to the role they play in bringing together the talented students of the school.

Even by the second year of the school, students and staff had participated in an assortment of experimental clubs, ranging from standard high-school fare like student government, newspaper, math, science, literary journal, and music clubs, to groups whose possibility at an online school are suggestive of the uncommon and experimental nature of the school and its students, such as the philosophy, culinary, investment, Asia, cross-cultural, service, 3D graphics and animation, and engineering clubs. In 2011-12, the register of clubs reached over thirty, followed by more than forty in 2012-13. The following sampling well represents the tradition of clubs at SOHS and their role in the school community, encompassing the idiosyncratic and frivolous, the expertise of serious hobbyists, and the sustained and focused efforts of academic teams and school institutions:

TABLE 6.1 Clubs at SOHS, 2012–13

Academic clubs:	Astronomy Club, Book Club, Chemistry Club, Chinese Club, El Circulo de Mate, History Club, Latin Club, Linguistics Club, Maths Club, Physics Book Club, Psychology Club, Steam Group, The Problem Creators
Arts and cultural clubs:	Circleline, Dead Poets Society, Film Club, Gastronomy Club, Literature Journal, The Argo
Service and school-service clubs:	Les Ecologists, Middle School Science Club, Music Gives Back, Newspaper Club, Operation Smile, The OHS Oracle, Yearbook
Interests and Entertainment clubs:	Chess Club, Explorer's Club, For the Birds, Lego Guild, Medieval Club, My Little Pony Club, The Tolkein and C.S. Lewis Club, Dominion Club
Preprofessional clubs:	Business Club, Leaders in Training, Pre-Med Club
Team clubs:	FTC Robotics Club, Mathermatical Modeling Club, Model United Nations, Science Club, University Level Math Problem Solving Club

These clubs have accomplished much over the life of the school, in ways that highlight SOHS students' ability to work closely, creatively, and productively across physical boundaries and differences in their own backgrounds. A few examples help to distill the ways in which clubs bring together individual students and the larger school community.

In the first year of the school, students and instructors collaborated to charter clubs around student and teacher interests and to explore creatively ways to collaborate in an online environment. SOHS has always had its share of culinary enthusiasts, so a culinary club seemed appropriately audacious for the online setting. Students (and instructors!) had a lot of fun meeting regularly to share recipes around a theme or ingredient, photos, test-tastings of others' recipes, cookbook reviews, and culinary exploits. The club developed a number of recurring games: identify that culinary object or strange food or spice, spot the missing ingredient, identify a food from its recipe, and on and on. On occasion, students would also wage online Iron Chef competitions, with several students preparing dishes around a single ingredient, on camera, and with appropriate narration. During holidays, members would reach out beyond the screen and exchange regional candies (including some from France and Canada) or favorite baked goods through the mail. At the end of the year, several students gathered with the instructor-sponsor to make a variety of recipes; as it happened, with students from California, Korea, and Hong Kong, the menu was as diverse as the school population. Many of those students are *still* sharing recipes and other stories online with one another, eight years later.[10]

Another longtime SOHS club, the Literary Journal, exemplifies well the ways in which a fun, collaborative club in which students work together around a shared interest can create both transformative experiences and enduring community. The Literary Journal club was formed by students passionate about creative writing as a forum for sharing and discussing their own work, as well as favorite texts. In the course of their regular meetings, characterized by the sometimes personal process of sharing their own work, and in their production of biannual compilations of SOHS students' creative writing, the members develop a closeness and history that enrich their time at the school, and long after. Several alumni of the club recently planned and attended a club reunion, held in the ongoing virtual classroom that has hosted the club for years and enshrines years' worth of student work and club activities, to visit with one another and their club sponsor and revisit some of their time together.

4 'In Person'

'I'm going [to summer session] this year (this is my first year), and I am super excited to meet all of my friends.'[11] This frequently repeated sentiment, paradoxical on its face, is suggestive of the place of

[10]This club has received particularly strong endorsement from the faculty of the school, with clear guidance to students to concentrate on baked goods, particularly those with long shelf lives.

[11]*SOHS Accreditation Student Survey* (2013).

physical meetings in the SOHS community: students form and build rich, meaningful, and durable friendships in the online environment of the school, so much so that they really love to be together in a physical setting. These physical encounters can also serve as touchstones for future interactions and collaborations—shared experiences that establish relationships, extend them, and provide reference points that frame collaboration down the road. Accordingly, the school, students, and families work together to develop programs and events that balance accessibility with the various functions of these meetings.

4.1 Graduation Weekend

Students might, with some honesty, attest that graduation weekend is enjoyable and meaningful primarily in the extent to which it gives them time to be together with their friends. Indeed, as suggested earlier, this is much of the social function of the event. However, there are a number of features of this particular social gathering that serve important, if somewhat secondary, purposes in the life of the community and in the relationships that make up that community.

Any commencement program is at its core a ceremony marking achievement, milestones, and transitions. The SOHS graduation weekend is replete with events and traditions in this vein, including the commencement itself, the awards ceremony and middle-school promotion, a senior-faculty dinner, prom, and grad-night celebration. Surely, these events are part of what it is to be a high-school student (or a high-school teacher). But in the context of the graduation weekend, they are also part of what it is to be an SOHS student: participating in graduation weekend after a year at the school, and eventually having it be *your* graduation weekend, is a singular shared experience that visibly binds SOHS students to one another.

The ceremonies and celebrations that distinguish graduation weekend from other gatherings are, to an extent, shaped to accomplish additional community goals. These events have a natural function of valorizing the educational objectives of the school in the celebration of the graduates and distinguished performers themselves. In making the relevant qualities of graduates and award winners explicit in their celebration, these qualities are emphasized to the community at large. Awards recognizing critical contributions to the community, such as collegial leadership in discussions or innovative leadership in clubs, reinforce in this public context the importance of community-building activities to the educational objectives for each student. Comments offered by instructors articulating the accomplishments of seniors in the commencement, and those of award winners in the awards ceremony, serve both this function, and also have the effect of identifying the strengths of particular students as they establish their place within the community.

But students are not wrong to think that graduation is very much about spending time together. Graduation weekend furnishes students, and all members of the community, with a range of settings and interactions in which to become better acquainted. Open-ended opportunities like exploring the campus or San Francisco complement dances, game nights, and formal ceremonies. Throughout all of these events, though, what is most striking (and perhaps most important) about the dynamics of the community interactions is their pervasive inclusiveness. Whatever the underlying causes, the shared experience and meaning of being a student at the SOHS is enough, in this context, to motivate a general and mutual enjoyment of each student's participation. It is an important testament to the strength of this inclusiveness that even in the most socially fraught circumstances, even at prom, the students welcome and encourage the inclusion of each of their peers. This phenomenon not only allows students to take full advantage of the unique interactions that occur in a physical setting, but also validates the inclusive and respectful spirit that is essential to the dynamic interplay that prevails when everyone is back in the online seminar.

4.2 Meetups

Schoolwide events and gatherings, such as the graduation weekend and summer session, are inevitably subject to limits of time, expense, and availability of facilities and participants. While the school seeks to expand these all-school opportunities and to do so in a manner that does not exclude students by cost and geography, a range of considerations call for additional modes of physical gathering. Most vividly, students so deeply enjoy the physical meetings they do attend that they view these school-wide occasions as occurring too infrequently. In September of 2009, the third year of the school, the first experiments with regional meetings, which have come to be called 'meetups', were initiated. This smaller, distributed format came to make sense as the school developed. With growth in enrollment, clusters of students have emerged across the country, often around metropolitan areas. With assistance from student-life staff in publicizing the events, students and families were empowered to plan and host events in their own areas, drawing on local interests and attractions to meet perceived needs and opportunities in a timely manner. Regional coordinators—volunteer parents who serve as local points of contact for families—have additionally helped to improve awareness of events and other families in a given geographical area. While meetups help to replicate some of the physical socialization and activities that would be common at a brick-and-mortar school, they also serve a special function in the unique context of the SOHS: in creating a local culture within the context of a larger school, the regional interactions exemplified by meetups create connections among students at the school who might otherwise have little in common (such as students in different years, areas of interest, or circles of friends). As such, facilitated by meetups, regional networks can serve as a unifying commonalty absent in more conventional school settings. Indeed, possibilities of the model are still being tested and pushed, as in the case of a group of about ten students in Southern California who have established a monthly routine of meetups, gathering most recently to experience the Getty Museum and the Griffith Observatory, to tour rare books collections at UCLA (joined by half of the SOHS English department), and to enjoy Manhattan Beach.

The first meetups were organized as nearly simultaneous meetings in four regions: Northern California, Southern California, New York, and Washington D.C. Hosted at family homes, they attracted about five or six students each, with some faculty and staff attending. Activities consisted primarily of conversation; in a gesture to the normal mode of interaction at SOHS, the Northern California and Washington D.C. groups Skyped one another. In the following months, students in New York and New Jersey orchestrated trick-or-treating at the American Natural History Museum and another group celebrated Halloween with a costume party in Northern California, with students attending from Idaho, New York, and Southern California. Occasional meetups developed in the following year to center around functions like individual college visits or organized precollege events like MIT Splash, recreational trips like a coordinated visit to Universal Studios Orlando, or international travel, such as a two-day visit to Elsinore Castle in Denmark, hosted by students living overseas, and a visit in Katsuura, Japan.

The frequency and geographic diversity of meetups truly began to accelerate in 2011-12, as the format and mechanisms for hosting and publicizing them became more streamlined and well known, and as school support for such events developed into a dedicated position of Director of Student Life. A partial list of gatherings in 2012-13 characterizes the extent and variety of these events:

TABLE 6.2 Meetups in 2012–13

Oct 2012	Boulder, CO	Picnic and hiking; instructor attended
Nov 2012	Cambridge, MA	Meetup during MIT Splash; instructor attended
Dec 2012	Northbrook, IL	Bowling, bocce, pizza
Jan 2013	Glendale, CA	Food and shopping at post-finals meetup
Jan 2013	Redlands, CA	Visit at student's home
Feb 2013	Baltimore, MD	Brunch at market
Feb 2013	Palo Alto, CA	Celebration of Science Bowl team; instructors attended
Feb 2013	Frisco, TX	Visit at student's home
Feb 2013	Anchorage, AK	Pizza making and games
Feb 2013	El Segundo, CA	Games and potluck
Mar 2013	New York, NY	3D printing class and dinner in Little Italy
Mar 2013	Pasadena, CA	Tour of CalTech
Mar 2013	Bedford, NY	Picnic, hiking, and games
May 2013	Irving, TX	Visit at student's home
May 2013	Holland, MI	Beach, bonfire, BBQ, and tour of Univ. of Michigan
July 2013	Carlsbad, CA	Pizza and swimming (2nd Annual)
July 2013	Central Point, CA	Fishing and camping

Students attest that such meetups make an important contribution to the growth of community at SOHS, with an impact on social connectedness just behind summer session and non-school social media.[12] Still, they have not been a panacea, at least historically, given the limited number of these events that any one student is likely to have been able

[12] Of students responding, 147 (90%) rated the effectiveness of meetups 'in creating social connections with [their] classmates' as excellent (63), very good (38), or good (32). In *SOHS Accreditation Student Survey* (2013).

to attend.[13] However, the increase in events, coupled with the overall enthusiasm of students who have attended such events, supports the assessment that meetups make a positive contribution to community and that increased accessibility is desirable. While the nature and limitations of that contribution bear more investigation, meetups appear to fit within the generally successful strategy of proliferating points of in-person socialization in support of the day-to-day interactions among students in the virtual setting of the school.

4.3 Summer Session

Since the inception of the school, summer session has been envisioned as a unique opportunity for SOHS students to build community as they gather in residence at Stanford. It also presents an opportunity to have students and instructors collaborate on intellectual endeavors that extend beyond what is possible in the academic year and online environment. Students and instructors can draw on and benefit from the physical resources of the University, the serendipitous meetings and activities of living together in a dorm environment, and the exclusive and intense focus on more limited topics than is common in the regular academic program. By any measure, summer session has proven a unique and seminal social experience in students' lives at the school throughout its different manifestations.[14] Plainest, perhaps, are the words of students speaking at a closing campfire, in which nearly every student spoke in the vein of this sampling:

> I just love you all so much.
>
> These have been the best two weeks of my life.
>
> Now I know I'm more than a nerd.
>
> I'm so glad I decided to come, and I can't wait for next year!

In its first iterations, summer session encompassed three weeks, giving students options from among science lab courses (first physics, then biology, and later chemistry as well) and session-long focused courses in historical research, literature, or writing. An additional course focused on reviewing and enhancing study skills across the various disciplines, interspersed with introductions to the methodologies and instructors in

[13]Curiously, only 28 (48%) of responding students who attended middle school at SOHS considered that meetups had contributed a lot (15), some (10), or a little (3) to their middle-school experience. It is possible that negative ratings flow from the infrequency of these events, or from the effectiveness of the format itself in creating social connections.

[14]Summer session most recently received a rating of excellent, very good, or good effectiveness in creating social connections with classmates from 127 (93%) responding students.

the disciplines. Outside of formal class time, a leadership program incorporated discussions and presentations about the nature and strategies of leadership, geared toward different ages and experience levels. Not unexpectedly, however, the most impactful component of the program for students was the opportunity to live and work with their classmates. Anecdotes repeatedly suggest that summer session provides an unparalleled occasion for the formation of friendships, the creation of bonds among all members of the school in attendance, and the sharing of experiences that connect students throughout their time at the school and beyond. Preserving and supporting this element of the summer session experience through the transformations and growth of the program has been a consistent focus of planning.

Experimentation in the structure of the offerings in the program has focused on better using the unique in-person and on-campus opportunities presented by summer session. In the school's fourth year, the emerging two-week courses were reconceived as a sampling of 'mini-courses' spanning three or four days. Here, the idea was to resist the temptation to accomplish *more* academic content of the type students receive during the regular year, but rather to embrace the short, in-person setting to engage a topic or subject not as accessible in the regular academic program. Examples of such courses include History of Computers, Philosophy East and West, Geometry and Art, and Introduction to Android Apps. These courses provide students a glimpse of how various different subject matters are engaged at SOHS, draw on Bay Area resources, and connect students with different instructors and fellow students than they might encounter during their normal academic program. Local events have included trips to the Silicon Valley Computer Museum, the rare books collections of the Stanford Libraries, local productions of classic dramas, and the Stanford linear accelerator.

A second transformation of the summer program, in the summer of 2012, featured a formal division of the program into curricula for incoming and returning students, as well as the creation of a session-long themed multidisciplinary course for returning students. Both changes reflected developing thinking about the function of an on-site summer program in a virtual school. Building on the training in study skills offered in previous years, the program for incoming students more intentionally served to orient new students to academic norms and practices at the school, technological systems and tools, and features and opportunities of the school community and culture. Staff and instructors developed this material in the mini-course model, with groups of students rotating through each of the three-to-four day orientation courses. In the afternoon, orientation students would move to a select set of academic mini-courses, gaining a feel for SOHS-style academic engagement in a range of subjects.

Returning students, meanwhile, are now able to participate in a two-week themed academic program during summer session that approaches a single topic using the tools and methodologies of a wide range of disciplines. This multidisciplinary style of study is consistent with and inspired by the approach to research and teaching at the heart of university initiatives at Stanford, and which President Hennessy has described as essential to future advances.[15] In its initial manifestation in 2012, the interdisciplinary program focused on a theme of 'The Problem of Food'. Students came to campus having read Michael Pollan's *The Omnivore's Dilemma*[16] to establish a common acquaintance with a host of issues surrounding modern food production and culture. Led by instructors but drawing on local resources, students then began work on a larger project in which teams of students developed recipes for a course in a full meal ultimately prepared and served to the all of the participants in summer session. The courses themselves represented the fruit of the students' work and reflection in activities as diverse as experimenting in molecular gastronomy, learning to design web pages, tasting locally-grown tomatoes, examining centuries-old recipes in rare books collections, talking with farmers, calculating carbon footprints, and debating the merits and difficulties of eating organically and locally. This particular project, and its multidisciplinary approach, nicely spoke to summer session's goals of providing a context for collaborative and socially stimulating work by showcasing the special skills of individual students and the model of teachers collaborating across disciplines. And it did so through projects that could only happen in-person, on the Stanford campus. Consistent with the SOHS mission, though, what was innovative about the program was not the medium or space in which it occurred, novel as it was for our school in that regard. In addition to bringing together different disciplines, the food program also brought together different populations in new ways, drawing upon food services staff as teachers and the students as cooks.

While students identify summer session as the forum that is most effective in fostering social connections, its impact is still limited by the same factors that complicate most physical interactions at SOHS. In one recent survey, only (69) 35% of responding students had attended

[15] D. Farber, 'AlwaysOn: Lessons from Stanford President John Hennessy', *ZDNet*, July 25, 2006, http://www.zdnet.com/blog/btl/alwayson-lessons-from-stanford-president-john-hennessy/3378.

[16] M. Pollan, *The Omnivore's Dilemma: A Natural History of Four Meals* (New York: Penguin Press, 2006).

summer session, though many of the students surveyed reported looking forward to attending, especially those who would have their first opportunity in the coming summer.[17] Most graduating SOHS students attend summer session at some stage in their careers, but enrollment did not support a dedicated middle-school program until summer of 2014. Among students who had not yet attended, commonly cited obstacles include other summer commitments (60%—78 students) and financial considerations (38%—49 students). Only 11 students (9%) had not attended due to the program's lack of appeal. Given the formative role the program plays in supporting and enriching the life of the community, all of these issues—expense, conflicting obligations, and eligibility—are points of focus in planning for future years. With a new high of ninety-seven students attending the summer session program in 2013, and with nearly150 students registered for the summer of 2014, efforts particularly in extending eligibility and highlighting the program's importance to families appear to be meeting with significant success.

5 Out of School

However important periodic physical gatherings are in the creation, expansion, and cementing of friendships and a sense of community, they are unlikely to be robust or frequent enough to sustain SOHS students, let alone enrich and challenge them, throughout the course of the year. And while in-class interactions are often cited by students as thrilling and substantial, they are constrained enough in their focus and academic agenda that they are also inadequate to both the social needs of students and the educational goals of the school. For students to find the school something other than an activity that alienates them from their local social community, their connections to their fellow students need to have some daily meaning or significance outside of the classroom. In order to collaborate productively and openly as a community in discussion sections, students must develop relatively nuanced understandings of their peers—pictures that are the accretion of diverse interactions and exchanges over time. And to extend learning beyond the classroom to a schoolwide community, where common academic and cultural experiences underwrite spontaneous discussions, collaboration, tutoring, mentoring, joking, support, and real friendships, students must have daily means of spending time together in the unstructured environment in which personalities unfold.

SOHS students have proven extremely resourceful in adapting social media and other electronic resources to this purpose, driven by the

[17] *SOHS Accreditation Student Survey* (2013)

promise of the interactions they find in their initial connections in class and other events, physical or otherwise. One veteran student was fond of telling prospective students that unless she turned off every single device, her SOHS friends would be in near-constant contact with her. Even in the second year of the school, another student captured a similar flexibility and constancy of electronic interactions (even with some dated technical references):

> I use Skype to talk to E in Canada, MSN to video chat with MC in Florida, and meebo to video conference with L and R in California and K in Connecticut. I talk to so many people on Gchat everyday that when I went on vacation I missed each and every one of them. That's something I think you do not get in a public or private high school. It's a strong bond you develop with your peers, that overcomes obstacles like distance, and physical contact.[18]

Despite the variation over time and in individual practices, SOHS students have developed a de facto set of practices and norms that are notably inclusive, flexible, and adapted to the peculiarities of their interactions and their needs. Particular tools do gain and lose favor, and new forms of interaction emerge; however, a sketch of the current suite of practices helps to characterize the more durable network of needs and functions that electronic media serve in the school culture.

5.1 Skype

By all accounts, Skype is the centerpiece of the non-school electronic community, and has been for some time. But while the video-conference capabilities of the application are of some use to the social and academic interactions of students, they are by no means the predominant focus of activity on Skype in the SOHS context. Students certainly video-chat in one-on-one or small group contexts (though Google+ is often favored for its free and larger group video-chats), but Skype is used primarily for its text-chat functionality, which can be channeled into topic-based groups of varying size and permanence. In addition to private messaging, students have formed essentially schoolwide groups, groups of classmates or grademates, groups of friends, study groups, and temporary groups for meetings or class projects.

While group chats spring up around most courses, discussion in those (and other groups) frequently strays away from class topics; in this sense, groups often form around school-based functions and intersections, but foster socialization of that unique group, greatly and uniquely contributing to the community identity of a given collection

[18] *SOHS Viewbook* (2008).

of students (for instance, the students in a given course or discussion section) while also occasioning the development of new friendships that might not develop in groups delineated by existing friendships. In one group, formed around a homeroom, the chat was used to coordinate some of the student-driven activities of the homeroom, including short-story writing, math problem-solving, and votes on various subjects. But these conversations spawned discussion of interests in literature or brief commentary on shared courses, as well as low-grade back and forth throughout the week, effectively extending the homeroom's function of giving students an additional forum for social connection and collaboration outside of the weekly meeting.

Interaction in the Skype groups is closely fitted to the nature of the medium, and also to the logistics that shape the students' contact. By its nature, the group chat in Skype straddles the boundaries of synchronous and asynchronous interaction. Discussions can extend throughout an entire day, driven by an ever-shifting subset of participants as students come and go from respective classes, extracurriculars, meals, studying, and sleep (shaped by timezone and habits). Some threads of a chat, such as focused exchanges, personal interactions, or passing jokes and hilarity, are tied to the moment (though they remain on record), while others can run for hours or days, with students catching up and weighing in on a topic raised earlier. In this manner, study sessions can run for hundreds of comments over several days, with the full complement of students never convening at any given time. This sort of opt-in, ongoing exchange is tailored to the distributed nature of the community: students can get what they want from the group, when they want it.

Skype therefore serves as the central, informal network for SOHS students. This is where students go to hang out with one another, collaborate, ask questions, and communicate in 'emergencies' (usually involving connectivity). Its central status in the community came about largely through critical mass, driven in part by the application's well-suitedness to need. Other more formally organized groups, such as Ning groups created by students, have come and gone, but Skype has achieved a measure of indispensability that is quickly communicated to and recognized by new students.

Beyond the good fit it provides to the needs of the SOHS community, Skype may appeal to students in its similarity to the interface of the virtual classroom (discussed in Chapter 4) and the patterns of interaction developed there. Students are thoroughly familiar with easy and robust interaction in synchronous text chat in virtue of their easy and robust interaction in the classroom text chat, such that Skype group chats are essentially an extension of that mode of interaction in a group setting. And, just like the text chat that is a secondary thread subordinate to the audio and visual conversation of the classroom, Skype group chats transpire slowly or intermittently, while students are occupied with other tasks.

5.2 Facebook

Inevitably, a large proportion of SOHS students use Facebook, and accordingly, use it to connect with one another. In many ways, their conduct on Facebook reflects that of their peers at brick-and-mortar schools: it is simply another medium in which they interact, though primarily in an asynchronous manner. There are, however, several features of their interaction in this forum that, if not entirely unusual, are significant for the growth and nature of their community.

Like many of their peers anywhere else, SOHS students use Facebook to craft and showcase their public identities. The verisimilitude of these personae is surely just as fraught and nuanced a matter as authors such as Turkle have shown it to be for most users of such media, especially the young.[19] Balanced as they are, though, by interactions outside the realm of Facebook, these profiles are particularly potent in the SOHS setting, where they can be used to offer one's fellow students a glimpse of the rest of one's life—pictures, friends, sports, and hometown. Students frequently engage in activities with a similar function in other SOHS venues: the student-run newspaper regularly profiles individual students in a 'Stories of an OHS Life' column, students in class take careful note of pets or an occasional younger sibling who might scurry through the camera view, as well as any other personally significant features of the others' 'classroom' setting, and homeroom activities or other class assignments involving stories or sharing about hometowns or extracurricular activities are always among the most popular.

As a working community, students have generated a wide range of special-purpose Facebook pages. The variety and activity of these pages may be somewhat more significant than in brick-and-mortar contexts. But of greater interest is the distinct role that these pages play for students in the network of other tools they have cobbled together for their interactions. Again, the nature of the medium attracts use for particular functions. In contrast to Skype, for instance, where a large chat can scroll on for hours, straying from one topic to the next, Facebook's post-and-comment structure affords more purposive threading of topics and discussions. While these exchanges are hardly serious in

[19] Turkle, *Alone Together.*

the typical case, they do allow for more focused planning of events or decision-focused interactions. The student government can gather opinions on a project or measure, alumni can answer a question about SOHS experiences or weigh in on a reunion proposal, and the students at large can offer collective advice about exam preparation or course selection. These behaviors, of course, are hardly ordained at the outset, but emerge as norms through collective experimentation as the optimal fit to focused needs.

The resulting web of contact points, forums, and resources is much more robust and dynamic than a cumbersome apparatus that the school might implement for this purpose. The students' ownership of this feature of their community life simultaneously empowers them to effect the changes they experience as needful, while fostering a sense of responsibility and pride in making *positive* contributions to the school culture that *they* have inherited and built.

5.3 Syncronous activities

Many electronic activities common among SOHS students are fundamentally approximations of physical interactions made impossible by distance. Video chats, the electronic classroom, and group text chats all would be, to some extent, unnecessary were students able to gather physically. Some of these mechanisms are extremely good approximations, and some have their own distinctive virtues beyond their physical model. At the same time, students in a brick-and-mortar environment are not necessarily together at all times, either. After school hours and apart from dedicated time, students make use of many of these same electronic media to spend time together, bridging much shorter physical distances.

However, students in a conventional setting do have the physical environment in which to *be together while doing other things*—they are able to go to movies, share a meal, take a trip, go to the beach, play a game, and so on. It is this type of interaction that is not as robustly supported by electronic media; clearly the most dynamic common endeavor SOHS students are able to participate in online is in their classrooms, where they are together while learning. Outside of class, however, they have also developed practices and traditions for spending time together and interacting while doing something else. A peculiar instance of this genre of interaction that has developed at SOHS over time is the practice of co-watching movies and other events while exchanging comments online. Students have coordinated large-scale sessions in which many students, and sometimes teachers, watch events like the presidential inauguration, presidential debates, or the Oscars. In the most formal versions, the school will open a virtual classroom to facilitate broad engagement, and a host will lead the games, contests, or analysis typical of such viewing parties. Smaller events, such as movie viewing, are orchestrated by individual students. Another example is the karaoke night organized by the student government, featuring a full gamut of performances by the assembled thirty students (including an interesting duet navigated online and an SOHS-style rendition of 'The Elements'). In these activities, the school community is hardly monolithic: different segments of the population do different things, and more or less of it, to meet their specific needs. Middle-school students, for instance, much less likely to be active or allowed on many social networking sites, connect meaningfully in the context of interactive gaming networks. Strikingly, this particular mode of online interaction surrounding a shared activity hardly different in the widely distributed SOHS community than it would in a local community of friends.

6 'Just Like Other Schools, Only More So'

More broadly, it is worth noting that many of the online forums and activities common at SOHS are essentially the same as those that occupy students at conventional schools when they go home for the day. As the role and capabilities of online tools have expanded in the life of every teen community, the nature of those communities has moved closer to life at the SOHS. It is increasingly at the interstices that there are significant differences: SOHS students do not physically bump into each other in the halls (though they do meet early ahead of class); they do not congregate in small groups to eat lunch (though they do have running chats on Skype in groups of various sizes); and they do not go over to one another's houses, go to Starbucks together, or go out on the weekend (though to some extent, they go to meetups, call/video-chat, and go to graduation and summer session together). Just like kids anywhere, and possibly more, they *are* actively and robustly present with their peers in class, and they are thoroughly enmeshed in a rich and dynamic network of online connections.

What is it, then, that determines whether the community at one school, whether online or brick-and-mortar, is a real community that meets the social and educational needs of its student-members? Our experience at SOHS suggests that it is not the shrinking (if not insignificant) line between physical association and mainly online interactions of the right sort. Some who are particularly attentive to the significance of embodied interaction resist this bridging of a divide commonly expressed in language—of 'virtual' and 'real'—that begs our question, asserting, 'Most of what needs to be done has to be done face to face, person to person—civic engagement means dealing with your neighbors in the world where your body lives.'[20] Claims like this one that the body is vital to community, whether in civic life or in education, are largely shorthand for other dynamics that are not essentially tied to onlineness.[21] Critics in the vein of Dreyfus are concerned that a lack of investment and personal stake in an online, *or any*, community undermines the ability of that network to create the dialogue that responds, challenges, and transforms its members. Dreyfus again, along with critics attuned to our emotional and cognitive needs such as Turkle and Nass, worry that online interactions are not close enough to 'in-person', 'face-to-face', or real, in ways that deprive us of depth of connection, responsiveness, and emotional connection that we critically need. These concerns are all well founded; community depends upon these things, and education depends upon community. But the example of SOHS testifies that whether or not a community creates investment among its members, and whether or not rich online presence fulfills cognitive and social needs depends on the depth, quality, and context of these connections, not their electronic medium.

At the Stanford Online High School, students are gathering online in a genuine school context. They go to classes where they engage directly, responsively, and collaboratively with their teachers and fellow students. There they share interests and experiences that drive them to engage one another in a broader set of interactions: in project-driven clubs, in casual exchanges and experiences, and in close personal interactions. These interactions and friendships are validated and strengthened in occasional physical gatherings that cement bonds that grow further back online. Students (and teachers and parents) are deeply invested in the actions and contributions of other members of their community, both in their own educational experience and in their career prospects as graduates of a relatively small, new, and unique independent school.

There is still a ways to go, and there are still real issues that merit watchful attention and study. Students simply want more of one an-

[20] H. Rheingold, *The Virtual Community: Homesteading on the Electronic Frontier*, rev. ed. (Cambridge, MA: MIT Press, 2000), chap. 11.

[21] Dreyfus's own focus on embodiment is part of a philosophical project, based in theories of perception, that rejects the Cartesian discounting of the body's contribution to perception, experience, and meaning, beyond mere sensation. However well motivated this project with respect to mind and body, Dreyfus himself backs off of its decisive stake in his assessment of the internet, acknowledging the potential of developments in telepresence and avatars (such as those in *Second Life*) to address some of his concerns about the medium.

other. The school is still in a phase of growth, both in the depth of students' enrollment (as part-time or full-time) and in total enrollment; can the intimate and supportive student culture in the school be preserved with more students, new students, and students who see the school as less of a risk, and less of an experiment? While the school culture is remarkably inclusive, is it the case that any particularities of *this* school culture underserve the educational or social needs of certain types of students?

At the same time, the discussion about community at SOHS need not be strictly about adequacy and shortcomings. On display in this description is a supportive and affirming community that is difficult to achieve among diverse and extremely talented students. The students' diverse backgrounds and ongoing experiences are powerful realities for students who might otherwise live more insulated lives. And the worldwide and self-selecting pool of students makes for a rare collection of like-minded students bound not only by their passions but also by the full knowledge of how precious that is.

7

Outcomes

1 Introduction

How do you measure your effectiveness as a school on students who are phenomenally talented? They already do well on tests. They are likely to improve over the course of their high-school careers. They are interested in learning. They are creative and they think outside of the box. They are often accomplished already. They have families that value education. They know their way around a book and have often taught themselves a good deal outside of school.

There are, of course, ways to do it. It would be a tidy study indeed to pair similarly situated applicants, deny and accept one of each pair, and compare their outcomes. When our numbers are large enough and student backgrounds more comparable, we might someday consider the efficacy of certain programs in the school by comparing part-time and full-time students in those programs. And eventually, our graduates will have moved through college and into careers sufficiently to chart trends, if not with comparative rigor. But it is not the goal of the school to experiment with our students. The Stanford Online High School is not a laboratory school. It is not the function of the school to alter its program or to treat individual students differently in the interest of investigating a particular hypothesis. Rather, SOHS is a demonstration school—a school whose curriculum, structure, and medium are intended to show what can be done in these areas, and how one might do it. As any school interested in continual improvement ought, we will adjust the curriculum and our practices to improve student results within the general framework of the school's mission. So when it seems best for students, we will increase the frequency of language course meetings, change graduation requirements, adjust workload, introduce new programs and courses, alter prerequisites, adopt new strategies in the classroom, and alter enrollment types or admissions guidelines.

These changes are based on experience and emerging best practices in what appears to yield the best results in our environment. Standardizing our curriculum and directing students to more standardized tests to provide external validation of our choices, rather than because doing so would be in the interest of our students, is neither a priority nor would it be consistent with the mission of the school.[1]

Traditional metrics do not provide entirely informative measures of the school's success as an academic program. Schools with comparable student profiles are not common and do not provide a robust target for comparison of outcomes. And the school's contribution to its students is simply difficult to study quantitatively at this point in our development. However, the school's founding mission casts some light on where to look even now to evaluate progress. That mission directs the school to 'afford gifted students everywhere an education ideally suited to their needs', specifying such an education as 'one which sets high expectations and challenges them to reach their potential; one which cultivates creativity, fosters analytical reason, and refines argumentative skills; one in which students pursue intellectual passions, and engage in philosophical reflection; one which builds the foundation for success in future academic pursuits and in life itself.' The premise of the school is that these goals are inadequately served and poorly measured by standardized curricula in any case. Better measures are the markers of the engagement and intellectual development of these students. Students' needs are met when they find a home in the SOHS academic program after having searched repeatedly for an academic challenge. They are well served when their school environment—peers, teachers, and curriculum—helps them to find, and fosters, academic passions. And their needs are met when they are uniquely prepared to matriculate and succeed at outstanding colleges with the resources to challenge them further. In these regards, the SOHS has built a strong record to flesh out the story of the strengths of our students in conventional measures.

2 Preparation of Graduates

In the school's 2009-10 accreditation visit and report, the visiting accreditation committee suggested that oral communication might be further stressed across the curriculum. In many ways, this recommenda-

[1]The SOHS is reviewing the College Work and Readiness Assessment (CWRA+) and other developing assessments that attempt to measure critical thinking skills, mindful of challenges such as those discussed in R. Ennis, 'Critical Thinking Assessment', *Theory into Practice* 32, no. 5 (1993): 179-186.

tion was apt for a school that did very little by way of explicit training in oral communication, and indeed, this recommendation was based in part on our own reflections in the preparatory self-study. Oral argumentation is a component of our goals for graduates, but to that point, there was no speech and debate team, no more than a supplementary summer session course on public speaking, and no formal component of the curriculum focused on oral communication. The ensuing discussions and planning led to more assignments including an oral component, as well as the formation of a debate team and crafting of other opportunities for leadership and speaking. But our sense that the school was underserving an important skill turned out to be misguided. While the school did not have many well-articulated programs focused on oral communication, what we did have were pervasive; at the time we did not fully appreciate the impact that consistent argumentative participation in discussion might have on students' oral presentation, in addition to their argumentative skills more generally. Anecdotes to this effect are powerful: SOHS graduates regularly demonstrate a polish and focus in their formal speech that allays any doubt that an online school can produce complete students.

At the level of achievement envisioned for SOHS students, the educational goals of the school are similar to oral argumentation in their contribution to a broad construal of a well-educated student. One formulation of the school's objectives in this regard are the 'Expected Schoolwide Learning Results' (ESLRs) developed in the initial years of the school.[2] These goals for students upon graduation are, notably, assembled from both the academic objectives in individual disciplines as developed in the context of individual courses, and schoolwide considerations. In this sense, they reflect the teaching staff's detailed vision of the foundations of scholarly preparation for advanced work in their disciplines, coupled with broader views about what an education must impart for general citizenship:

Upon graduation from SOHS:

- Students will possess theoretical and applied knowledge of the essential concepts, principles, processes, and facts of diverse subject areas and disciplines.
- Students will have mastered the reasoning skills necessary for abstract and practical problem-solving. These skills include modeling,

[2]This terminology comes from the school's accrediting agency, the Western Association of Schools and Colleges (WASC). ESLRs are intended to further refine a school's vision and inform the educational program. The current terminology refers to 'Schoolwide Student Goals'.

testing, induction, deduction, interpretation, criticism, formalism, and analysis.
- Students will be able to interpret and understand materials from diverse sources and disciplines.
- Students will be able to employ effective written and spoken language considering purpose, message and audience; and students will be able to communicate effectively across disciplines and through a variety of media.
- Students will have acquired the requisite tools, knowledge, and perspective to be responsible and productive citizens in a global community, with an understanding and appreciation of diversity and its implications.
- Students will possess the necessary skills, independence, and motivation to pursue life-long learning.

The model of graduates that emerges is one of independent learners who have mastered the disciplinary material and skills sufficient for a productive understanding, who are capable of critical reading and analysis, who are skilled in the tools of discovery and thinking, who on this basis are capable of constructing arguments and adducing evidence in support of these views, and who can present their work clearly and persuasively. Graduates should be equipped and inspired to do this all in a variety of contexts, on their own, and in global community as constructive citizens. Still more concretely, the school is dedicated to the formation of scholars who know enough and how to argue, and then how to communicate their work as productive participants in public and professional discourse.

The goals that the SOHS takes as essential and distinctive features of its program are not easy to quantify. They exceed the level, scope, and nuance of standardized assessments. There are notoriously few good measures, for instance, of the recondite but much-desired capacity for critical thinking; it is hard to test what you cannot consistently define.[3] And poise, presentation, and resourcefulness are not amenable to standardized studies. Anecdotal testimony and student self-assessment are therefore helpful direct indicators. But somewhat more objective are the indirect markers of the target skills and mentality—the achievements and undertakings that these abilities facilitate or engender. In the context of high-school graduates, the most immediate measures are associated with college. It is the goal of any high school to prepare students for success in a college that is a good and challenging fit; the more substantive aims of the SOHS are very much an interpretation of what

[3] See the discussion of critical thinking in Chapter 3.

such a preparation consists in. And the subsequent early careers and plans will speak to how students trained in these ways are positioned to work toward their goals.

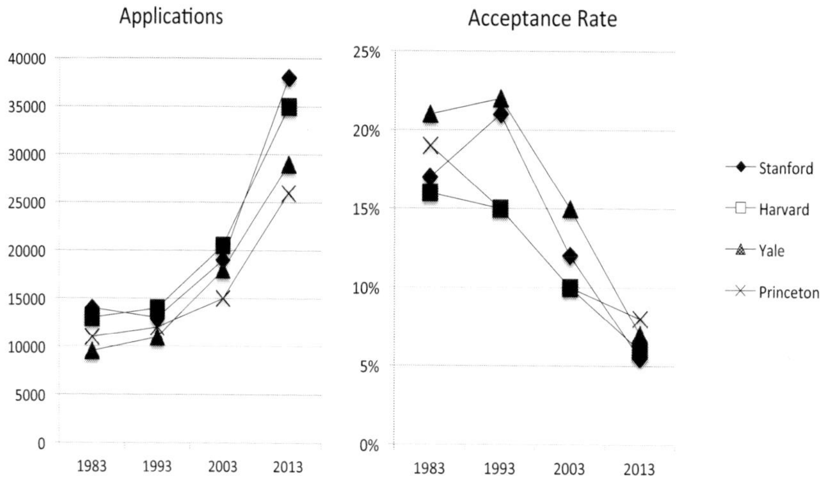

FIGURE 7.1 College applications have increased almost three-fold over thirty years, while admissions have remained flat, resulting in ever-declining rates of admission.[4]

3 College Acceptance and Matriculation

The same combination of talent and intellectual passion that drives students to seek out the SOHS similarly interests them in highly-selective colleges. In many cases, the major research universities would indeed make great fits for SOHS students; other students are ideally served by the smaller community and undergraduate teaching focus of liberal arts colleges. In the hyper-competitive (See Figure 7.1, e.g.) and status-driven admissions environment our students face, it is incumbent upon the school to give our students every advantage in preparation and placement, while also helping them to navigate the unavoidable arbitrariness of a process with so much variation at such a scale. In such an

[4]Figures are adapted from I. Maisel, 'What It Takes', *Stanford Magazine*, November/December 2013, https://alumni.stanford.edu/get/page/magazine/article/?article_id=66225.

TABLE 7.1 Stanford Online High School graduates, by year

Year	Graduates	Year	Graduates
2006–7	2	2010–11	29
2007–8	9	2011–12	23
2008–9	16	2012–13	29
2009–10	20	2013–14	34

environment, students are well served to identify schools that provide them the right resources and setting in which to pursue their goals. And it is the SOHS's goal to help them obtain the right opportunities and to overcome any preconceptions they might have that are grounded in a received understanding regarding college rankings.[5]

So while admission to the well-known schools is a natural objective for many of our students, admission to one or some is not an outcome that each student can trust in, even when they have scores and profiles comparable to typical admits. The situation is similar at any independent school. The challenge at SOHS, as at other schools, with respect to college admission, is to put students in the best possible position for a process that makes minute and sometimes unpredictable distinctions in the absence of complete information. This is an elaborate, multifaceted effort that occurs both at the level of individual students and at a schoolwide level over time.

Where does the school stand now, with respect to this important but highly volatile indicator of the outcomes it achieves for its students? Our list of college acceptances for SOHS graduates is one very rough measure (see Table 7.2).[6] While such a list says little about the quality of fit between individual students and the schools to which they are accepted and matriculate, it supports several large-scale observations. First, the array of acceptances (and applications) represents a diversity of student interests. Students apply and are accepted to national

[5]For a treatment of this topic, see R. Ehrenberg, 'Reaching For the Brass Ring: The *U.S. News & World Report* Rankings and Competition', *The Review of Higher Education* 26, no. 2 (2002): 145-162, doi:10.1353/rhe.2002.0032.

[6]It is important to note that this list represents acceptances by students who receive SOHS diplomas—roughly 110 graduates over the four-year period reflected in the table. Non-graduating students also have very strong results, but as they are graduating from other schools, their college results reflect less consistently on the impact of the SOHS on student results, given the variety of other factors involved. The strength of results for non-graduating students does, of course, reflect on the caliber of student at the school.

TABLE 7.2 Stanford OHS College Acceptances, selected, 2011–2014

Institutions with four or more students admitted:

Carnegie Mellon University, Columbia University, Cornell University, Dartmouth College, Drexel University, Emory University, Massachusetts Institute of Technology, New York University, Northeastern University, Princeton University, Reed College, Rensselaer Polytechnic Institute, Stanford University, University of California at Berkeley, University of California at Davis, University of California at Los Angeles, University of California at San Diego, University of Colorado at Boulder, University of Illinois at Urbana-Champaign, University of Michigan, University of Oregon, University of Pennsylvania, University of Southern California, University of Washington

Institutions with two or more students admitted:

Amherst College, Baylor University, Boston College, Boston University, Bryn Mawr College, Carleton College, Case Western Reserve University, Fordham University, Georgetown University, Harvard College, Johns Hopkins University (and Peabody Institute), Macalester College, New College of Florida, Northwestern University, Rice University, Rochester Institute of Technology, Santa Clara University, Sarah Lawrence College, Southern Methodist University, Swarthmore College, The University of North Carolina at Chapel Hill, The University of Texas, Austin, Tufts University, Tulane University, University of British Columbia, University of Maryland, College Park, University of Minnesota, Twin Cities, University of Notre Dame, University of Rochester, University of Virginia, University of Wisconsin, Madison, Vanderbilt University, Washington and Lee University, Washington University in St. Louis, Wellesley College, Williams College, Worcester Polytechnic Institute

Institutions with one student admitted:

Barnard College, Brandeis University, California Institute of Technology, Claremont McKenna College, Davidson College, Georgia Institute of Technology, Hamilton College, Harvey Mudd College, Lewis & Clark College, Mount Holyoke College, New England Conservatory of Music, Purdue University, The American University of Paris, The University of Georgia, University of Chicago, University of Redlands, University of St. Andrews, Vassar College, Wesleyan University, Whitman College, Yale University research universities, smaller liberal-arts schools, schools with historical STEM focuses, public and private colleges, and schools with national and stronger regional draws. Indeed, there is presumably some effect in this diversity of the demographic fact that SOHS students are selecting schools and applying to them from regions across the country. Also apparent in this list is a high level of achievement by students. Strong records have been established at Ivy League schools, with multiple acceptances to Columbia, Cornell, Dartmouth, University of Pennsylvania, Princeton, and Harvard. Students have matriculated frequently to outstanding liberal arts schools, including Amherst, Reed, Williams, Haverford, Bryn Mawr, Smith, and Sarah Lawrence. Superlative research universities like Stanford, MIT, and Johns Hopkins have accepted numerous students over the life of the school, while acceptances throughout the University of California system are also very high. While strong college results are not the highest validation of a student or a program, they demonstrate that students at the school are succeeding in a variety of rigorous admission processes. Strong continued results also demonstrate that college admission offices recognize that our students are coming to them well prepared for the rigors of even the most challenging post-secondary environments.

3.1 Building Awareness and Reputation

Online education has undergone a series of seismic transformations since the start of the school that have to some degree shaped the lens through which the Stanford Online High School and its students might be seen. At the time of the school's launch, the field was relatively pristine, such that skepticism regarding the program might consist mainly in uncertainty that a meaningful education could be executed in the online environment. The emergence of MOOCs and their subsequent loss of some of their original luster has helped to flesh out part of the picture of what an online education might look like, but among observers of secondary education might raise concerns about student engagement, depth of material, validity of results, and lack of a comprehensive academic program and school experience. Large-scale online high schools catering to disaffected students, or generic online curricula developed by corporations and implemented by individual schools have similarly and not without reason shaped attitudes toward online learning at the secondary level. And some of our students face an additional layer of scrutiny consequent to their unorthodox transcripts, reflecting as they often do an assemblage of coursework from a variety of programs and institutions prior to work at the SOHS. Here, though, may be a less ambiguous benefit from the expansion of online education: it is far less uncommon to find transcripts of intellectually curious and driven students that testify to a conscientiously constructed body of work leveraging available and sometimes experimental opportunities. It is in this context that the school and its students must work to stand apart.

SOHS students' results in Stanford University admissions are representative of the general strength and potential growth in admissions outcomes. While the Stanford Online High School is a part of the broader University, there are no admissions agreements or special considerations given to students of the high school. To be sure, the Stanford University admissions office knows the strength of the program and quality of SOHS students. And SOHS students have historically been accepted at about three times the national rate. Similar long-standing records of acceptance at schools like Reed, Columbia, and MIT, which each have accepted and matriculated several SOHS students over the life of the school suggest that an acquaintance with the school and an understanding of the rigor of the academic program and the quality of the students who graduate from the program have positive results for subsequent applicants.

Achieving a broad and accurate understanding of the school among admissions offices nationally has accordingly been an important part of the school's development. In particular, it has been important to differentiate the SOHS from other online programs and schools, in its standards, its college-style courses, and its talented students and staff. To facilitate this communication, SOHS has looked to college counselors with experience in college admissions offices to help build awareness of the school and its students in an appropriate manor. The counseling office has maintained a presence at the events of the National Association for College Admission Counseling, presented at the College Board Regional Forum, traveled to colleges of central interest to our students, and established relationships with those schools. In addition, they have worked with all aspects of the SOHS program, considering academic advising, curriculum development, graduation requirements, and representation of student performance on transcripts and in recommendations, in order to ensure that the nature of students' talents and work at the school are as legible as possible. Visits to the school by college admissions officers are one measure of the counseling office's success. In the most recent admission cycle, representatives of thirty colleges spoke with SOHS students, reflecting a real interest in SOHS graduates. That this number has been increasing shows that the interest has been steadily increasing as well.

The critical accomplishment in building relationships with colleges for the SOHS is communicating the essential schoolness of the program, that its academic program is uniquely challenging and formative, and that students who flourish at the school are talented enough and sufficiently prepared to contribute in any college environment. The best evidence in this regard is the accomplishment of our students at those colleges. Students who are honored for achieving all As in their freshman years at Stanford, who immediate flourish in advanced courses, who go on to medical school or to law school at Stanford, Cornell, and Yale, or graduate school at the University of Chicago and MIT are all early signs to their respective colleges of the preparation these students have attained at the SOHS. As students begin to establish records in their careers, this narrative will be clearer still.

4 Preparation for College

A primary immediate goal of the SOHS academic program is to prepare students to succeed in challenging college curricula, where the standard for success is not just high performance, but also quick entry into upper-level material and development of mentorships and other opportunities. Advanced coursework certainly facilitates this transition. But the broader schoolwide goals articulated in the ESLRs also represent a distillation of the skills and abilities viewed as critical to college success. The success of these measures in the view of alumni helps to frame the discussion of elements of the program that are particularly effective.

Alumni report that by the end of their time at the SOHS, the school had helped them to broad achievement of the expected learning results for graduates. Indeed, for each of the six goals for graduates, over 90% of responding graduates reported that they had achieved the standard well or very well (See Figure 7.2).[7] In this context, there is only minimal variation to consider. 'Preparation for lifelong learning' and 'employing effective written and spoken language' exhibit particularly high reports of being achieved 'very well', as does 'ability to understand diverse materials', which all respondents also reported achieving either very well or well. Strong correlations also exist between years a student has spent at the school, on the one hand, and reports of achieving ESLRs concerning content knowledge, reasoning skills, preparation for citizenship, and preparation for lifelong learning, on the other hand. There is some indication, then, that the school achieves a significant impact on all its graduates, and quite quickly, though some goals are

[7] *SOHS Alumni Survey* (2014).

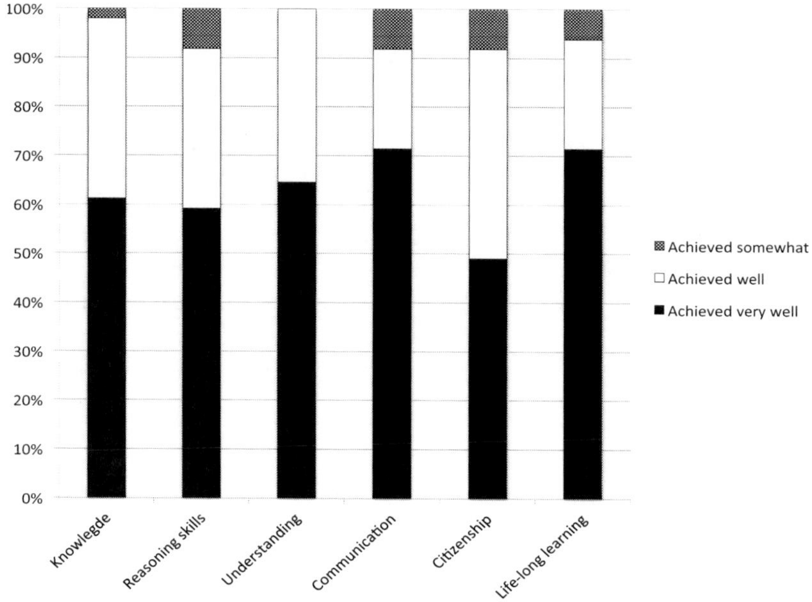

FIGURE 7.2 Alumni reports of achievement of Expected Schoolwide Learning Results (ESLRs)

felt to be achieved more widely and forcefully among graduates who spend more time at the school.

4.1 Academic Preparation

Perhaps more telling, though, are themes in the reports students make in unguided contexts. Throughout the alumni survey, graduates reflecting on their preparation emphasized their training in writing and critical thinking at the school. Several students drew similar connections between a strong foundation in writing from rigorous training in writing at the SOHS and an easy transition to college-level work.

> The essay assignments I receive in college are of similar caliber to those I received at OHS, so the transition from high school coursework to college coursework was not the struggle it was for so many of my peers. Thanks to my writing foundation, I get to focus on what I'm writing more than how I am writing it.

> I entered college with the ability to write, and to write well[...] While most of my peers struggled with writing, I was able to spend more time on crafting my own original ideas instead of spending time learning how to write.

> I was really surprised when we started having discussions and writing papers, because they felt so much like the things we'd been doing in the OHS. It was a lot less of a jolt than I'd thought it would be.

> AP courses can be taken at most any brick-and-mortar high school. However, the OHS's advanced English and Core courses can't. This is because these courses train OHSers to read, write and think in a way that not even most college students will ever learn. The knowledge and perspective that these courses give to OHSers is not only useful in the classes themselves, but in any college class and life in general. Thanks to the humanities courses at OHS I am now able to write persuasively in any context and cast a critical eye over any paper, article or argument instead of blindly accepting it as fact.

Students who attempted to characterize what it was about their training in writing that served them well in these ways emphasized quantity of writing, feedback and revision, as well as techniques of close reading and use of sources. Thus equipped, students felt well prepared to concentrate their efforts on the substance of their written work rather than the mechanics.

Students also single out critical thinking, and particularly the Philosophy Core courses that focus on critical thinking skills, as both significant among their high-school accomplishments and also broadly applicable to their college work.

> The philosophy coursework was particularly helpful in developing my ability to participate in an academic environment.

> I learned a lot of calculus and physics and biology, and that serves me well when I need to use those subjects, but the reasoning (somehow both critical and open-minded) I learned in DFRL [the Core course Democracy, Freedom, and the Rule of Law] still serves me much more often.

> I feel that it was the Core more than any other set of courses that taught me how to write argumentative papers with precision and depth.

As with writing, training in critical thinking aims to equip students with foundational skills that are central to college-level and professional inquiry. Strength in this area—a central part of the intellectual framework that the academic program prioritizes for its graduates—enables students to do more than master the concepts they encounter. As at the SOHS, such inquiry, scrutiny, and creativity, are, of course, the standards of distinctive work in college. Students well practiced in such thinking should feel its significance in a range of disciplines.

Reflections by alumni regarding what their school did well during their tenure are inevitably framed by an assessment of their own preparation for college relative to that of their peers. Responses to questions in this vein are informative and positive where the school expects to find its strengths, and generally positive but more nuanced in areas—like social preparation—in which the school is shaped more forcefully by the online medium. With respect to academic work, 94% of responding alumni reported having felt very well prepared (69%) or well prepared (25%) for academic work in college compared to their peers. With respondents from the most selective schools in the country, whose peers in college hail from some of the nation's best college-preparatory schools, these are telling results. More detail, however, is apparent in student responses regarding the nature of their preparation. In addition to the mentions of writing and critical thinking skills discussed above, several more general themes emerge in these comments, with significant focuses on the preparation derived from the difficulty of the SOHS curriculum and the imperative to develop strong organizational and study skills. One graduate captures several frequently expressed sentiments:

> Honestly, I think the most important aspect is just the academic rigor. Compared to my previous school experiences, OHS demanded a level of knowledge far deeper than was ever required of me before. In addition, high expectations and the structure of classes resulted in a second, more unique effect. Students were led to go beyond just simple knowledge and instead draw more complex connections and conclusions, resulting in true original thought[. . .] In addition to the more obvious academic benefits, I would say that OHS also stood out as a great creator of life skills, which may sound shocking to some when they think of any type of 'homeschooling' program. I, however, believe that the OHS helped educate me beyond just books, largely because of the time management skills and general responsibility that are required of a student attending OHS. With its flexible schedule and relatively high out-of-class to in-class work ratio, the OHS experience is reflective of a college atmosphere.

Many graduates echoed the theme of preparation for college through difficult work, some emphasizing the rigor or depth of expected inquiry, others the advanced topics and skills covered in SOHS courses:

> [H]aving advanced science and math courses under my belt, as well as the background in writing and critical thinking that the English and Core courses offered definitely gave me a leg up on my peers.

> The high standards and quality of peers and teachers served to give me an expectation of the sort of intellectual stimulation to seek at college.

> The emphasis on independent research and original thought is unlike anything I've experienced in any other school system. I think perhaps this was the strongest educational aspect of OHS. I am often struck by the fact that my coursemates at university have not has as much experience with research.

Advanced courses in physics, English, philosophy, history, and computer science received specific mention for the preparation they provided students for courses covering equivalent or significantly overlapping material in college. While some graduates expressed frustration at not being permitted to advance more quickly in college in light of their high-school coursework, no respondent reported struggling with the difficulty or rigor of college courses.

Nearly as prevalent as comments concerning the difficulty of SOHS coursework were references to the preparation for college provided through the skills and habits of organization and time management acquired at the school. For some graduates, it was simply the volume of work that inoculated them against surprises in college, while others appreciated the strategies they developed for managing such work, uniquely among their college peers:

> Since the OHS class [and] homework structure and workload is very similar to college, I already knew what to expect entering my freshman year.
>
> I felt that after attending the OHS full-time, I had very little difficulty transitioning to university classes and schedules. I was already accustomed to very challenging material and managing my time well.
>
> The OHS instilled in me a great deal of self-discipline, teaching me the importance of keeping a schedule and staying on top of my priorities without external pressures.
>
> The independent time management skills that the OHS fosters have saved me in college.

For many of these graduates, these skills were indeed 'acquired' or 'fostered' in their time at SOHS, often through the personal adjustments they made to the college-style schedule and strenuous workload. The manifest centrality of these skills to success at the SOHS, both among immediately successful students and students who encounter initial struggles, has led to an ever-expanding suite of formal programs at the school focused on enhancing and supplementing these skills.

4.2 Social Preparation

As one might expect for a school, online or otherwise, that students choose primarily for academic reasons, rather than for social ones, alumni assessments of the social preparation for college provided by the SOHS are more mixed than those of the academic program. Asked to assess their preparation for the social aspects of college (as pertains to interactions with peers), relative to their fellow students in college, nearly half of respondents reported feeling very well prepared (18%) or well prepared (31%), while 24% felt equally prepared, and another 24% felt less well prepared. That a quarter of students felt a deficiency in their preparation for peer-based social elements of college certainly indicates areas for possible improvement; it will be telling to observe the trajectory of views on this topic as students who have experienced the school in the expansion of its opportunities in community life move into the alumni ranks. Still, the reflections prove to be complex, highlighting variations in student preferences and personalities, expectations, and outside activities. Several comments are representative of general contentment with the social preparation afforded by the life of the school, couched in an alertness to their own particular interests and situations:

> On one hand, the OHS helped me realize the importance of actually making a clear effort to talk to people. On the other hand, I'm not the most social person in the world to begin with, so my idea of being socially prepared might be different than that of someone who desires a more elaborate social life.

> I'm not sure how it was for OHSers in general but I felt that I had a very active and full social life in high school and that that continued into college.

> I entered college with the ability to carry on a conversation with my peers, but not necessarily the ability to blend into a 'mosh pit'.

A number of students, meanwhile, voiced a pragmatic strategy and a set of expectations that are well founded in the experience of the school and compatible with the diverse activities of SOHS students—namely, supporting their SOHS social development with rich interactions outside of the school:

> Since I was doing things outside of the OHS I had no problem.

> I had the good fortune of having a decent circle of friends outside of the OHS, so I wasn't lacking in any social skills. I arrived at [college] somewhat overwhelmed by the sheer number of new people, but no more so than everyone else.

> I think most of my social preparation came from outside of OHS. Probably an important skill that OHS can confer is the ability to speak up—OHS can also foster good listening skills, if responding to classmates' opinions and comments is encouraged and valued.

Like this last student, graduates frequently identified unique contributions that their SOHS experiences made to their social preparation, though not relying exclusively on these experiences:

> I didn't feel at a social disadvantage at all in college. I think much of that was due to extracurriculars I had already been doing before the OHS (speech/debate, helping at youth camps, etc.), but I do think

> the OHS helped me in a few key ways. The main way was in making me comfortable discussing ideas honestly, critically, and respectfully with my peers. Much of my freshman year of college was spent discussing philosophy, religion, science, sociology—you name it. That can be tricky do in a constructive (rather than purely argumentative) way if you've never done it before.
>
> OHS class discussions made me have a great respect for peers' intellectual thoughts, and this has made me seek friends, activities, and conversations that are intellectually stimulating.
>
> OHS always sounds antisocial, but it (and especially summer session) prepares you for being independent and figuring out your life on your own. Many others I know struggled with that.

Clearly, and as one would expect, socialization is complicated at an online school. For some, it is natural and fulfilling; others supplement it deftly with outside activities and relationships; and some do find it to be an incomplete preparation for the social demands of college. In the right context, though, there is no doubt of its potential to provide students with a rich opportunity for personal and social development:

> The OHS truly changed my life. It allowed me to make a handful of lifelong, deep friends who I know will be at my side forever. It prepared me for a lifetime of learning, and it gave me the confidence to go out into the world, confident in who I am, with the knowledge that I have the power to be a positive force in the lives of those around me. For that I will be forever grateful.

While it is preparation for social interaction with peers in college and beyond that is the focus of any consideration of the social setting at SOHS, there are other meaningful social experiences at the school whose efficacy in preparation for college are of interest. In particular, the interactions SOHS students have with their teachers bear some unique resemblances to potential interactions with college professors that might serve students well. In their coursework at SOHS, students regularly encounter teachers with extensive academic backgrounds in a field. Through the seminar setting and the emphasis on communicating with one's teachers in and out of class, students are positioned to overcome some of the hurdles that often prevent college students from proactively engaging their professors.

> OHS emphasized getting to know your professors and meeting with them to ask questions or go over topics you need help with. That is something that a lot of university students do not do. I try to meet with each of my professors to ask them questions about what they look for in papers, etc., and I think it really helps me succeed in school.

In the course of these interactions, students develop skills and habits of fruitful engagement with their teachers, learning to ask the kinds of questions that lead to helpful guidance, to prepare for productive meetings, to discuss a topic of interest in depth in an individual setting, and to defend a position with confidence and care.

> Developing a relationship with your professor in college is not that much different from doing so with teachers in high school. In both cases, you have to ask good questions, meet them outside of class, and just show that you care about their subject and about learning. Any decent professor will appreciate and respond to a student who shows interest.
>
> The OHS educational model provides for rich and highly personalized intellectual collaboration with instructors, especially in the Core and other paper-writing classes, making it the perfect foundation for developing close relationships with professors later on.

And indeed, alumni have reported good success in developing mentors and securing participation in labs and research projects in college. More generally, 76% of responding alumni felt themselves very well (51%) or well (25%) prepared to develop good working relationships with their professors, compared to their peers.

In responses throughout the alumni survey, alumni indicated relatively high confidence in their preparation for social aspects of college. But students expressed still less hesitation regarding social skills and experiences more securely academic in their nature and function. Students feel well and uniquely equipped to engage one another and their teachers in college in virtue of their training at SOHS. When confidence is less pronounced, and this is less frequently than one might expect in this environment, it is with respect to the development of robust social lives in high school, and the skills to do so in college. One hopes that the intensive efforts at expanding social opportunities at the school over the past several years have begun to address these uncertainties in substantive fashion, but also that best practices among students for whom this environment works without issue can be more broadly employed.[8]

5 Beyond College

For a school that has graduated eight classes of seniors, including an inaugural group of only two students, a consideration of the career preparation and trends among alumni will not draw primarily on actual career outcomes and experiences. Alumni who have graduated from college are now occupied in graduate school, law school, medical school,

---

[8] See Chapter 6 for a detailed discussion of these efforts.

and in positions in consulting, software engineering, and marketing. So early on, however, these outcomes serve primarily to authenticate the career plans and developing specializations reported by alumni who are still in college.[9]

The unusual structure of the SOHS, with its diversity of enrollment types, unconventional medium, and focus on gifted education, suggests conflicting hypotheses regarding patterns of student interests. One might assume, for instance, that an online school would attract more technically-inclined students than not. Alternately, the curriculum of advanced courses might appeal to talented students wherever they find themselves unchallenged—whether in the humanities or in STEM. Further, the mix of student interests that are manifest in the school environment are colored by part-time and single-course students, who often exhibit intense interest and specialization in a given field. It might seem to some students and observers, then, that the school population has a tilt toward the sciences, or math, or English and the humanities, but for all of these reasons, appearances are not necessarily reliable. The eventual specialization of graduates, then, is data without clear predictors, and might conceivably speak both to the general demographics of SOHS students and to relative strengths within the academic program.

In the event, the reports from alumni of projected majors are sufficiently balanced that they do not ground claims about an unusual bias in the school for one field (See Table 7.3). Indeed, the balance itself is perhaps what is most evident: 28% of reported majors fall under the rubric of the sciences, 23% are fields in the social sciences, 27% are humanities, and 22% are engineering specializations. Within these somewhat arbitrary delineations, top majors include computer science, English, arts, economics, and engineering. Some perspective on these figures can be had in comparison to top majors at schools like Stanford University, where STEM fields clearly hold sway: undergraduate enrollment in majors at Stanford in Fall of 2013 was highest in Computer Science; Human Biology; Engineering; Science, Technology, and Society; and Biology.[10] At Yale, by contrast, top majors include Economics, Political Science, History, and Psychology, with 30% of juniors and seniors majoring in the arts and humanities, 37% in social sciences, 25% in biological and physical sciences, and 7% in other areas.[11] What

[9] Of survey respondents, 97% have matriculated into four-year college programs, and those who have not plan to do so as well. No student has graduated from the school expressing a plan not to attend college.

[10] Stanford Facts 2014, 'Other Undergraduate Education Facts', http://facts.stanford.edu/academics/undergraduate-facts, updated April 23, 2014.

[11] '2013-14 Yale Factsheet', http://oir.yale.edu/yale-factsheet.

is apparent in these limited figures is that while SOHS produces quite a number of students who go on to major in STEM fields, it also attracts and nourishes students inclined to English and the humanities.

TABLE 7.3 Planned majors of alumni[12]

Majors	Students
Computer Science, English	7 each
Arts, Economics, Electrical Engineering, Mathematics, Psychology	4 each
Biology, Cognitive Science/Neuroscience, Engineering (Other), Pre-Med/Medical, Undecided	3 each
Business/Finance, Chemical Engineering, Classics, Creative Writing, Ecology/Environmental Science, International Relations/Political Science	2 each
Anthropology; French; History; Philosophy; Physics; Science, Technology, and Society	1 each

Given the commitment to learning embodied in graduates' choices to study and succeed at SOHS, it is not surprising that many envision careers involving advanced degrees beyond the undergraduate level. Over 50% mention graduate or professional school among their career plans, while numerous others are pursuing careers that may well lead them back to school at some point. While in many ways, plans of this sort simply reflect modern expectations and requirements for the sorts of demanding careers to which talented students aspire. But it is also to be hoped that the school and its instructors have played a role in nurturing the love of a discipline that graduate school requires, and also that long acquaintance with teachers who have also studied at this level has both helped to open these possibilities to students and equipped them better to complete their graduate work.

The careers for which SOHS students are preparing, meanwhile, are not too far removed from students' academic plans in college, though they suggest somewhat the underlying interests and rationale behind

[12]One might have feared that the Core would drive students into further study of philosophy in college. Rather it seems largely to have inoculated them against the lure, giving them the knowledge that they can pursue whatever intellectual interest they have in an authentic and meaningful way, confident that the philosophical impulse can travel with them across the disciplines.

those plans. Behind varied involvement in business, careers in medicine (medical technology as well as medical care), technology, law, and science slightly outstrip career plans in the arts, engineering, academia, and publishing. Perhaps most striking among alumni's characterizations of their career plans is the prevalence (20%) of interest in entrepreneurship, and not exclusively in software. The future of this trend, and of these students themselves, bears observation in a school which is itself a venture. Careers involving significant research elements, including academic work and both basic science and medical research, are also relatively common (19%) among alumni who reported some career plans.

It will take some time before clear messages emerge regarding preparation for careers, informed by experience in those careers. Many of the school's unique features—its medium and format, the global diversity and caliber of its students, the rigorous and advanced curriculum, the background of its teachers, and the student and teacher community—bear plausible import not only for college, but for success in careers. Questions of whether alumni reliably find, as does one working alumna, that the global community of the SOHS engenders valuable fluency in the global environment of business, or whether focused training in critical thinking translates profitably into a range of career paths, will await future assessments.

6 Further Questions

Even from the vantage point of life in college, and despite all the challenges and hard choices posed by the SOHS, from the hard work and technical challenges to the flux of a new and experimental school and distance from their school friends and teachers, 96% of alumni responding to our survey reported that the school was a very good (76%) or good (20%) choice for them. Given all of these hurdles, this is indeed a positive affirmation of the school's ability—and the ability of an online school—to meet its educational mission. But the alumni also spell out the meaning of their endorsement in addressing the question of whether they would recommend the SOHS to a prospective student. Of responding alumni, 90% said they would definitely (47%) or probably (43%) recommend the school, while 8% were unsure. Given the chance to elaborate, many qualified their responses in a way that made sense of the greater uncertainty about recommending the school. Indeed, just as the school advertises that it is not the right fit for every student, alumni expressed the same caveat, with a full nineteen of twenty-seven written comments explaining that the school is not the right fit for everyone, though most avow that it was the right fit for them. The decisive factors in determining the goodness of fit, according to these alumni, are the extent of the student's personal motivation and the student's particular social situation and needs.

> It's difficult, and if you aren't willing to put forth the effort then you won't do well. But the classes are informative and if you find the right people, you will become the best of friends.

> OHS isn't for everyone. The coursework is challenging, very similar to college—academically, the prospective student would need to be of a certain caliber. Also, the difference in the OHS's social dynamic compared to brick-and-mortar schools could be challenging for certain students to adapt to. That being said, I enjoyed my experience at OHS and would recommend it to a prospective student as long as they are the right fit.

There is surely important and informative truth in these reflections: the school is difficult, it demands independent motivation and discipline, and it requires thoughtful calibration of social experiences. But the detail of the comments also helps to frame several questions going forward, many of which the school has been probing for a number of years.

While most of the graduates mention the rigor of the workload with a certain pride, and some of them warn against or lament any real diminishing of that aspect of the difficulty of the school, one could ask whether the school has in some ways overachieved its goal of preparing students for college. When students at Ivy League schools indicate that college is no more difficult or strenuous than high school, it is reasonable to ask whether this is as it should be, or if an outstanding preparation for college might be accomplished with less of a demand on students. As the comments suggest, students are cognizant of some sacrifice they are making with respect to other endeavors, made in the interest of a strenuous academic program. Would more academic diversity—the ability to take more courses, for instance—or more opportunity to pursue social or athletic practices, be attainable in an academic program that did not make college sometimes feel like a dropoff in intensity? The school has, as described in Chapter 3, pursued a reflection on workload within the parameters of the existing academic goals of its courses and overall curriculum: initiatives to make the workload somewhat more manageable are mainly focused on efficiency and effectiveness of assignments and assessments in achieving the established goals. But there is a different conversation that could be had centering on the necessity of all of those existing goals to the overarching aims of the program.

Just as being well prepared for the rigor and intensity of college work may not automatically justify all of the measures leading to that preparation, there may also be some space between a school being 'the right choice' or being 'ideally suited for the needs of gifted students' and the practical preparation it offers for all aspects of all college academic environments. Such a gap may be visible in the comments of a very small but thoughtful minority of respondents to the survey who, in particular, highlighted the transition from the small school environment of the SOHS into larger university contexts. One former student who found the SOHS preparation for college to be 'poor' in some regard pointed to an adjustment in college to a more methodical content-absorption focus in some courses in the sciences, at least early in college. The college emphasis on memorization, rather than engagement with material in homework and class discussions, the student attests, required cultivating different skills than those emphasized at SOHS. The student notes the irony of the concern, and also acknowledges the subsequent development at the school, suggesting that the SOHS 'was more optimized for the life of the mind' than for some of the more practical aspects of college success. But the challenge the student poses is one worth examining for any small, independent school: how best can a school dedicated to the intellectual and academic ideals of a personalized school environment balance the benefits of that environment with preparation for the inevitable realities of more impersonal, routinized settings? In a similar vein, two students found the benefit of their experience engaging their teachers at SOHS to translate somewhat unevenly into college courses:

> For me, it was easier to develop good relationships with professors at the OHS than in undergrad. At the OHS, the class sizes are small, and the professors go above and beyond to make themselves available. In undergrad, though, I had many large classes (>100 students) where meaningful interaction with the professor was much more difficult. I think the OHS did a good job of teaching us how to interact with professors, but those skills don't necessarily translate easily to large classrooms.

> I'm good when it comes to smaller classes, but the professors of 100+ person lectures are still a bit intimidating to approach.

One of the authors is reminded of a former online student (from before the creation of the SOHS), who quipped that his first real distance learning was not the online course he had taken at Stanford, but was a freshman lecture course in a large auditorium he took after matriculating at Harvard. To some extent, these limitations of the preparation for college that a school like the SOHS provides are structural results of its strengths. But they do draw useful attention to the role of preparation for some of the less-than-ideal features of university study, in addition to preparation for its opportunities.

In addition to the adjustments the school can and continues to make to address phenomena highlighted in surveys, other changes are built into trends tied to the growth of the school. While the community life of the SOHS has expanded dramatically over the past several years—for some of the alumni, too recently to have made much of an impact on their experience—it is a peculiarity of the school to this point that ninth grade is not the most common point of entry for graduating students. And even entering ninth-graders did not, as is customary in brick-and-mortar environments, come from a limited set of feeder schools; it is the norm for students to come to the school knowing no other students. At boarding schools and colleges, the antidote for social development in such a context is the intensity of the experience of living together. At SOHS, such experiences are inevitably limited; but friendships and acquaintances of far longer term are increasingly afforded by developments in enrollment. In 2013-14, one quarter of the total school enrollment is in the middle school: these students will have been with one another in class for five or six years by the time of graduation. Similarly, the largest class in the school in 2012-13 was the ninth grade class. As classes form early in the middle school and high school, with more students and for longer careers at the school, students will find at the school a strong basis for collegiality, and, to credit the alumni, for friendship.

Growth in the middle school and at the early high-school level addresses the caveats noted by alumni in two additional ways. In addition to giving students more time together over which to build stronger and more rewarding relationships, a longer tenure at the school creates a deeper investment among students in developing those relationships, as well as the social situations outside of school that supplement life in the school community. The intensity of efforts by middle-school students and families in this regard are indicative of this investment. And when more students at the school are enrolled for extended periods, all students feel the implications of their efforts toward interaction.

A second genre of benefit from a larger middle-school population accrues directly to the students themselves, but also speaks to the qualifications expressed by alumni. Many students, in all manner of testimony, reference the significant adjustment in difficulty and intensity of work experienced at the start of their SOHS careers. Indeed, the middle-school program was initiated partly to cushion this transition and to move it to a period in students' careers during which their academic prospects were less at stake. Part of that cushion consists in developing, more gradually and with greater support, the skills of time management, planning, and self-directed learning cited by alumni as essential assets for success at the school. However precise the content-based placement processes at the school are or become, new students at the advanced levels will necessarily be compelled to make rapid adjustments to expectations at the school. At the middle school and in early parts of the high-school program, though, there is more room for error and adjustment; entry into the school at this juncture might be feasible for a broader selection of students possessing the requisite academic qualifications.

In many ways, however, the mere prospect of making further adjustments along these lines is a sign of significant success in achieving the school's founding mission. By many diverse measures, and most vividly in the mature, talented, and sophisticated thinkers who graduate from the school, SOHS has succeeded in envisioning and implementing a rigorous, advanced, and unique academic program for gifted students. This program equips them for entry, rapid advancement, and success in college, and also nourishes the love of learning that is the typical motive to seek out the school. That the intellectual life of the community has proved an asset to students, and that broader social life is robust and rewarding enough to be compared to that of a brick-and-mortar setting, ranks among the most significant results of the school to this point. Building on that achievement, both for its own value and as part of broadening the range of students for whom the school is the right fit, is a newly incorporated element of the school's mission.

8

Looking Forward in All Directions

1 Overview

Throughout the book we have seen the important role played by the different components of the school. We have seen how the 'secret sauce' does not consist in technology but in bringing students and instructors together in an environment designed to let learning happen naturally. In doing so we have returned time and again to the image of Socrates with his students in the Agora and the fact that what students crave more than anything else is the opportunity to be engaged in a community of fellow learners that challenges them to develop their potential. We have seen that crucial to developing educated students is engendering the right ways of thinking and habits of mind and we have seen the role that the curriculum and pedagogy play in making this happen. We have seen the impact of technology throughout, and throughout technology has been in a supporting role, rather than on center stage

As we come to this final chapter, we return to looking at the school and discuss how it can be that an online school is a real school. Next we step back and look not just at the actors in our drama but at the stage itself. We turn from Socrates and his students to the Agora. We look at how the campus of the school plays an essential role in the life of the school not just as a container, but as an enabler of accidental learning and the sense of possibility. We also explore new technological tools, and while we still eschew allowing these tools to drive the pedagogy, we explore how they might be harnessed to deepen the fundamental experience of schoolness. Finally we look at the potential that this model of highly personalized online learning has for other populations and the implications it has to the wider community of schools and to the future of education in itself.

2 Real School, Virtual Space

We have stressed throughout the book that the fact that the SOHS is online is not an essential feature of the school. By this claim, we do not mean to deny that our students spend a great deal of time in front of a computer, because they do. Rather, we have in mind facts of the following sort: if one were to turn off the servers at Stanford, the SOHS would still persist because the school is not coextensive with its online presence. In the same way, a brick-and-mortar school would still exist even if its building burnt down. Schools are more than their infrastructure. In fact, sometimes the servers do get turned off and the school does not come to a grinding halt. Students and teachers still find ways to connect, if in suboptimal settings, to continue their work until the situation is resolved. This suggests that there is more going on than just the class; otherwise when the class went off, the school would be off too, by definition. One wonders how many brick-and-mortar schools can say the same on days when a snowstorm cancels class.

In stressing that online is not an essential feature, we mean to draw attention to the school's unrelenting focus on another matter entirely: providing an environment in which talented and motivated students can be pushed, can excel, and can flourish in unparalleled ways. Part of the story of the founding and early development of the SOHS has been an account of the institutional discovery that the environment in which this kind of education is possible is a school environment. We think this message is important at so dynamic a moment for online education: that at its best, online learning happens in a school. As the field explores the myriad possibilities and formats of online learning, then, it should be mindful of what is gained and lost when programs approach or stray from a true school model.

If it has not been misguided bravado, the claim that SOHS is a 'real' school is of further significance for how the experiences of our school should be read. The other half of the story, of course, is about what school for talented students can be at its best, whether it is online or not. If our school is not primarily about technology and teaching online, its findings extend beyond online endeavors. Entirely outside of its online capacity, the SOHS illustrates an implementation of flipped classrooms in a high-level academic environment; it affirms the place of college-style seminars and schedules in facilitating dynamic and inspiring collaborative learning among talented students; it models a challenging curriculum centered on critical thinking and training in professional academic methods and norms; it furnishes strategies for acceleration and differentiation among talented students; and it speaks to the contributions that teachers with advanced academic backgrounds and pedagogical orientations can make to the education of such students. That these things happen in a school that is online does not mean, automatically, that they have no bearing on brick-and-mortar counterparts.

That the SOHS is rightly considered a school, above all else, means finally that online tools and formats are not irretrievably inimical to a school environment. Schools that prize the collaboration, interaction, and rigor of an independent school environment, but that seek to capitalize on the possibilities of online elements, have some reason to believe that they do not (necessarily) imperil their schoolness for onlineness. To these schools, the SOHS models not just logistical flexibility, but the pedagogical benefits that can come from real geographic diversity; it illustrates the advantages of flexible scheduling and flipped instruction; and it demonstrates that demand for uniquely advanced courses can be assembled across a broader pool of students and schools. To schools interested in these prospects, the experiences of our school point to the keys of accomplishing this all in a school context. SOHS has found its way to an understanding of the qualities and skills essential to students and teachers who succeed in online work in a school setting; we have identified the unique strains that the environment places on students and teachers, as well as ways to protect against, detect, and mitigate them; and we have explored ways to stitch together diverse students and school norms to create effective classrooms and communities. From this example, brick-and-mortar schools might calibrate their own strategies for integrating online tools into their own school environments.

All of this, however, assumes that there is no fundamental oversight implicit in understanding an online program to be a real school. We believe that we have made the case, in the particulars, that the SOHS is indeed a real school. But it is also important to know why this is true. Innovations that stretch a concept can often compel a better understanding of the essential qualities of the members of that class. In a tradition exemplified by Alan Turing, for example, the mere prospect of a 'thinking' machine has prompted a more careful, and fruitful, assessment of what it is to think. If the SOHS is a real school, what does it show us about what is and is not a school such that the SOHS clearly is one?

Educators readily affirm that a school is far more than a building. Facilities matter of course—they can make the project of a school easier, more supportive, and more dynamic, or they can be an obstacle that makes everything harder and slower. But these are factors that operate *on* a school, rather than *within* it; a school must happen some place, but the essential qualities of the place are determined by what needs to happen there, rather than by the features of the buildings that have so far been built to house this function. But if bricks and mortar do not make a school, what is the stuff or matter of a school? When we cannot know a school by its building, how do we know a real school when we see one? The picture we have developed in the course of this book understands a school as stretching far beyond the courses it offers.

The Stanford Online High School is a real school in that it engenders and draws upon an active community as part of its educational mission. The interactions and relationships of this community serve a range of critical functions. In the classroom, and to some extent, outside as well, students and teachers provide one another the excitement of engagement and collaboration, but also the resistance that even the smart kid with lots of books knows is necessary to keep her from a 'frictionless spinning in the void'[1] of private learning. Importantly, though, the community means that there is a lot of stuff that matters going on outside the classroom as well: students organize and undertake their own projects, they develop friendships and arbitrate conflicts, adults (teachers and parents) exchange expertise and experiences, and there is a 'space' where these exchanges can occur and propagate without excessive design.

Understood in its fullest sense, the community, in conjunction with the curriculum, entails much of the remainder of what makes the SOHS more than an imitation of a school. It is the community, for example, that embodies the source at SOHS of the accountability of a real school. To be sure, SOHS attends to the familiar suite of external accreditation and certification processes that guarantee a level of formal accountability. And the school surely courts and engages in a collaborative relationship with parents. But the core of the school's accountability for its students is the responsibility of each adult at the school, and particularly in the classroom, to assess and develop the talents of each student. Far from being an online course-distributer that merely certifies the work of those students who do not fall by the wayside, the SOHS focuses on connecting individual students not only with courses, but also with other students, teachers, advisors, counselors, mentors, and other staff who know them, understand their goals, talents, and weaknesses, and who work over time to help them flourish.

The SOHS community is also a locus of the school's essential task of teaching more than content. The curriculum, for its part, stresses the development of intellectual skills and habits of mind in addition to

[1]This image comes from J. McDowell, *Mind and World* (Cambridge, MA: Harvard University Press, 1994). The image appears there in a quite different context; it is used to represent a process of thinking that is unconstrained by sensory experience of the objective world.

mastery of content. But even these academic skills are perhaps most effectively honed in discussions, in seminar and out of class, with teachers and peers who are immersed in the same norms. As members of a community whose health and projects are significant to each member, however, students are in a position to develop ethically. Whether appreciating how the dynamics of class discussions affect their peers, or in working through the schoolwide significance of a planned podcast, they experience the implications and demands of their dealings with others.

In establishing a real school, online or anywhere, the members of the community matter, too. Students, of course, can sign up to take courses *à la carte*, just as easily as they can sign up to be part of a school; having students does not make an educational program a school. But their instructors can make the difference between a school and something less. SOHS instructors are teachers—that is their profession and their calling. They are happiest in the classroom with students, and even grading their work; dealing with sometimes balky technology is the price they accept to work with SOHS students in the context of the school's academic program. Indeed, sometimes we bungle the non-teaching stuff, because we are not technologists who are trying to teach, or reform-minded administrators trying to cook up a data-driven, scalable exercise in efficiency. Rather, teachers are focused on teaching students in a class setting, engaging in inquiry with the group, and developing the talents of each individual student.

It is ironic that as we measure our success at being a school, independent from our success as a school, one of the best indicators is provided by the nature of the problems we experience—not by our avoidance of problems, for problems are unavoidable, but rather from the fact that we increasingly have the same sorts of problems that traditional brick-and-mortar independent schools have. As the school has evolved, the questions have become less and less about what technology we use and how to recover from flaws in software and more and more things like why someone's son or daughter should not have to attend homeroom or PE, or how they should be allowed to skip prerequisites, or be exempted from attendance requirements.

It is important in determining whether something is viable to look at the problems it solves and does not solve in the broader context of which freedoms it enables and which it takes away. Many times the cure is worse than the disease, and the efforts to fence out all problems can result in making the suboptimal the norm. It is in this context that the SOHS is best viewed: it is a school that solves more problems than it creates, and that enables more freedom than it restricts.

Most importantly, it embraces ambiguity and is comfortable leaving in place unsolved exactly those problems that should be unsolvable in a community of highly engaged and highly determined students and families.

3 Accidental Learning and Intentional Spaces

Trying to fence off problems, trying to enforce rigid conceptions of how students learn, trying to keep people focused and on task via narrow structures, are all manners of over-engineered views of learning that have the potential to preclude the type of accidental learning that has long been an essential component of growth and discovery. This is perhaps the greatest risk faced by an online school or by online-learning efforts in general.

Discussions of the potential of online learning often point to the image of students wanting to learn a certain subject and then being able to use their computer to find someone who can teach it to them, or to find resources that will let them learn it on their own, perhaps connecting with instructors only when necessary, and ultimately earning a certificate or badge that proves that they have acquired the knowledge in question.

Contrast this with the following experience that one of the authors had. An enthusiastic seventeen-year-old shows up at the University of Chicago for an eight-week summer mathematics camp. The camp is loosely structured so that students have courses in the morning and more or less have free run of the University in the afternoons. The student studies number theory and complex analysis. Outside of class the student plays bridge and soccer, and spends countless hours discussing philosophy. The students interested in philosophy discover a wealth of used bookstores and read voraciously. By the end of the summer the student returns home with a deep and abiding interest in things philosophical as well as mathematical and a determination to learn more about both.

The difference between taking courses and being at a school is well illustrated by this example. In the context of a school, the learning is not just limited to the courses in which one is enrolled, but carries over to the discovery that occurs in virtue of being in a community where learning is occurring and where one can stumble into what is going on. One sees this play out in preschools and in universities: students are provided with a panoply of options and allowed to discover their interests, or students are required to take distribution requirements in part to ensure that they are exposed to things beyond what they think they are interested in. Universities and schools embrace diversity for exactly this reason, both in their selection of students, but also in their academic offerings, for they know that students will develop a better understanding of themselves and what is possible if they are exposed to a wide variety of people and courses.

One of the great joys of being on a campus like that of Stanford is the ability to stumble into wonders that pique one's interests. What is being lost in online-learning efforts that embrace a course- and content-centric view of learning is just this sort of wandering into things unexpectedly, whether it is by talking to students in one's space who are studying different things or whether it is in the chance wandering into the wrong class by mistake or the standing on the eves listening to what another class is discussing. The rigid categorization of what is to be learned into learning objects of particular types and into content delivered just as needed and only when relevant leaves students inherently impoverished.

These are risks that we have tried to mitigate in a variety of ad hoc ways at the SOHS, using Skype groups, research colloquia, homeroom, assemblies, and so forth. (We once tried a lunchroom, but no one came, and despite this fact the students said the food was terrible.) These are all attempts to establish some of the accidental, in-progress nature of productive existence in space. It is easy to get lost in the particulars of how things work at the SOHS and to forget that as with any school, in addition to the actors in this drama—in this case the instructors, the students and their families, the curriculum they are studying, and the community that has emerged—there is also the stage on which the drama occurs, which in this case is the campus. The campus plays a definite, and often defining role in determining just what the experience of being in the school is. This is not to say that relationships between people are not front-and-center, but rather to say that the space in which these relationships occur inevitably informs the relationships, imbuing them with a particular sense of possibility.

Much of the discussion in this book has been about the interactions that occur within the virtual space or outside the virtual space and less about the space itself. What about the space and the impact it has on learning? We have seen throughout how the students see the space they occupy as being a real space. In listening to students at the SOHS talk about being in class, about what happened in class the other day, or about seeing each other in class or after class, the discussion is always of 'being in class' and never of 'watching class', unless they are viewing a recording for a lecture or seminar that they missed. When the events are happening live, they are happening in a space, and not on a screen. The language that they choose to use reveals that to them, what is happening is real and that they are in a real classroom, even if it is not one that they are physically residing in.

That students are able to bridge from the experience of using a computer to participate in a virtual classroom, to being with one another in a virtual space, is an important component of the schoolness of the SOHS. A campus provides students a rich space in which education can occur. What the Agora provided to Socrates and his students was a similarly rich space. Both of these are very different than the image of a student working home alone with his electronic tutor. The richness of the education the students receive comes from the interaction they enjoy with one another and from the opportunities afforded by the space in which the interactions occur.

As we noted in our discussion of the role of community in Chapter 6, anyone who has ever attended an orientation at a university like Stanford will have inevitably heard someone say something along the lines of 'Ninety percent of what you learn at this university you will learn outside the classroom. You will learn from each other in the dorms and walking the halls.' The message is clear: learning neither stops nor starts when one enters the classroom, nor does it come just from the prescribed materials of the class or the prescribed expert. And yet, if one looks at the structure of most online courses, even those that have virtual classroom components, one will see that very little thought is being given to the space outside the classroom. And this is something that both these reflections on traditional environments and our own experiences at SOHS have shown to be unfortunate.

If one observes students in a school, one will see that the space that the students are in has a subtle but definite influence on how the students act. The way students act during class differs from how they act in the classroom before or after class, and this differs from how they act in common spaces like the lunch room or the courtyard, which differs from how they act on the periphery of school waiting for their parents or for the bus, which differs from how they act in the café across the street or in a café downtown. In each of these spaces students will manifest themselves and their personalities differently, being more or less guarded in what they say, more or less open about who they are, and more or less receptive to new ideas and friendships. Each of these spaces plays an important role in students' educational experience in the traditional brick-and-mortar environment, and unless analogous spaces are provided in an online school, students will miss their absence. If they are missing, the school will feel less of a school, even if the students cannot identify the reasons why this is so.

A few years ago, during a conversation with a publisher who was trying to convince us that their combination of learning management system (LMS) and student information system (SIS) provided a turnkey solution for online schools, one of us said frustrated, 'You're missing the point, technology has no place in an online school.' Prima facie absurd, and yet somehow resonant. In the same vein we added 'We don't need a learning management system, our instructors all have advanced degrees. They can manage their own learning. What we need is a virtual campus.' This really is what is most needed. It is not sufficient to have an LMS and an SIS and a virtual classroom; this will leave one with merely a *virtual* school.

What is most often missing in an online school is the sense of a place where things occur and which exists outside of any particular thing occurring. What students need is a place to go to attend their seminars, to find their friends, and to work on projects and the like. Rather than thinking of their computers as providing the door into the each of the rooms, the ideal would be for them to have access to a space which is the campus and from which they can wander naturally to the room in which their classes meet. Such a virtual campus would ideally provide the analogs to overhearing other classes, stumbling into people, getting to know those who have their lockers next to one's own, and all of the other accidental encounters that individually seem insignificant but that together constitute the fabric of being in school. This is an essential insight and this is something that is sorely missing in the commercially available systems today.

When space does not work right, when we trip on a curb, we feel the stress. We need to have all of the various spaces and the types of personality that belong to them. We also need to have the ability to move through space and discover things around us that we are not necessarily part of in the narrow sense. The design of learning management systems and virtual classrooms has largely been driven by an idealization of what learning should be, as opposed to careful observation of what it actually is. These systems try to bring artificial clarity to what should be a fuzzy image. By overthinking structures and making determinations about what is needed, the designers of educational software environments build their assumptions about what is or is not essential into the systems. This inevitably leads to things being missed or overlooked. Sometimes the motivation for this is a decision about what is important. Sometimes it is a desire to fence off certain types of behavior as undesirable. But as we discussed throughout this book, many times facets that seem extraneous turn out to be missed when absent, and forcing students or instructors to do things in certain ways will far more often than not result in worse outcomes.

4 The Technologies We Crave

Besides a good virtual campus, and the expected incremental enhancements to the tools we have already discussed, there are a number of technologies on the horizon that properly adapted will have substantive beneficial impact in the coming years. While a full discussion of this would merit a book of its own, we call attention to a few that could improve our students' experience of the school and our ability to respond to our students while they are in school.

4.1 Immersive Spaces

As we prepare this book for publication, Facebook has just purchased the virtual reality headset manufacturer Oculus Rift for two billion dollars, citing among other things its potential as a tool for education. This news story reminded us of an article we had envisioned writing in the style of a *Time Magazine* cover story back in the late 1990s. The photograph accompanying the article was to have been of an old-style schoolhouse, with wooden desks sitting two children per desk, the teacher standing at the front of the classroom in front of a chalkboard, while the students would all be looking forward wearing virtual reality helmets. On the chalkboard would be written 'The future of education?'

Throughout the book we have stressed that the SOHS is about schoolness first and foremost and that we are not about building an island somewhere and having our students come to class as avatars. But this said, we are interested in the spaces that our students occupy and the richness of the interaction that a well-crafted space affords. Moreover, the potential synergies between video games and education are worth noting, not for the issues of gamification so often discussed, but because of the way video games make it easy for people to engage and play each other rather than to just play by themselves. This is the same experience that makes education in the SOHS so much more compelling for our students than the typical asynchronous course.

The easier the technology makes it for people to have rich interaction with each other in video games when coming in from remote locations, the more potential there will be for achieving rich interaction in a multitude of ways among students coming together online from remote locations. The idea that students engaged in learning might be wearing virtual reality helmets and meeting together in a virtual space makes it even easier to visualize our students coming together with the instructor, all outfitted in modified togas, in a recreation of the actual Agora. Perhaps the instructor can lecture on geometry using a stick and the dirt *à la* Socrates and the slave boy.

4.2 Awareness of Students in Offline Spaces

One of the facts of the Stanford Online High School is that our students and instructors are able to attend class from anywhere, and often do. We have students who join in from boats on the open sea and from land yachts on the open highways. If someone's connection is poor or the space she is working in is ill suited for discussion, or potentially distracting to other students, the instructor will tell the student to come back later when better prepared to attend class. Because the online classroom is a synthetic space, it pulls in aspects of the spaces in which students are situated, and students making poor choices regarding the suitability of the location from which they choose to join class will adversely impact not just themselves but others in the classroom.

The same influence of space on the ability of students to concentrate certainly plays out when they are working on their assignments, reading their books, or writing their papers. Traditionally where students are working when they are not at school was not information one had available unless students were at a boarding school. We often tell families that we are more of an online boarding school than we are an online day school, because our students are living in the context in which they are going to school and they do not go home from school at the end of the day. In the same way that boarding schools have structures in place to make sure that students are getting their work done in an appropriate manner, our school might benefit from technologies that make it easy to keep track of where students are working as well as how effectively students are working when they are working. This is not something for which we have unique needs; in fact, online schools are often better positioned to keep tabs on what their students are doing, if only by making design decisions that force their students to do everything within a narrowly constructed online system. The challenge is finding a way that lets students work in a natural-seeming manner, using the tools and techniques that they naturally gravitate toward, but to still be able to gain insight into not just what they are producing, but how they are producing it, since as we discussed above, good education pays attention to process.

With the rise of e-readers, geolocation, eye tracking, smart paper, and other technologies, the potential to understand how students are working when they are working individually, as well as when they are in their lectures or seminars, is emerging. While we have yet to systematically implement any of these technologies, we have begun to think about how they might be promisingly deployed.

E-readers, especially if coupled with eye-tracking capability, can let us know not only if the students did the reading, but what passages they lingered on. Knowing which students are doing the reading and when, also creates opportunities for impromptu study groups and for students to interact with each other. Geolocation can take this a step further, letting students keep tabs on their friends, not to mention letting our instructors identify that students are doing their work in cafés even if online papers do not have tell-tale coffee stains. Smart paper could greatly facilitate the production and distribution of mathematical proofs, engineering diagrams, and all manner of work that requires more than what is easily produced at the keyboard. This opens up new avenues for student collaboration around the whiteboard, and also can provide insight into which team members are doing the work on group projects.[2]

Each of these aspects of paying attention to our students provides an opportunity to deepen the feeling of connection between the students and the school, which in turn will drive engagement and schoolness.

4.3 Awareness of Students in Online Spaces

From the inception of the SOHS we have viewed having rich video seminars as essential for creating the proper sense among the students that they are in fact students in a school surrounded by peers who constitute a community. As we move forward with the technology, one of the things we have most frequently wanted has been a virtual seminar environment that makes it possible and easy to see all of the participants in the seminar in a natural way.

The ideal system would have continuous video feeds of the students while they are in class, but would give the teacher the flexibility to configure how these feeds are experienced. A defect of a system modeled on a 'camera follow the mic' approach is that when the instructor is talking the only person the instructor sees is himself. This provides little information to the instructor; the important data for the teacher is in the faces of the students. Being able to have all students visible at all times would sometimes be useful and other times could be distracting, especially if one is trying to attend to everyone. More useful in some contexts might be to have the camera auto-switch around the attendees so that the teacher could serially gaze across the faces of her students while teaching. What is essential is having the flexibility to conform the system to the pedagogical goals of the activity, and not to have to bend pedagogy to fit the limits of the technology.

[2]Clearly, there is a debate to be had here concerning appropriate mixtures of monitoring technology, privacy, and autonomy. Our students and our school are well positioned to explore these issues.

Tracking the reactions of one's students becomes even more difficult when they are in breakout rooms and the instructor is able only to be in one place at one time. Interestingly enough, such may be possible to do in an automated way. Companies are beginning to explore the use of video recognition of facial microexpressions to provide real-time analysis of the emotional states of users of software. This same approach could be applied to all of the student video feeds, whether or not the instructor is able to see the video feeds, to gather information on how students are responding to a presentation or discussion. Being able to tell if students are bored, frustrated, anxious, eager, and the like, is important, and good instructors naturally factor this in when teaching. The absence of this sort of information in the virtual seminar environment is one of the great challenges in teaching online, and finding ways to incorporate it in a manner that does not require students to self report or require instructors to pay undue attention has great promise. Moreover, such a system promises an ability to gauge reaction among students to material, to tell who is attending and who is not, and to reveal interpersonal dynamics and other aspects that are prevalent in the classroom, but not readily identified online. Each step that we can take that restores aspects of being in situ to being online will serve only to deepen the schoolness of the school.

4.4 The Proper Use of Technology

More immersive spaces, more attention to our students and their experience of the course, the opportunity to drive engagement and responsiveness, and other tools that would deepen the relationships formed and advance the educational project: these are the technologies that we crave at the SOHS. This is not to say that there would be no place for interactive textbooks and other types of asynchronous materials in our courses, anymore that we would say that there is no room for traditional textbooks in our courses. All we are saying is that such things are no more relevant to the SOHS than they are to any other independent school. We are much more interested in the technologies that bring our students and instructors together, and that blur the distinctions between being online and in situ. We are much less interested in the technologies that are inherently designed to drive students apart.

5 Applicability and Implications of the SOHS Model

In writing this book, we have kept our focus on our school and as such on our population of students. By all measures they are a special population, but that said, they are not needles in haystacks. On measures of ability they are clustered in the top five percent or so of the population, but are not uniformly more rarefied than that. And while they may have more focus and determination than the average student, they are not outliers in this dimension either. Similarly, the superior study skills and focus that our graduates exhibit are often lacking in our entering students. What our students have had in common is a combination of need and desire that has made the SOHS the right school for them.

There are a number of ways to approach the question of how our school's experience might be applicable to other populations. The most obvious, and certainly the one we are most frequently asked about, is whether or not we could build the school not online. More specifically, would it be possible to develop a version of the school that followed the course structure and curriculum of the SOHS, but that did so on a physical campus with students in front of each other and their instructors during the day? Such a school would be operated on a college-like schedule, using a flipped-classroom model, blending asynchronous online materials with in-person seminars, and featuring a rigorous philosophy-based Core curriculum. We have no doubt that such a model would certainly work. As we have argued throughout this book there is nothing essential about the SOHS that requires it to be online. In fact, when we have shown the documentary short filmed at our 2012 graduation to peer independent schools the most common reaction is 'Hey, those are our students.'

If we limit the question to the applicability of the SOHS in its onlineness to other populations, there are again several possible answers to the question. One of the compelling characteristics of the SOHS is the diversity of its student population. Students come in from across the spectrum of states and countries such that there are few dominant subgroups outside the ones that all students would expect, namely, the school is about 80% composed of students in the United States. One could imagine adapting the model to different geographies, taking a broadly similar approach but making subtle changes to bring the curriculum in line with the local climate. Along these lines it has been suggested that a version of the SOHS would be ideal for certain Asian countries, but only if it had a certain amount of localization, particularly replacing the Core course on Democracy, Freedom and the Rule of Law with a course entitled 'Morality and Authority'. More sympathetically, we could present the Confucian ideal in contrast with the Socractic ideal. Such a school could be developed autonomously, or a series of such schools could be developed, with a type of sister-school relationship and with formal cooperation enshrined in their charters. Alternative approaches, particularly if one had a goal of building a network of schools, would be to establish satellite campuses in different localities with cross-registration available to students, or even develop the satellites as a farm system with the best students promoting and transferring to the main campus. While the possibilities are myriad, they are not ones that we are exploring, as such directions fall clearly outside of our mandate as a demonstration school. But as a thought experiment, once can easily see how once one removes the limiting factor of physical location from one's thinking about a school, one loses a principal constraint that has traditionally informed school design.

5.1 Applicability to Students of Differing Abilities

The SOHS came into being to solve a particular set of problems faced by a specific group of students. While aspects of this solution—technologies, methodologies, and so forth—may be applicable, the curriculum certainly has a particular sort of student in mind. So another question regarding applicability is one that varies neither the onlineness, nor the cultural context, and that keeps the methodology in place, while setting aside the curriculum to see whether this style of online school is suitable for use with students whose academic ability would not qualify them for admission to the SOHS itself. This is an open question and not one that we are likely to answer empirically, for the nature of the SOHS, like that nature of Stanford University itself, is to focus its instructional energies on a small group of students in a fairly narrow ability band.[3]

Now there is certainly nothing intrinsic in the approach we have taken that requires students to be of high ability as much as it requires students to be of comparable ability and to have the requisite comparable need and desire for being in the school. As the preceding chapter on student outcomes discussed, SOHS graduates are clear that the school is not for everyone, and those whom it is for must be well matched academically and motivationally. While we can imagine courses being taught in this matter to students with less academic ability—and of course we have students in the school at present whose ability outside their areas of strength is middle of the road—it is hard to imagine the approach succeeding with students who are bored or unmotivated. This is the critical factor for keeping track of all the balls in the air, and being responsible for getting work completed and submitted when not in front of a teacher every day. As we have discussed throughout, the great challenge faced by an online school is that it is too easy for students who do not want to be there to not be there.

[3]The probable limit of enrollment for the SOHS is roughly 600 FTE students and roughly 1,000 headcount. As with the University itself, just because something is successful and in demand does not mean that it should increase its numbers, only its selectivity.

The other factor that may come into play in the possibility of online work with other populations is the ability of students to settle into the abstraction of space constituted by the school. We do not know whether there is anything special about the population of students in the SOHS when it comes to their ability to perform the abstraction and to view the virtual classroom as a classroom, nor do we know if these students enter the school particularly adept at making and sustaining relationships in an online environment. These are questions that will merit further investigation in the next volume.

Ultimately the applicability to other populations boils down to the same factors that make a school successful for its students in any context: the mission of the school and the talents of the instructors must be well matched to the population of students the school intends to serve, and there must be a clear problem being solved by the school. Without alignment of vision and clarity of purpose, it is impossible for any school to be successful.

5.2 Applicability to Lower Grades

A natural companion question to that of the applicability of the SOHS model in other spaces or to other secondary-school populations is that of the applicability to the lower grades. We are frequently asked by parents when and if we will create an Online Elementary School or expand the Online High School down to the Kindergarten level. This is a question that merits a nuanced answer.

When we started the SOHS, we were initially a three-year school. We avoided calling ourselves a 'tenth grade to twelfth grade' school, as we were less interested in the traditional definition of grade and more interested in catching students roughly at the high-school-sophomore level of attainment and providing them with a rigorous academic program that would take that level as the starting point. In retrospect, the motivation for this was a mixture of correct intuition and naïve assumption. The correct intuition was that there would be a significant number of students who would want to make the jump to the SOHS once they hit tenth grade. That this was the case is substantiated in the discussion in Chapter 6 about the distribution of grade levels among entering SOHS students. The naïve assumption was that the real need among students was in the end of high school and that the freshman year was not a problem we needed to solve.

Regardless of whether that was true (it was not, as was illustrated by our addition of middle-school grades the following year), it is the case that many students looking for high schools conduct that search while in eighth grade. And being a school without a ninth grade leads to students deciding that they can jump straight from eighth grade to tenth grade. To address this problem and the corresponding problem of students looking to start in independent schools at seventh grade, we added the ninth grade in the third year of the school, and then added grades seven and eight the following year.

What we had not fully anticipated in adding the lower grades was that one of our fundamental premises in the design of the school would fall flat. This was the assumption that students of this caliber, if treated in the manner in which one treats good undergraduates, would rise to the occasion. So when bringing new instructors into the school, most of whom were coming from a college context, often without any explicit prior experience teaching high-school-aged students, we would stress to them to just forget about the age of the students and teach them the way you would Stanford undergraduates. Indeed, one of the selling points to the instructors has always been that they can work at Stanford and teach their specialties to students who are every bit as smart as Stanford undergraduates, but just happen to be younger.

This approach had worked well for us for a number of years prior to the creation of the SOHS during residential summer programs we operated on the Stanford campus, and this approach continued to be successful for students in the higher grades of the SOHS. It has been less so in the middle-school grades, primarily because in those grades, student age-related developmental issues are simply more prevalent. Nor does it work, by analogy, to just say 'Treat these students like high school students.' Middle-school students require specific attention to their needs as middle-school students. Middle school has presented a set of unique challenges, some of which we have addressed in the curriculum, some of which we have addressed in choice of instructors, and some of which we have addressed in overall design and function. But our approach continues to evolve, and ultimately the middle-school program may wind up looking different from the high-school program in a number of more significant ways—more frequent seminars, shorter seminars, fewer asynchronous lectures, more interventionist monitoring of student performance, and specifically trained middle-school counseling staff, to name a few.

It is from this vantage point that we address the question of whether the approach we have taken at the SOHS would lead to a viable Online Elementary School. And to this we add a few more observations. First of all, it is certainly possible to offer courses on this model to students who are in elementary school. We have done so successfully for a number of years, teaching a course on Shakespeare to a group of students in fourth grade as part of an outreach program. But these students were participating not as students in a school, but on an *à la carte* basis and only for courses that were intended to be enrichment falling outside of any core academic course of study, and as we discussed at length in the first chapter, there is a significant difference between the two.

It is also certainly possible for students younger than twelve to be successful in the SOHS, even as full-time students. We have had a handful of students in the school on a part-time basis younger than this and they have been successful. While not something that we actively seek out, if a qualified student with a clear need presents, and meets the admissions requirements, we have been willing to take her. These cases are, however, fundamentally limited in number.

The question of whether the model applies to the lower grades ultimately has two answers. Everything in our experience suggests that it would be possible to make a myriad of changes and create something that would, for a targeted group of students prove effective. Whether the result would be similar in any manner to the SOHS is an open question. It is rather much like asking if any school targeting students in grades seven-to-twelve could add a lower school. Since lower schools exist, the answer is certainly 'yes'. But whether it would be a school that would imbue students with the indelible mark that signifies having received an SOHS education, the answer is almost certainly 'no', for the SOHS is as much about the Core and the culture and the relationship as it is about the application of a technology or the inhabiting of a certain virtual space.

5.3 Applicability to Existing Schools—Schools Working Together

The most pressing question regarding implications of the SOHS for other populations is in the applicability of the SOHS model to existing independent schools.[4] Here is where some subtlety is required for other schools. Since they already exist as schools, with their own space and students, they do not find themselves in the starting point that the SOHS did. Typically this question comes up either because a school feels compelled to do something online so that they are not left behind in the event that online turns out to be important, or because they have a particular population of students with academic needs that they are unable to meet.

For institutions contemplating going online, our strongest advice is to stay focused on your mission and core values and to remember that

[4]We frame this discussion in terms of independent schools because these are the ones whose underlying economic models most closely parallel that of the SOHS. The discussion in suitably modified form will apply to public schools as well.

online learning is a tool and not an end in itself. For it to be a tool worth using, all stakeholders must understand the goals and objectives behind its introduction and must understand how this tool will advance the mission of the institution. This is particularly important when technologies in question are being heralded as disruptive and the individuals being impacted by the technologies are unsure where they will land. The biggest threat from technology is not the intrinsic disruptive nature of the technology but the potential that the promise of cheap technological solutions has for causing schools to wander away from their missions.

In the independent-school world tuition has been increasing at CPI plus two percent for years.[5] No one questions that this is unsustainable, but few answers have been put forward. One of the fundamental problems for these schools is the challenge of what to do with students whose interests or abilities put them on the tail of the distribution, so that there are not enough of them to justify teaching a course. In the first chapter we discussed how twenty-five years ago we built an online AP calculus course with the goal of having this course used to address the needs of students at schools without a qualified teacher or without enough students to justify offering a course. This problem persists for students at the upper end of course sequences, as well as for students in languages or subjects that have passed out of vogue. The example of the SOHS can serve as a model for solving what is a fundamental problem of anyone who is dealing with tails of distributions while trying to constrain costs. But one needs to be careful in how one approaches this problem.

There are two ways that schools find themselves in this situation. The first is when the students are simply outliers. This may be the first time the school has ever had to address this need. It may be part of a trend or it may be an anomaly. The second is when the group with the need is actually a dwindling population. It may be that the school used to have enough kids for a course and has a perfectly good instructor on site, but for whatever reason enrollment has dwindled and it is no longer cost effective to offer the course. So maybe there used to routinely be eight kids in AP Physics, or maybe it used to be the case that five students were enough to justify teaching a course, but for whatever reason this year there are only four kids and the minimum necessary to offer the course would be ten. In the first case the need is for a course. In the second case the problem is not that the school

[5] S. Jeynes, *ISM Trustee Handbook* (Tempe, AZ: Independent School Magazine, 2008), 53.

needs a course, but rather that it has empty seats it needs to fill. When viewed in this way the problem is essentially one of an imbalance of need and capacity within the system. This is the type of problem that calls out for a technology-driven solution.

If the schools were next to each other, it would be easy enough for students to cross-register at different institutions. This sort of collaboration has been prevalent among neighboring universities for years, but is generally not seen at the high-school level because of logistical complexities. Of course, if we had teleporters, we could beam the students into seminars and the distance would not matter. Or we could take the approach we have been using in the SOHS to accomplish something similar.

Instead of looking for someone on the outside who can use the technology to teach their students, we would encourage schools to come together and work collaboratively to use this technology to solve their own problems. Such collaborations can be done in a manner that keeps the focus on what makes independent-school education great, and this is the interaction between instructors and students.

A number of such efforts have emerged in recent years whereby schools are working together to offer courses online to each other's students, though in most cases they are doing so via asynchronous models that suffer from all the problems of content-centrism described above. One notable exception is that of the Malone Schools Online Network, which comprises sixteen schools that have come together to adapt the SOHS model of synchronous courses for use on a room-to-room basis, whereby small groups of students at schools are stitched together through high-definition video conferencing in a manner that facilitates rich student-student and student-instructor interaction and that does not require students who are in a room together to sit back-to-back looking at their laptops rather than each other. In this environment, we have made available our Core course in Democracy, Freedom, and the Rule of Law, while other schools have offered Organic Chemistry, The Ottoman Empire, and Meteorology.

The alternative and more common approach is to outsource the education to an external vendor. In this case the school finds an external entity, be it a university or a private company, and pays it to teach the students. The online calculus course we developed at Stanford in the early 1990s was done with just such a use in mind. And while there is much that may be appealing to schools about working with universities, the results are often better if they work with each other, as then students are working with those who understand what is involved in teaching high-school students, something often lacking at universities.

Of course, looking to universities to provide instruction can be merited when students are taking courses that are legitimately beyond the high-school level, and universities and high schools are both mission-driven institutions.

The slippery slope begins when schools look not to each other or to universities, but instead to commercial providers that are for-profit companies and whose objectives are necessarily very different than those of a school. Likewise, when schools look to online tools and techniques not as means to an end but as an end in itself, or when the technology is adopted for the purpose of driving down costs rather than as a means to drive up quality, they run the risk of losing sight of their missions. As long as a school remains focused on its mission, on the teaching and learning and the communal experience of education, the ancillary instructional resources will remain just that.

While cost is always an important factor, it cannot be the deciding one for independent schools. After all, there is already a host of good free alternatives on offer in the form of the public school system. But if one can remain focused on quality and deliver that quality at fair value, then the same facts that have historically driven families to independent schools rather than the public schools will continue to obtain. If schools lose track of why they provide value to their families and how their education programs flow from their missions, one cannot expect the families to remain. If one relies on others to solve one's problems, parents and students will begin to wonder why they rely upon the school at all, and a world in which a school just outsources its instructional needs to vendors will cause the parents at the school to wonder why they should not just do the same thing.

5.4 Implications for Quality Standards

During our initial accreditation visit from the Western Association of Schools and Colleges in the first year of the SOHS, the question was raised about classroom observation opportunities. We replied that since all the class sessions were recorded they could review any class they wanted from any point in the past year. This is one of the strengths that the SOHS has compared even to traditional schools: there is an ability to look under the hood to review what is happening in the classroom in a manner that is typically not possible in the traditional school context.

The ability to record, review, document, and analyze opens up a number of possibilities. At its simplest, recording class sessions affords instructors the opportunity to review their own work and that of their peers to identify ways to improve instruction. This allows for rapid prototyping and an iterative development that drives a process of ongoing improvement. It also provides a basis for continuing professional development, both for the instructors inside the SOHS and for instructors from other institutions who wish to learn from example.

More interesting than this, perhaps, are questions surrounding classroom and discussion dynamics and the factors that make a seminar successful. How is engagement produced and maintained during seminars? How interactive are seminars? How does the multithreaded nature of the online seminar (providing both the main audio-visual channel of communication, coupled with text chat and shared accessible whiteboard space) promote and maintain this engagement? With everything recorded, it is now possible to analyze exactly how much each student has contributed to the seminar. We are only beginning to look at this type of information.

Two areas where we hope to see the work of the SOHS have broader impact are in the development of standards for quality instruction and standards for what constitutes advanced courses.

Much of the discussion about quality and efficacy in online instruction begins at a starting point that assumes that substantial changes have been made to courses and modes of instruction to adapt the curriculum to the online environment, especially when the online environment is impoverished in some way, either by being purely asynchronous or by restricting student-instructor interaction to narrow channels such as email. Such studies tend to focus on questions of 'no discernable difference', hoping to show that the online course is comparable to what it is replacing. Unfortunately, showing that one mediocre solution is no different than another is on par with claiming that all men look like Socrates when viewed at night from a sufficient distance. What we hope to do instead is work with peer institutions, be they online or brick-and-mortar, to define objective characteristics for what constitutes high-quality instruction. This is a question that is important to answer, especially when people are confronted by cheaper alternatives. This is also a question that can, perhaps, best be approached in the laboratory of an online school. By working online in a seminar model, we are in some sense working with the essence of the seminar—we are working in an environment where we can see what conditions are necessary and sufficient for a good seminar, stripped of the particulars of physical setting. In this sense, we can see what should make a seminar work in any environment—we see what it is qua seminar that makes it work.

We believe that the types of features we have identified in the SOHS that substantiate its claims for schoolness, taken to their logical extreme, will help to tease out the characterization of quality schoolness. Part of this will be identifying the habits of mind that are essential components of what students should be learning and determining what practices or activities are essential for their inculcation. We believe that regular substantive interaction between students and instructors is a key, particularly interaction that models what we are trying to teach. Similarly, regular substantive work produced by students, reviewed by instructors and other students, and that is returned and revised, is another. What is important here in determining quality and the ideal is to stay focused on what should be and to worry less about what is or what is currently possible. This should be a standard to which all aspire even if it is one that few will achieve.

As regards objective standards for advanced coursework, many schools these days find themselves in a catch-22. On the one hand, the AP has lost much of its credibility as a viable mechanism for teaching advanced subjects to students. The number of universities accepting AP exams for credit, and the subjects where credit is accepted, has been steadily declining since the 2000s.[6] The criticism most often hurled at the AP is that it is a mile wide and an inch deep. And while the SOHS continues to offer a number of AP courses, as the discussion above in Chapter 3 made clear, we approach these courses in a way that makes them distinctly our own, serving our own pedagogical objectives, even if they have as a secondary benefit the effect of preparing students to take the AP exam. The same holds true for many independent schools, which would love to move away from the AP, but believe that by doing so they will hamper the chances of their students when it comes to college admission. In the same way that the SOHS model of course delivery, coupled with archival storage of syllabi, student work, and recorded class sessions provided documentation beyond the expectations of our initial accreditation committee, and which made their job far easier than it would have been otherwise, we believe that the system could be used to provide substantiation regarding course design and execution as a basis for a new standard for advanced courses. This is not to say that schools would adopt and teach the SOHS courses as an alternative to the AP; rather, schools would use an SOHS-style flipped classroom, live-seminar model as a way of providing substantiation for their courses, even if the seminars were taking place in a face-to-face seminar room. Coupled with student portfolios to deepen the documentation of what happens in the class, some process of peer review of the online artifacts could be used to establish quality and provide

[6]Lewin, 'Dartmouth Stops Credits for Excelling on A.P. Test'.

a level of documentation allowing college admissions officers and academic departments to make more informed decisions about student achievement in these courses. That there is a need for an alternative currency is clear. Whether the SOHS system could be coopted and implemented to serve this purpose in physical schools is less clear, but the models of institutional collaboration mentioned above may provide a way to approach this problem.

6 Why is this Interesting?

As we reach the conclusion of the book, it is natural to be confronted by the following questions: There are hundreds of millions of students out there, how will you serve them all? We understand why an electronic Aristotle would be interesting, but you abandoned this in favor of Socrates and the Agora. How can this model serve more than a handful? Why is this interesting? How is this relevant?

The focus of online learning efforts for the past few years have been on their potential to radically transform education, whether by disrupting the status quo, changing the role of the teacher, or reaching the vast multitudes. There is a feeling that unless you can reach millions, you cannot have an impact. And while the need to reach millions might be compelling for those looking to make their fame or fortune, examples abound of those who have had a profound effect on the education of millions without themselves educating millions.

In the eight years that we have been operating the SOHS we have seen numerous big online projects come into being. Most of these suffer from the same sort of problems we uncovered in our own efforts along these lines in the 1990s and 2000s, and that we discussed at length in the first chapter. The simple fact remains that these big courses are no closer to solving the problem of delivering excellent education than the mass production of textbooks has been. While they are tools that can have their place in the solution, they are not the solution. Nor were our attempts to create an electronic Aristotle the solution. While there remains much that can be fruitfully explored in trying to create such a system, there is little to show that courses built around such systems develop within students the level of engagement and commitment that are hallmarks of excellent education, not to mention the frustrating rates of attrition we had all those years. While the operation may be successful at times, the patient dies far too often.

Measuring the worth of a project only in terms of the number of students it can directly serve is a very narrow perspective. When the question of how the SOHS fits in with the mission of Stanford University was raised at a meeting of the Stanford Board of Trustees in February 2012, Stanford President John Hennessy stated that if the SOHS can provide an independent-school education comparable in quality to [*name of a prominent independent school close to Stanford – ed.*] for 40% of the tuition, then this has tremendous significance both for the nation and the world. In the same vein, when Theodore Sizer left his position as Dean at the Graduate School of Education at Harvard to take the job of Headmaster at Phillips Academy, it was with a realization that he could accomplish a great deal taking one venerable institution and showing what could be done, how the institution could be made to work for the students and faculty and the broader community, and to serve as a beacon of what is possible.[7]

Sometimes we solve the problem, other times we show a way towards a solution. Sometimes we change the world by reaching into it and actually changing it, while sometimes we build our perfect little world and serve as an example. As Voltaire said, we cultivate our garden.

This book has provided a detailed look at just how we have come to cultivate our particular garden over the past eight years. We hope that our story shows how others, who share our objectives, can do the same.

[7]F. Hetchinger, 'To Let Some Air into the "Hothouse"', *New York Times*, October 1, 1972. See also, 'Phillips Andover Names New Head', *New York Times*, February 23, 1972.

Appendix and Ancillary Materials

A variety of ancillary materials and supporting documents can be found online at http://www.bricksandmortarbook.com.

References

Bazelon, E. 2013. *Sticks and Stones: Defeating the Culture of Bullying and Rediscovering the Power of Character and Empathy.* New York: Random House.

Bergmann, J., and A. Sams. 2012. *Flip Your Classroom: Reach Every Student in Every Class Every Day.* Washington, DC: International Society for Technology in Education.

Cain, S. 2012. *Quiet: The Power of Introverts in a World that Can't Stop Talking.* New York: Crown Publishers.

Cyranoski, D., N. Gilbert, H. Ledford, A. Nayar, and M. Yahia. 2011. 'The PhD Factory'. *Nature* 472: 276–279. doi:10.1038/472276a.

Dewey, J. 1916. *Democracy and Education.* New York: Macmillan.

Dickens, C. 1854. *Hard Times*, Illustrated edition. London: Heritage Illustrated Publishing, 2014.

Dipaolo, A. 1995. 'The Stanford Instructional Television Network: A Partnership with Industry'. *European Journal of Engineering Education* 20, no. 2: 243–246. doi:10.1080/03043799502002l7.

Dreyfus, H. 2009. *On the Internet*, 2nd ed. New York: Routledge.

Dweck, C. S. 2006. *Mindset: The New Psychology of Success.* New York: Random House.

Ehrenberg, R. 2002. 'Reaching For the Brass Ring: The *U.S. News & World Report* Rankings and Competition'. *The Review of Higher Education* 26, no. 2: 145–162. doi:10.1353/rhe.2002.0032.

Ennis, R.H. 1989. 'Critical Thinking and Subject Specificity: Clarification of Needed Research'. *Educational Researcher* 18, no. 4: 4–10. doi:10.3102/0013189X018003004.

Ennis, R. H. 1991. 'Critical Thinking: A Streamlined Conception'. *Teaching Philosophy* 14, no. 1: 5–24.

Ennis, R. H. 1993. 'Critical Thinking Assessment'. *Theory into Practice* 32, no. 5: 179–186.

Emanuel, E. J. 2013. 'Online Education: MOOCs Taken by Educated Few'. *Nature* 503: 342. doi:10.1038/503342a.

Etchemendy, J., 2012. 'Online Education'. Presentation to Stanford Board of Trustees, February 7, 2012.

Gross, M. 1999. 'Small Poppies: Highly Gifted Children in the Early Years'. *Roeper Review* 21, no. 3: 207–214.

International Association for K–12 Online Learning (iNACOL). 2011. *National Standards for Quality Online Courses,* version 2. Vienna, VA: iNACOL.

Jeynes, S. 2008. *ISM Trustee Handbook.* Tempe, AZ: Independent School Magazine.

Khan, S. 2012. *The One World Schoolhouse.* New York: Twelve.

Maisel, I. 'What It Takes'. *Stanford Magazine*, November/December 2013, https://alumni.stanford.edu/get/page/magazine/article/?article_id=66225

Mayadas, A. F., R. Gomory, and W. Patrick. Unpublished manuscript in production. Hudson Whitman/Excelsior College Press.

McDowell, J. 1994. *Mind and World.* Cambridge, MA: Harvard University Press.

McPeck, J.E. 1984. 'Stalking Beasts, but Swatting Flies: The Teaching of Critical Thinking'. *Canadian Journal of Education* 9, no. 1: 28–44.

McPeck, J. E. 1990. *Teaching Critical Thinking.* Routledge: New York.

Office of the University Registrar of Stanford University. *Stanford Bulletin.* Updated August 1, 2013, http://exploredegrees.stanford.edu/undergraduatedegreesandprograms/#transferworktext.

Ophir, E., C. Nass, and A. Wagner. 2009. 'Cognitive Control in Media Multitaskers'. *Proceedings of the National Academy of Sciences* 106: 15583–15587. doi:10.1073/pnas.0903620106.

Plato. 1997. *Complete Works*, edited, with introduction and notes, by John M. Cooper. Indianapolis, IN: Hackett.

Plutarch. 1927. *Plutarch: Moralia,* Volume I, trans. Frank Cole Babbitt. Loeb Classical Library. Cambridge, MA: Harvard University Press.

Pollan, M. 2006. *The Omnivore's Dilemma: A Natural History of Four Meals.* New York: Penguin Press.

Ravaglia R. 1995. 'Design Issues in a Stand Alone Multimedia Computer-based Mathematics Curriculum'. In *Fourth Annual Multimedia in Education and Industry*, 49–52. Asheville, NC: Association for Applied Interactive Multimedia.

Ravaglia, R. 2005. 'Founding Proposal for Online High School'. Unpublished submission to the Malone Family Foundation, August, 2005.

Ravaglia, R. 2007. 'An Online High School at Stanford University'. *Understanding Our Gifted,* 19 , no. 4: 6–9.

Ravaglia, R., P. Suppes, C. Stillinger, and T. Alper. 1995. 'Computer-based Mathematics and Physics for Gifted Students'. *Gifted Child Quarterly* 39: 7–13.

Ravaglia R., T. M. Alper, M. Rozenfeld, and P. Suppes. 1998. 'Successful Pedagogical Applications of Symbolic Computation'. In *Computer-Human Interaction with Symbolic Computation*, edited by Norbert Kajler, 61–87. New York: Springer-Verlag.

Rheingold, H. 2000. *The Virtual Community: Homesteading on the Electronic Frontier.* Cambridge, MA: MIT Press. Kindle edition.

Roberts D. F., U. G. Foehr, and V. Rideout. 2010. *Generation M^2: Media in the lives of 8–18 year-olds.* Menlo Park, CA: HJKF Foundation.

Ryle, G. 1949. *The Concept of Mind.* Chicago: University of Chicago Press.

Skinner, B. F. 1951. 'How to Teach Animals'. *Scientific American* 185: 26–29.

Sousa, D. and C. A. Tomlinson. 2011. *Differentiation and the Brain: How Neuroscience Supports the Learner-Friendly Classroom.* Bloomington, IL: Solution Tree Press.

Suppes, P. 1966. 'The Uses of Computers in Education'. *Scientific American* 215: 206–220.

Turkle, S. 2011. *Alone Together: Why we Expect More from Technology and Less from Each Other.* New York: Basic Books.

Index